THINKING PALESTINE

edited by
Ronit Lentin

Zed Books
LONDON & NEW YORK

Thinking Palestine was first published in 2008 by Zed Books Ltd,
7 Cynthia Street, London N1 9JF, UK and
Room 400, 175 Fifth Avenue, New York, NY 10010, USA

www.zedbooks.co.uk

Editorial copyright © Ronit Lentin 2008
Copyright in this collection © Zed Books 2008

The rights of Ronit Lentin to be identified as the editor of this work have been
asserted by her in accordance with the Copyright, Designs and Patents Act, 1988

Designed and typeset by Long House Publishing Services
Cover designed by Andrew Corbett
Printed and bound in the EU by Gutenberg Ltd, Malta

Distributed in the USA exclusively by Palgrave Macmillan, a division
of St Martin's Press, LLC, 175 Fifth Avenue, New York, NY 10010, USA

A catalogue record for this book is available from the British Library.
Library of Congress Cataloguing in Publication Data is available.

ISBN 978 1 84277 906 4 hb
ISBN 978 1 84277 907 1 pb

Contents

Acknowledgements

This book is the collaborative effort of an interdisciplinary group of Palestinian, Israeli, American, British and Irish scholars who got together at the conference 'Palestine as State of Exception – A Global Paradigm', held in Trinity College Dublin in September 2006. I owe them my deepest gratitude. In particular, I owe an intellectual debt to Honaida Ghanim, whose theorization of Palestine as 'state of exception' inspired this project. I also thank Nahla Abdo, Sari Hanafi and Alina Korn, who came on board for the book. Thanks to the Institute of International Integration Studies (IIIS), Trinity College Dublin, and in particular to Adrienne Harten and Caroline Bolster of the IIIS, and to David Landy, for their assistance. Special thanks are due to the University of Dublin Fund for its financial support for this book. Thanks to Susannah Trefgarne and Ellen McKinlay of Zed Books for their editorial support. Finally, I am grateful, as always, to my soul sister Nitza Aminov.

Ronit Lentin

Introduction: Thinking Palestine

Setting the object of the debate[1]

Not a state but rather a territory, a national entity, perhaps a state-in-becoming, Palestine occupies a central place in the contemporary political imagination. That 'the question of Palestine' is debated above and beyond other contemporary political questions is most probably due to the central position of 'the Jews' in the post-Holocaust West and to Palestine, the territory, being 'the Holy Land' of the three monotheistic religions; but it is also due, as Gargi Bhattacharyya argues in this volume, to the fact that the Palestinian struggle is regarded as the unfinished business of a previous imperial era and that 'the struggle for a free Palestine has been popularized, pop-culturalized, and added to the style pantheon of the global left'. For the late Palestinian intellectual Edward Said, however, Palestine is above all a *consciousness*, built on the uniqueness of Palestinian history, which has taken a different course from Arab history due to the dialectics of its traumatic national encounter with Zionism.

This dialectic connection arguably makes Palestine a unique case study. Said's book *The Question of Palestine*, which re-introduced the Palestinians into English-language academic and political debate, was not intended as a value-free account. It rather described 'our night and our slow awakening', always dialectically setting the Palestinian experience against Zionism, which 'has meant as much to us, albeit differently, as it has to Jews. What we need to inform the world is how it

1

meant certain concrete things to us, things of which we collectively bear the living traces' (Said 1980: xv). This book does not aim to discuss the question of Palestine in its entirety, nor Israel or Jewish history. The object under consideration is rather the Palestinian conception of Palestine and the representations of Palestine, the consciousness, the political idea, the territory, the history, seen, above all, as a dialectical experience positioned against its perennial other, Zionism. The starting point for this book is an analysis of Palestine in light of Giorgio Agamben's 'state of exception' (Agamben 1998, 2005), debated from different angles by contributors to this collection. This introduction briefly outlines Agamben's concept of the 'state of exception' based, among other things, on the work of the Nazi jurist Carl Schmitt, the German Jewish cultural theorist Walter Benjamin, and the French theorist Michel Foucault, who in *Society Must be Defended* (2003) posits a theory of the birth of state racism. To complete this theoretical exploration, Israel is theorized, after David Theo Goldberg (2002, this volume), as a 'racial state'. I do take on board, however, Goldberg's warning against using racialization as a vague analytical tool, and the need to anchor it in regional models or mappings, rather than ideal types or broad generalizations, and in 'contours of racist configurations, each one with its own material and intellectual history' (Goldberg 2005: 88).

In view of the relationship between racial states and resistance, and because, like the other contributors to this volume, I am politically committed to Palestinian self-determination, I face a dilemma in presenting a seemingly abstract theorization of Palestine (and dialectically, Israel) in light of Agamben's state of exception. My dilemma is that – notwithstanding Agamben's positing sovereignty's subject as *homo sacer*, or 'bare life', at the mercy of sovereign power (1998) – such analysis runs the risk of erasing the active agency of the Palestinian subject, represented as either passive victim of Israeli dispossession or aggressive insurgent, but with interpretative control wrested away. As illustrated in the collection of autobiographical narratives of dispossession of Palestinian and Israeli women that I co-edited with Nahla Abdo (Abdo and Lentin 2002), I am deeply committed to the de-objectification of the Palestinian subject. I am, however, also well aware of my problematic position as (an exiled) citizen of Israel, and as such a member of the perpetrator group, in relation to representing Palestinian subjectivity.

Indeed, the question has to be asked why so many Israeli scholars are preoccupied with researching Palestinians. While in some cases it has to do with empathy, or solidarity, it may also have to do with the tendency to orientalize the Palestinian other (Said 1978), epitomized as the orient-at-home – exotic, sensual, chaotic but also the desired 'colonial fantasy' (Yegenoglu 1998). In some cases an education in Arabic and Middle Eastern studies trains Israelis for intelligence work: many Israelis researching Palestinians are security services veterans (Rabinowicz 1998: 134), contributing to the colonial power/knowledge regime. The close cooperation between the security services and Israeli universities and research institutes is no secret.

Like many anti-Zionist Israelis, whose 'road to Damascus' tales often date back to the wake of the 1982 Lebanon war, I too have my account (Lentin 2007). In recounting these Israeli anti-Zionist Damascene tales, the moment of conversion is crucial and how this is recounted indicates our sense of self and current political positionality. However, auto/biographical accounts are ultimately about the teller rather than the told, regardless of our conviction that *our* personal auto/biography is about empathy and solidarity. Thus, despite the good intentions, in much Israeli research on Palestine the Palestinians often get erased, their voice subsumed by the voice of the powerful colonizer, leading to a degree of appropriation that we are all guilty of (see my chapter in this volume).

In this light, and in light of the chapters in this volume, I want to propose a theorization of 'Palestinians' not merely as victims, or as spoken for and about (although, of course, to theorize is always also to objectify). I am inspired by the Jewish Israeli sociologist Yehouda Shenhav's (2006) re-reading of Frantz Fanon's *The Wretched of the Earth* (1961) and of Agamben's interpretation of Benjamin's 'Critique of violence' (1921), and Shenhav's critique of Agamben for ignoring, unlike Schmitt or Hannah Arendt, the role of European imperialism in conceptualizing European sovereignty. Shenhav's postcolonial reading of Fanon and Benjamin may lead to the missing link in thinking about Palestine and Palestinian subjectivity, even though, surprisingly, he stops short of theorizing the State of Israel as a 'racial state'.

I begin this introduction with a brief theoretical outline of the state of exception, state racism and the racial state. I then posit Israel as a racial state, where the state of exception with reference to its Palestinian other was instituted from its very establishment through a series of emergency laws, not yet repealed. I then read the Palestinian active agent through a discussion of Fanon, Benjamin and Shenhav. I conclude by outlining the contents of the book, including, inter alia, a contestation of the applicability of Agamben's theorization of the state of exception to the State of Israel.

State of exception

According to Carl Schmitt, who posits the contiguity between the state of exception and sovereignty, a sovereign is one who determines the 'state of exception', which Schmitt understands not as a state of emergency or as merely responding to necessity (as do the Roman jurists cited by Agamben), but rather as a general concept in political science. The state of exception must be understood as a response to a condition of superior danger to the continuing existence of the state. The sovereign, according to Schmitt, is constructed by the state of exception, which the sovereign him/herself determines. But although the sovereign's action is not controlled by the legal order of the state, it becomes clear that it is the sovereign who decides both whether a state of exception exists and which action to take to overcome it (Schmitt 2005: 25–7). However, the state of exception is difficult to define precisely because of its proximity to civil war, insurrection, and resistance. Civil war, which is the opposite of normal conditions, lies in a zone of undecidability in relation to the state of exception, which is 'state power's immediate response to the most extreme internal conflicts' (Agamben 2005: 2).

Schmitt was a trenchant critic of Weimar liberalism, which he saw as 'Jewish', and he later became a Nazi ideologue who theorized sovereignty at the point of transition from Weimar to the Nazi Reich. It is tempting to link the theorization of the state of exception to the Nazi state. As Agamben reminds us, soon after Hitler took power, he proclaimed the Decree for the Protection of the People and the State, which suspended the articles of the Weimar Constitution concerning personal liberties. The decree was never repealed, making the Third Reich a state of exception which lasted twelve years. Modern totalitarianism can therefore be defined as the establishment, by means of a state of exception, of a legal civil war that allows the physical elimination not only of political adversaries, but of entire categories of citizens not integrated into the political system.

Agamben insists, however, that this voluntary creation of a state of emergency is not merely a description of the Nazi Reich. Through the state of exception, the sovereign 'creates and guarantees the situation' that the law needs for its validity – and this circularity characterizes not only extreme regimes such as the Nazi state, but also the voluntary creation of a permanent state of emergency that has become one of the essential practices of contemporary states, including so-called democratic states (Agamben 2005: 2). This involves, on the one hand, the extension of the military authority's wartime powers into the civil sphere, and, on the other, the suspension of constitutional norms that protect individual liberties (as argued by Zreik in this volume in relation to Israeli constitutionalism).

One example Agamben gives to illustrate the biopolitical significance of the state of exception as the structure in which the law encompasses living beings by means of its own suspension is the 'military order' issued by the US president on 13 November 2001, which authorizes the indefinite detention and trial by 'military commission' of non-citizens suspected of terrorist activities. The US Patriot Act enacted on 26 October 2001 already allowed the attorney general to take into custody aliens suspected of activities endangering the national security of the United States, though within seven days the alien had to be either released or charged. What was new about Bush's order was that it erased any legal status of the individual; thus not only did detainees not have POW status, they did not even have the status of persons charged with a crime according to American law. As in the Nazi camps, detainees lose any legal identity (Agamben 2005: 3).

Agamben's reading of Schmitt's state of exception theory rests not only on sovereignty declaring a state of emergency in which the sovereign both stays outside the law and enacts it, but also on the notion that it is the nation (in the sense of *Volk*, rather than citizenry or residency within the state's territorial borders) which needs defending from its others. Crucially, the state of exception is a *security* state, instituting 'an unprecedented generalization of the paradigm of security as the normal techniques of government' (Agamben 2005: 14).

In *Homo Sacer: Sovereign Power and Bare Life* (1998), Agamben argues that the constant state of emergency or exception enables the state to turn the lives of those under state rule into what he calls *homo sacer* or 'bare life'. A Roman concept, *homo sacer* (sacred man) is he who may be killed but not sacrificed. While useful in theorizing the 'bare life' of Nazi concentration camp inmates, Agamben extends this to the lives of detainees, to whom, according to the US Administration, the American Constitution does not apply, even though the US Supreme Court ruled otherwise in 2004. Agamben argues for the general applicability of the state of exception: 'At once excluding bare life from and capturing it within the political order, the state of exception actually constituted, in its very separateness, the hidden foundation on which the entire political system rested' (Agamben 1995: 9).

The questions Agamben teases out in *State of Exception* are whether we are talking of a territory which exists outside the rule of law, and whether the state of exception is inside or outside the law. Judging by Israel's intricate regime of emergency regulations and the play between the judiciary, the legislature and the executive with regard to both Israel's Palestinian citizens and those Palestinians living under occupation, it does not take a major leap of the imagination to extend the analysis to Palestine and Israel.

Racial state

Michel Foucault (1990) argues that when life becomes included in mechanisms of state power, politics turns into biopolitics, the territorial state becomes a 'state of population', and the nation's biological life becomes a problem of sovereign power, which he terms 'biopower'. Through a series of governmental technologies, biopower creates 'docile bodies' and the population – its life, welfare, longevity, health – becomes the ultimate object of government. Foucault dedicated his 1975–6 Collège de France lecture series to the birth of state racism (2003), charting the transition from sovereignty's power to kill unwanted people in the regulatory modern state, which directs its biopower at living beings and, more specifically, at their mass – as population. Put simply, Foucault posits a transition from the sovereign power of the old territorial state, 'to make die and let live', to modern biopower, 'to make live and let die'. The duty to defend society against itself (and by extension defend 'the nation' from its indigenous and immigrant others) means that the state can scarcely function without racism, which Foucault sees as 'the break between what must live and what must die' (Foucault 2003: 254). According to this analysis, racism has two functions: the first is separating out the groups that exist within a population; the second is making it possible to establish 'a relationship between my life and the death of the other that is not a military or warlike relationship of confrontation, but a biological-type relationship: the more inferior species die out... the more I – as species rather than

individual – can live, the stronger I will be' (Foucault 2003: 255).
Rather than serving one group against another, race – understood not
in biological but rather in classificatory terms – becomes a tool of social
conservatism and state racism – a racism which society practices against
itself. As opposed to scapegoat theories of racism, which argue that sub-
populations are cordoned off under economic and social duress,
Foucault sees racism as an ongoing social war, nurtured by biopolitical
technologies of purification. This sheds light on the ongoing plans,
since before the establishment of the State of Israel, to 'transfer'
Palestinians outside the state's borders (see e.g., Pappe 2006).

In Goldberg's (2002) theorization of all modern nation-states as racial
states, the state is a state of power which excludes in order to construct
homogeneity. Through governmental technologies – such as constitutions, border controls, the law, policy making, bureaucracy, population
census, invented histories and traditions, ceremonies and cultural
imagining – modern states, each in their own way, are defined by their
power to exclude and include in racially ordered terms, aiming to
produce a coherent picture of the population by keeping racialized
others out and by legislating against the 'degeneracy' of indigenous
minorities. In constructing homogeneities, the state not only denies its
internal heterogeneities, it is also a normalizing biopower state.

If we concur with Goldberg's theorization of all modern nation-states
as racial states, and with Foucault's view of racism as intrinsic to all
modern, normalizing states (through the use of biopolitical technologies
ranging from social exclusion to mass murder), there is little doubt that
Israel can be theorized as a racial state par excellence, where the state of
exception was instituted prior to its establishment in relation to its
Palestinian other. As Shenhav reminds us, 'In Israel there is a constant
state of emergency. The state inherited the British Mandate's "Emergency Regulations" under which it continued the anomalous suspension
of the law, within the law... We must remember what this system
enables: one rule (life) for the majority of the state's citizens, and another
(death, threat of death, threat of expulsion) for the state's subjects, whose
lives have been rendered "bare"' (Shenhav 2006: 206–7).

Israel as a racial state

Goldberg writes in this volume that 'Israel cannot live with the
Palestinians, purging them persistently from green-line Israel, but

cannot live without them, conceptually as much as materially, existentially as much as emotionally.' However, theorizing Israel as a racial state is not merely about its relations with its Palestinian other. Following Foucault's general idea about the need to defend society – interesting here also is Burleigh and Wipperman's (1999) theorization of the Nazi state as the ideal-type racial state, where the object was the *protection of the body* of the *Volk* – and remembering that Zionism was articulated as the imperative to protect the nebulous body dubbed 'the Jewish nation' from antisemitic persecutions, we begin to understand the inevitability of theorizing the State of Israel, from its very inception, as a racial state. Indeed, the prominent Israeli genetics professor Rafael Falk reads the entire history of Zionism as a eugenicist project, aiming to save the Jewish genetic pool from the degeneration forced upon the Jews by diaspora existence (Falk 2006: 25). Falk argues that understanding Judaism as a racial essence became an integral part of Zionist thought towards the end of the nineteenth century. While many European Jews struggled against the idea that Judaism is a race, just as the antisemites justified the persecution of Jews by biological reasoning, seeing Jews as a separate 'race', prominent Zionist thinkers such as Herzl, Hess, Bialik, Nordau and even the liberal philosopher Martin Buber adopted the terminology of *Volk* – a racial nation shaped by 'blood and soil' (Falk 2006, 18–19).[2]

This race thinking, albeit without 'race', has serious consequences. The prevalent thinking about racist discrimination in Israel rejects the notion of 'race', preferring, as does the influential geographer Oren Yiftachel, to theorize Israeli schisms in ethnic terms and the State of Israel as an 'ethnocracy' (Yiftachel 2006). However, in terms of the racialization of Palestinians,[3] such thinking supports the theorization of Israel as a racial state and Goldberg's 'racial palestinianization' argument in this volume.

Israel, constructed as the state of the 'Jewish nation', grants automatic citizenship to anyone who can prove s/he has a Jewish mother, while depriving of citizenship those Palestinians born on the land, who happened to be absent on census day – this applies to both 1948 and 1967. Palestinians not expelled during the 1948 Nakba, numbering some 160,000,[4] were re-dubbed 'Israeli Arabs' and put under military rule, based on British Mandate Emergency Regulations issued in 1945. These regulations virtually abolished basic rights of expression, movement, organization and equality before the law, though they left Palestinian citizens of Israel the right to vote and be elected. A series of laws, including the Law for Absentee Property (1950), the JNF (Jewish National Fund) Law (1953) and the Law of Agricultural Settlement (1967), barred – by legal means, demonstrating the salience of the state of exception – the selling, leasing, sub-letting and owning of land by 'non-Jews', for which read 'Palestinians'. Though officially abolished in 1966, to all intents and purposes the emergency regulations are still in place – controlling 20% of Israel's citizens (Pappe 2006: 220–2).

Contributors to this volume provide many examples – here as elsewhere – of this ongoing anomalous situation. One example is Ilan Pappe's discussion of the Jewish National Fund (JNF), the agency in charge of land ownership, forestation and the Hebraicization of Palestinian place names. Founded in 1901, the JNF was the principal Zionist tool for the colonization of Palestine, first buying Palestinian lands upon which it settled Jewish immigrants, before becoming the main instrument in the Zionization of Palestine. The JNF was entrusted with perpetuating the Zionist myth of Palestine as an 'empty' and 'arid' land before the arrival of Zionism. One consequence is that 93% of land in Israel, established on 78% of historic Palestine, previously owned by dispossessed Palestinians, is owned by Jews, while to this day Israel's Palestinian citizens are prohibited from establishing new settlements. In 1948 the JNF prepared the ground for the Nakba with the 'village files' – a complete mapping of each Palestinian village that served the actual plans, culminating in Plan D, devised by the Zionist leadership, aimed at killing the Palestinians' elite, damaging their sources of livelihood and water supply, and bringing about their systematic and total expulsion from their homeland. Pappe documents this process in *The Ethnic Cleansing of Palestine* (2006), putting paid to the argument, by so-called Israeli 'new historians', that the expulsion of the Palestinians was an unfortunate consequence of war, which today would be dubbed 'collateral damage'.[5] To illustrate further, Pappe highlights the central role of Israel's national parks, where forests of imported European conifers replace indigenous Palestinian olive, almond and fig trees, erasing the memory of the Nakba and of pre-Nakba Palestinian life. The parks, built on destroyed Palestinian villages whose ethnically cleansed inhabitants now reside in refugee camps or in exile, replace Palestinian sites of trauma and memory with Israeli ecologically correct spaces of leisure and entertainment (Pappe 2006: 229).

This is an example of the processes which have led Palestinian scholars such as Honaida Ghanim (2005, this volume) to posit the reduction of the occupied Palestinians to biological subjects. In a biopolitical regime, Ghanim argues, while the life of the subject-citizen is protected by the state, the life of the occupied subject is akin to 'bare life' that may be killed at the state's whim. Sari Hanafi (2005) argues that biopolitics is being deployed by Israel to categorize Palestinians into different 'states of exception' that render them powerless in a process he describes as spacio-cide intended to appropriate land, rather than eliminate people.

Agamben stresses the centrality of the security imperative to the state of exception. Security is indeed central to the self-perception of the Israeli state, where the military occupies a central place (Lomsky-Feder and Ben-Ari 1999: 3), leading Kimmerling (1993) to posit 'cognitive (Israeli) militarism' and argue that during times of war the system puts routine activities 'on hold', mobilizing all its resources to deal with what it sees as the ongoing 'existential threat'. As the State of Israel sees itself as a haven for the 'Jewish nation', the control of the Palestinians is viewed as an imperative born of necessity, and an ongoing state of emergency, which, to paraphrase Agamben, 'creates and guarantees the situation' that the law needs for its validity, enacted to defend (Israeli Jewish) society against its indigenous others.

Following Said's argument about the dialectical relationship between Palestinian consciousness and Zionist politics, it is crucial to reiterate that Israeli preoccupation with state security determines not only the prevalence of the state of exception in governing the territory occupied in 1967, but also the lives of Palestinian citizens in the Israeli state proper, as argued, for instance, in Sabagh-Khouri and Sultani's essay on the trial of the Israeli-Palestinian leader of the National Democratic Assembly, Azmi Bishara (2003, see also Pappe in this volume). According to Agamben, 'A state whose main preoccupation is security, and for whom security is the main legitimization, is a brittle organism; such a state will remain vulnerable to terrorism and will ultimately become terrorist itself.' Shenhav adds that the state of exception does not pertain only to the 'enemy', but refers to all social strata and institutions, making it ultimately undemocratic (Shenhav 2006: 217).

This analysis fits Israeli reality. Israeli obsession with state security is fed by a deep sense of Jewish victimhood and vulnerability. However,

Said reminds us in *The Politics of Dispossession* (1994) that 'the question to be asked is… how long are we going to deny that the cries of the people of Gaza… are directly connected to the policies of the Israeli government and not to the cries of the victims of Nazism.'

'Insurrection of subjugated knowledges'

In order to think beyond the objectification of 'the Palestinian' as either victim or terrorist, I want to consider Foucault's notion of the 'insurrection of subjugated knowledges' that he used during his lecture at the Collège de France in 1976 (Foucault [1976] 1980: 81–2).[6] Foucault insists that 'subjugated, local, regional knowledge' that stands in opposition to professionalizing, medicalizing, and state knowledge is the only way of enabling criticism to perform its work. This resonates with Goldberg's insistence that the racial state encompasses the potentialities of resistance, and Agamben's argument that the state of exception includes a potential right of resistance. While juridical theorists have debated whether the right of resistance should be inserted into the constitution, Walter Benjamin's and Frantz Fanon's theorizations of violence help us think the Palestinian subject not merely as *homo sacer*, but rather as active resistant staging an 'insurrection of subjugated knowledges' through both theory and practice.

In *Black Skin, White Masks* (1952) Fanon introduces the idea of the internalization of blackness by the black subject in a racist society, through dehumanization, invisibility and lived experience. Not content with constructing a history or an identity of the black subject, Fanon insists on 'lived experience' as the central focus of a politics of resistance (A. Lentin 2006). It is thus not surprising that his later book, *The Wretched of the Earth* (2001 [1961]), written while he was deeply involved in the Algerian struggle, posits violence as a crucial phase of decolonization.

Unlike Audre Lorde's well-rehearsed feminist dictum that 'the master's tools will not destroy the master's house' (2001), Fanon instructs his insurgent readers to use the master's tools to destroy the master's empire, since 'decolonization is always a violent phenomenon'. Fanon recognized that the prolonged establishment of large forces of occupation cannot last and that for the colonized natives the most essential value, because the most concrete, is first and foremost the land (2001: 34). The colonizer's argument, that the colonized understand only force,[7] means that colonial violence aims not only to keep the enslaved at arm's length, but also to dehumanize them. The settler's preoccupation with security reminds the native out loud that he alone is master. As a result, 'the settler keeps alive in the native an anger which he deprives of outlet; the native is trapped in the tight links of the chains of colonialism...' But the native's muscular tension finds its outlet in bloodthirsty explosions. 'Thus collective auto-destruction in a very concrete form is one of the ways in which the native's muscular tension is set free' (2001: 42), because violence, according to Fanon, leads not only to trauma and hence submission, but also to the colonized making violence their own: 'by their ever present desire to kill us... they have become men', according to Sartre's preface. As the colonist army becomes ferocious, as the country is marked out and there are mopping up operations, transfers of population, reprisal expeditions, and massacres of women and children, the colonized – becoming the child of violence – draws from violence his humanity' (Sartre 2001: 20). The colonized, according to Fanon, 'of whom they have never stopped saying that the only language he understands is that of force, decides to give utterance by force. Indeed, the argument the native chooses has been furnished by the settler, and by an ironic turning of the tables it is the native who now affirms that the colonialist understands nothing but force...' (Fanon 1970: 15–16; see also Abdo in this volume). As Europe and the West benefit from colonialism, the humanitarian chatter of the liberal intellectual obscures the fact that the European has only been able to 'become a man' through rendering the colonized slaves and monsters.

Fanon had probably not read Walter Benjamin's essay 'Critique of violence' (2004), which influenced Schmitt's work on the state of exception. According to Benjamin, the law cannot tolerate the existence of violence outside the law: 'if violence is also assured a reality outside the law, as pure immediate violence, this furnishes proof that revolutionary violence – which is the name for the highest manifestation of pure violence by man – is also possible' (2004: 252). Schmitt refutes Benjamin's notion of 'pure violence' as entirely outside the law, arguing instead that in the state of exception it is included in the law through its very exclusion. Schmitt's response to Benjamin proposes the state of exception as a figure that neither makes nor preserves the law, but suspends it (Agamben 2005: 54). However, according to Benjamin, it is precisely 'pure violence', that is violence which stands outside the

law, which is appropriated for the benefit of the sovereign by the declaration of a state of emergency, or a state of exception.

Fanon produces the colonized viewpoint in the spirit of the very
same 'revolutionary violence' that Benjamin speaks of: the colonial
sovereign declares a state of emergency, positioning himself outside the
law, while remaining the very incarnation of the law itself. But if the
colonial sovereign makes the state of exception a paradigm of the
normal – blurring exception and the law – there is little point in
obeying that law. Shenhav's postcolonial reading suggests that Fanon
enables us to locate the missing piece in the current European debate
about the state of exception.

Despite its usefulness, I want to go beyond Shenhav's postcolonial
argument that inserting 'vacuums of sovereignty in the colonies'
creates patchy sets of ad hoc, extra-territorial legal arrangements,
making the state of exception the paradigm of occupation. My
argument is that if we read the State of Israel as a racial state, established
in order to re-affirm the superiority of 'the Jew' over 'the (Palestinian)
native', reading Palestine as a state of exception (in terms of 'condition'
rather than 'nation-state') allows us to re-invest the Palestinian subject
with the potentiality of the 'insurrection of subjugated knowledges',
which includes, inter alia, violent resistance to colonial oppression as a
means of re-assuming subjecthood. While hugely disturbing for those
contemplating the arbitrariness of armed resistance, and for the victims
of such resistance, this reading makes way for discursive and interpretative control by Palestinian subjects who, even in empathetic readings,
have hitherto been theorized largely as mere victims, or 'bare life'.
That such a reading is no longer acceptable is evidenced, inter alia, in
the recent 'future vision' documents published in 2007 by leading
Israeli Palestinian organizations, calling for the abolition of the Jewish
character of the state, which, their authors argue, stands in the way of
their equality (see e.g., Ghanem 2007; and Pappe in this volume).[8]

In Edward Said's introduction to *The Question of Palestine* he articu-
lates his aim to put forward a representative Palestinian position,
'something not well known … even now, where there is so much talk
of the Palestinians and of the Palestinian problem' (Said 1980: xi). This
could have been written today, as talk of the 'Palestinian question' is
often limited to the 1967 occupation, and subsumed by the broader
neo-imperialist discourse of the 'new Middle East', and as the West (and
Israel) opt to empower the Fatah-led Palestinian Authority while

ignoring the elected Hamas government. On the fortieth anniversary of the 1967 war, Samera Esmeir calls for the reintroduction of 'the question of Palestine' by remembering that the 1967 occupation is but the latest cycle of occupation: 'although in many official narratives Israel uses the term "occupation" for the 1948 events, this has been largely omitted from the international vocabulary, legitimating the existence of the state of Israel and erasing the violence of its establishment' (Esmeir 2007).

Said bases *The Question of Palestine* on what he calls the Palestinian experience, which, he argues, 'became a self-conscious experience when the first wave of Zionist colonialists reached the shores of Palestine in the early 1880s' (Said 1980: x). Despite what he identifies as Palestinian weaknesses and failings as a people, and their inability to interest the West in the justice of their cause, Said identifies, already in the late 1970s, Palestinians constructing a political identity and will of their own. Furthermore, despite their geographic dispersal and fragmentation, Palestinians have achieved a degree of unity, because, as Said sees it, 'the Palestinian *idea* (which we have articulated out of our own experience of dispossession and exclusionary oppression) has a coherence to which we have all responded with positive enthusiasm' (Said 1980: x). This Palestinian idea, which relies by no means merely or even mostly on violent resistance, can be theorized – in that theorization is never closed or final but rather open-ended – as arising out of what Foucault calls 'the insurrection of subjugated knowledges' and of what Fanon calls 'lived experience', as is argued by the contributors to this volume.

The book

While offering original theoretical approaches to thinking Palestine, all the contributors to this collection – Palestinians, Israelis and internationals – are also politically committed to Palestinian liberation, beyond the currently advocated two-state solution (see Lentin 2005a, for discussions of the one-state solution), and to thinking 'the Palestinian' as active agent.

The book is divided into three parts: the first premised on Goldberg's concept of the racial state, the second developing and debating the notion of thinking Palestine along Agamben's theorization of the state of exception, and the third discussing some contemporary representations of Palestine.

In the first part, centring on the palestinianization of race, Goldberg develops his argument that all modern nation-states are 'racial states', each in its own way, to discuss first Israeli 'racial historicism' in presenting itself as modernizing in opposition to Palestinian pre-modernity. He then posits 'racial palestinianization', based on a 'revulsion and repulsion related to dispositions of abjection, horror, hatred, anger, inferiorization'. Racial palestinianization, he insists in the spirit of Foucault and Agamben, is the prevailing response to a state of perpetual war. Indeed, it *is* a state of war declared perpetual, a war made the normal state of affairs, enabling a state of emergency and suspending all rights for the target population. Goldberg's argument that Palestinians are treated by Israel not *as if* a racial group, not simply *in the manner* of a racial group, but *as* a despised and demonic racial group, puts paid to the theorization, by Yiftachel and others, of Israeli schisms as merely 'ethnic', an argument that considers 'race' to be ultimately biological.

Bhattacharyya develops the argument of the palestinianization of race to think of the contemporary impact of Israeli representations of terrorism on the politics of 'race' in Britain and other places. Her chapter considers the central role played by the figure of Palestinian terrorism in policy relating to the 'war on terror', the transferral of Palestinianized conceptions of minority communities into the racial politics of Britain and other European nations, and the convergence of renewed state racisms and participation in the 'war on terror'.

The second part of the book, which takes Agamben's 'state of exception' as its starting point, begins with Ghanim, who develops Foucault's notion of biopower, developed to analyse population management in the modern European nation-state, to suggest biopower's opposite – thanatopower – as the appropriate conceptual frame for understanding the management of colonized occupied spaces and subjugated populations. Ghanim posits thanatopower putting Palestinian activists and political leaders to death through targeted assassinations. In its more subtle form it exposes the Palestinians to the ongoing destructive power of the occupier through closures, curfews, the destruction of cultivated fields and agricultural lands, the bombing of cities and populated neighbourhoods, the operating of bypass roads and the separation by spaces of Palestinians and Jewish settlers. Following the second Intifada, Ghanim argues, the imaginative geography of these spaces of exception was activated through the construction of physical systems that include the construction of the Separation Wall, the establishment of permanent and temporary checkpoints and other obstacles that mark the Occupied Territories[9] as 'abnormal spaces', the antithesis of Israeli 'normal space'.

Hanafi's chapter takes the notion of the space of exception further to posit the refugee camps in Lebanon not only as a space of exception but also as an experimental laboratory for control and surveillance by several actors involved in the different modes of governance, who have been contributing to the suspension of this space under the cover of the law. Besides the Lebanese authorities, these actors include the PLO and the United Nations Refugee and Works Agency for Palestine Refugees in the Near East (UNRWA), but also Islamist groups and different local political commissars. While Hanafi differentiates between closed and open refugee camps, suggesting that the camp setting as a closed space is not a 'natural' setting but rather has its *raison d'être* in disciplinary power, control and surveillance, and in deploying the state of exception, he also suggests that the camps foster an urban rather than a national Palestinian identity.

Khalili's chapter, also set in Lebanon, focuses on the Ansar detention camp, which, she argues, is a relevant subject of study, not because of its uniqueness as a concretization of the state of emergency (or exception), but rather because of its very familiar ordinariness as an instrument of control. The wide array of the practices used at Ansar was perfected in past colonial settings. In a sense, Ansar was the historic outcome of a whole series of strategies of counterinsurgency, institutions of domination, and technologies of control perfected through decades of colonial rule, beginning in the late nineteenth century. Khalili concludes by arguing that philosophical discussions which see sovereign power over life and death replaced gradually by disciplinary power often obscure the fact that relocating the site of power beyond a state's own borders, as in the case of the Ansar zone of exception, ultimately enables the state to designate people outside the law, and to effectively appropriate liminal territories through re-definitions of sovereignty, which give agency to powerful colonial/imperial actors.

Drawing on the conceptual differences between prison and ghetto, Korn's chapter theorizes the Palestinian territory as a ghetto. Using the Oslo process as a turning point, she argues that from then onward a dominant form of Israeli control of the population of occupied Palestine has emerged, including ghettoization, spatial confinement and restriction of Palestinians to their villages and towns. This concept of ghettoization is understood against a backdrop of the decrease in the use of Israeli prisons and of mass incarceration to assure efficient control.

The debate on the applicability of Agamben's state of exception paradigm becomes acute in the chapters by Zreik and Pappe. While Zreik's highly theoretical chapter takes the State of Israel as an example of the state of exception, Pappe argues against the applicability of Agamben's model, positing Israel instead as a *mukhabarat* (security) state of oppression. Zreik argues that although Israel is an extreme case, it does nevertheless fall within Agamben's paradigm, and his chapter aims both to read the case of Israel in light of the paradigm and to read the paradigm in light of the case of Israel. Tracing the genealogy of the relation of rule and exception, fact and norm, chaos and order, Zreik first draws attention to the dark side of the modern liberal constitutional state, and then discusses Israeli constitutionalism in light of the nature of the 'state of exception'. In not wishing to conceal its (exclusively Jewish) ethnic nature, Israel did not manage to push the exception to the margins. As a result, what surfaces in other countries only in cases of national emergency appears in Israel on an almost daily basis. The persistence of the exception in Israel, the ongoing state of emergency, the violent moment of birth, and the persistence of its ethnic nature are features that one might find in some countries at some points in time. Israel is unique in that all of them are present within it most of the time.

Pappe, however, argues that although the dark side of democracy as described by Agamben seems to prevail everywhere in the oppressive Jewish state, including doomsday scenarios of persons stripped of any human or civil rights, the rule of emergency regulations and the overall state of siege, Israel cannot be theorized as or in a state of exception because its very inclusion within the parameters of this debate assumes that Israel belongs to the family of western liberal democracies dangerously deteriorating to the abyss dreaded by Agamben. Instead, Pappe posits Israel as a *mukhabarat* state of oppression, which exists mostly within the Arab world, characterized as a mass mobilizing state, run by an all-pervasive bureaucracy and ruled by military and security apparatuses. Pappe extends the analysis of Israel as a militarist state to the state within the State of Israel: the state of the Palestinians within the Jewish state. This, however, is a hybrid with another model, the settler-colonial state, which can be presented as a mixture between an Arab postcolonial model and a colonialist model such as South Africa during Apartheid, rather than as Agamben's western democracy descending into a state of exception.

The final part of the book concerns some contested representations of Palestine. Agamben, as argued by Hanafi, falls short of addressing the agency of the actor resisting the 'total institution', conceiving the camp as a paradigmatic place of modernity, using concentration camps such as Auschwitz as examples. Likewise, Agamben also fails to address the gendered implications of *homo sacer,* which, in view of his emphasis on the link between 'birth' and 'nation', I have termed elsewhere *femina sacra* (Lentin 2005b). In this book, Ghanim's chapter uses the gendered example of a Palestinian woman about to give birth at an Israeli check-point to discuss Palestine as state of exception. Abdo's chapter, based on interviews with female Palestinian resistance fighters, or *munadelat,* challenges the representation of Palestinian women by western feminists as 'uneducated', 'powerless', 'controlled by their men' and 'willing to die and be rewarded in the after-life in Paradise'. Using Palestinian women's own voices, experiences and narratives, Abdo powerfully explores the role played by the colonial state (Israel) in promoting Palestinian women's racialization with the aim of contributing to de-orientalizing and de-racializing Palestinian *munadelat* (see also Shalhoub-Kevorkian 2005a, 2005b).

Landy's and Lentin's chapters centre on the representations of Palestine by its western and Israeli supporters: in Landy's chapter, participants in activist tourism, and in Lentin's, Israelis dedicated to commemorating the Palestinian Nakba in Hebrew. Both chapters, each in its own way, suggest a degree of appropriation and silencing of 'the Palestinian' as active agent of Palestinian experience. Landy's chapter examines the representations made by activist study tours and their effect on participants' understanding and future activism. The representations these study tours make of Israel, Palestine and the participants themselves are important in framing political discourse in the Palestinian solidarity movements in Europe and America. While these tours succeed in their central aim of granting agency to foreign activists to speak in favour of Palestinian rights, the means by which study tours enable them to speak out may at the same time work to silence Palestinian subjectivity. Lentin's chapter locates the Nakba as a specific site of contested commemoration through an exploration of *Zochrot,* whose activities include 'Hebraicizing' the Nakba by creating a space for it in the written, spoken and public discourse of Hebrew Israel, and promoting an 'alternative discourse on memory'. Lentin asks whether *Zochrot* ultimately appropriates Palestinian memory and perpetuates

Palestinian victimhood, a position most Palestinians reject. The two chapters question whether both activist tourism and *Zochrot*'s activities serve in some ways to efface the Palestinian right of return, which, in the case of the former, goes largely unmentioned, and in the case of the latter remains on the level of the symbolic.

The final two chapters offer two further angles on the contested representations of Palestine in today's world. McCarthy's chapter is a detailed exploration of the attitude of the foremost Palestinian thinker, Edward Said, to the state, both in his literary-cultural work and in his more directly political work on Palestine. Importantly, McCarthy reminds us, Said was at different times an advocate both of the two-state solution to the Israel–Palestine conflict and of the bi-national state solution, famously saying that he wished to argue for the setting up of a Palestinian state, and that he would be its first critic.

Al-Hardan's chapter re-affirms Palestinian subjectivity in being articulated from her own 'Palestinian Arab ontological displacement and erasure, dual when gendered, which is only evident if rescued from the margins by the woman-narrator of an embodied, "situated knowledge"'. The chapter is a comparative historical study of the contemporary discourse on Palestine at the highest echelons of world power, as heir to a discourse born out of a specific Western European historical experience and world-view. Its justifications for the domination of Palestine, al-Hardan argues, manifested in the 1917 British occupation, continue to serve the exclusive colonial-settler Zionist Jewish rule at the expense of the indigenous Palestinian population.

Omar Barghouti (2005) argues that by constructing the Palestinians as 'relatively human', Israel, supported by the USA and other world powers, has managed to get away with its taken-for-granted assumption that the Palestinians cannot have equal needs, aspirations, or rights with Israeli Jews. This collection, through the political, but also theoretical, commitment of its contributors, is a step towards reversing this relative humanization and recognizing that the 'moral Palestinian challenge to their colonial existence' is not an existential threat for Israelis but rather 'a magnanimous invitation to dismantle the colonial character of the state' (Barghouti 2005: 43).

Notes

1 My thanks to Anaheed al-Hardan, Alina Korn and David Landy for their helpful comments.

2 Arthur Ruppin, director of the 'Erez Israel office', and Zionism's main 'colonizator', preached eugenicist selection of the racially dominant old-new Jewish 'human material' in the Zionist settlement of Palestine. Ruppin, who, like other race hygienicists, believed the state had a central role in 'improving the race' of the *Volk*, was instrumental in producing a Zionist repertoire of racial categories and *volkist* imagery (Bloom 2007).

3 But also of Arab Jews, see e.g., Shohat 2001; Shenhav 2003.

4 It is unclear why they were allowed to stay, some stayed because of local arrangements, some because they collaborated, others because it was not always possible to complete the expulsion (Pappe 2006).

5 Typically, the Israeli 'new historian' Benny Morris writes, in an article on Zionist historiography: 'In 1948 most of the Arabs were transferred from the new Israeli state… The transfer was *not premeditated or the result of a master plan*, as argued by Arab spokespersons later… but there is no doubt that the idea of transfer existed in the minds of the *Yishuv* leaders (headed by Ben Gurion) and the army commanders' (Morris 2000: 43, my emphasis).

6 My thanks to Festus Ikeotuonye for drawing my attention to this concept.

7 In 1956, the FLN's famous leaflet argued that 'colonialism only loosens its hold when the knife is at its throat' (Fanon 2001: 48).

8 For an Israeli Jewish response, arguing against the call to alter the exclusively Jewish nature of the State of Israel, see e.g., Saguy and Stern 2007.

9 Hanafi insists on terming the territory occupied by Israel in 1967 in the singular as 'occupied territory', while most contributors stick to the plural form.

References

Abdo, N. and R. Lentin (eds) (2002) *Women and the Politics of Military Confrontation: Palestinian and Israeli Gendered Narratives of Dislocation*, Berghahn Books, Oxford and New York

Agamben, G. (1998) *Homo Sacer: Sovereign Power and Bare Life*. Stanford University Press, Stanford

Agamben, G. (2005) *State of Exception*, University of Chicago Press, Chicago

Barghouti, O. (2005) 'Relative humanity: The fundamental obstacle to a secular democratic state solution', *Race Traitor*, no. 16, 24–48

Benjamin, W. (2004) 'Critique of violence', in M. Bullock and M. W. Jennings (eds) *Selected Writings, Vol. 1, 1913–1926*, Belknap, Cambridge, Mass.

Bloom, E. (2007) 'The German origins of Hebrew culture: On obscuring the nationalist role of Arthur Ruppin, "the father of the Jewish settlement in Erez Israel"', *Mita'am*, no. 11, 71–93

Burleigh, M. and W. Wipperman (1999) 'The racial state', in M. Bulmer and J. Solomos (eds) *Racism*, Oxford University Press, Oxford

Esmeir, S. (2007) 'Returning the question of Palestine', *Machsom*, 8 June 2007, «www.mahsom.com/article.php?id=5518»

Falk, R. (2006) *Zionism and the Biology of the Jews,* Resling, Tel Aviv

Fanon, F. (1970) *A Dying Colonialism,* Penguin Books, Harmondsworth

Fanon, F. (1986 [1952]) *Black Skin, White Masks,* Pluto Press, London

Fanon, F. (2001 [1961]) *The Wretched of the Earth,* Penguin, London

Foucault, M. (1980 ([1976]) 'Lecture One: 7 January 1976', in C. Gordon (ed.) *Power/Knowledge: Selected Interviews and Other Writings, 1972–1977,* Harvester Press, Brighton

Foucault, M. (1990) *The History of Sexuality, Vol. I: The Will to Knowledge,* Penguin, London

Foucault, M. (2003) *Society Must be Defended: Lectures at the Collège de France, 1975–76,* Allen Lane, London

Ghanem, A. (2007) 'The Arab constitution', *Ha'aretz,* 14 March 2007

Ghanim, H. (2005) 'Thanatopolitics: Dialectics of life and death under occupation', *Theory and Criticism,* Vol. 27, 181–6

Goldberg, D. T. (2002) *The Racial State,* Blackwell, Oxford

Goldberg, D. T. (2005) 'Racial Americanization', in K. Murji and J. Solomos (eds) *Racialization: Studies in Theory and Practice,* Oxford University Press, Oxford

Hanafi, S. (2005) 'Spacio-cide and bio-politics: The Israeli colonial conflict from 1947 to the Wall', in M. Sorkin (ed.) *Against the Wall,* The New Press, New York

Kimmerling, B. (1993) 'Patterns of militarism in Israel', *European Journal of Sociology,* no. 34, 196–223.

Lentin, A. (2006) 'De-authenticating Fanon: Self-organised anti-racism and the politics of experience', in A. Lentin and R. Lentin (eds) *Race and State,* Cambridge Scholars Press, Newcastle

Lentin, R. (ed.) (2005a) Special issue on Palestine, *Race Traitor,* no. 16

Lentin, R. (2005b) *'Femina Sacra:* Gendered memory and political violence', *Women's Studies International Forum,* Vol. 29, no. 5, 463–73

Lomsky-Feder, E. and E. Ben-Ari (eds) (1999) *The Military and Militarism in Israeli Society,* SUNI Press, Albany

Lorde, A. (2001) 'The master's tools will never dismantle the master's house', in K. Bhavnani (ed) *Feminism and 'Race',* Oxford University Press, Oxford

Morris, B. (2000) *Jews and Arabs in Palestine/Israel 1936–1956,* Am Oved, Tel Aviv.

Pappe, I. (2006) *The Ethnic Cleansing of Palestine,* Oneworld Publications, Oxford

Rabinowicz, D. (1998) *Anthropology and the Palestinians,* Institute for Israeli-Arab Studies, Ra'anana

Sabagh-Khori, A. and N. Sultany (2003) *Resisting Hegemony: The Azmi Bishara Trial,* Mada al-Carmel, Haifa

Saguy, A. and Y. Stern (2007) 'In the land of Israel the Jewish nation was established', *Ha'aretz,* 6 April 2007

Said, E. (1980 [1978]) *Orientalism,* Routledge and Kegan Paul, London

Said, E. (1980) *The Question of Palestine,* Times Books, New York

Said, E. (1994) *The Politics of Dispossession: The Struggle for Palestinian Self-Determination, 1969–1994,* Chatto and Windus, London

Sartre, J. P. (2001 [1961]) 'Preface', in F. Fanon, *The Wretched of the Earth,* Penguin, London

Schmitt, C. (2005) *Political Theology: Four Chapters on the Concept of Sovereignty,* University of Chicago Press, Chicago

Shalhoub-Kevorkian, N. (2005a) 'Voice therapy for women aligned with political prisoners: A case study of trauma among Palestinian women in the second *Intifada'*, *Social Service Review,* University of Chicago Press, Chicago

Shalhoub-Kevorkian, N. (2005b) 'Counter-spaces as resistance in conflict zones: Palestinian women recreating a home', *Journal of Feminist Family Therapy,* Vol. 17, no. 3/4, 109–41

Shenhav, Y. (2003) *The Arab-Jews: Nationalism, Religion and Ethnicity,* Am Oved, Tel Aviv

Shenhav, Y. (2006) 'The imperial history of "state of exception"', *Theory and Criticism,* no. 29, 205–18

Shohat, E. (2001) *Forbidden Memories: Towards Multicultural Thinking,* Bimat Kedem Lesifrut, Tel Aviv

Yegenoglu, M. (1998) *Colonial Fantasies: Towards a Feminist Reading of Orientalism,* Cambridge University Press, Cambridge

Yiftachel, O. (2006) *Ethnocracy: Land and Identity Politics in Israel/Palestine,* University of Pennsylvania Press, Philadelphia

PART I
The Palestinianization of Race

David Theo Goldberg

1 Racial Palestinianization

For Tanya Reinhart
1943–2007

Palestinians as a people, and Arabs more generally, regionally first emerged as a pan-national self-identification in *modern* terms in the earlier decades of the twentieth century as expressions of anti-colonial and autonomous sensibilities, interests, and commitments. The heterogeneity among Arabs living throughout the region sought a more cohering identity in the face of intensifying British and French colonization after World War One, the discovery of large holdings of oil, growing anti-colonial movements in Africa and Asia and ultimately the founding of Israel. The name 'Palestine' was reinvoked by the British in the early 1920s upon receiving a League of Nations mandate to rule over the territory after Ottoman imperial control in the late nineteenth century had folded it into the southern extension of Syria.

Thus British modernization, as Salim Tamari has pointed out (1999), transformed a complexly secular, cosmopolitan, broadly communitarian order under Ottoman rule – especially in cities such as Jerusalem and ports such as Jaffa and Haifa (but also more regionally in Beirut and Damascus) – into a more segregating, ethnoracially and religiously discrete and divided set of communities in contest with each other for resources, space, and political favour; in other words, classic colonial divide and rule, ethnoracially fuelled. This regional transformation of heterogeneity into the logos of an assertedly homogeneous ethnoracial ethnoraciality is what I trace here in the name of racial palestinianization.

Producing racial palestinianization

Israel was an anomaly at its founding, reflecting conflicting logics of world historical events between which its declarative moment was awkwardly wedged. On the one hand, it mimicked rather than properly mirrored the logics of independence fuelled by decolonizing movements, though perhaps curiously closer in some crucial ways to Pakistan than, say, to India or other decolonizing societies of the day. On the other hand, it embodied *in potential*, by the structural conditions of its very formation, *some* key features of what was coterminously emerging as the apartheid state. In what follows, I am less identifying Israel as representing the apartheid state as tracing the ways in which, in conception and practice, it has come not just to embody apartheid elements but to represent a novel form of the racial state more generally.

In the latter spirit, Palestinians were the indigenous inhabitants of Palestine. They were indigenous in the sense of being 'found' in the area, both by the nineteenth-century colonizing powers and by the increasing convergence of Zionist-inspired Jews in the territory after the Balfour Declaration of 1917, and especially in the wake of World War Two. Identified as the direct kin of biblical Philistines, Palestinians as a people were often seen as philistines as much in characterization as in scriptural name, conceived in the representational struggles as bloodthirsty and warmongering, constantly harassing modern-day Israelites, debauched and lacking in liberal culture. Terrorists, it seems, historically all the way down to the toe-nails of time, Goliath cut to size by David's perennial craftiness and military prowess.

Israel came to be seen as an exemplary instance of what Michel Foucault, though in a different context, memorably has called 'counter-history' (2003), as a historical narrative of insurrection, against the grain, establishing itself in the face of formidable and threatening power directed against it. Israel is forged out of a 'biblical history of servitude and exiles', as a 'history of insurrections' against state-imposed or -sanctioned injustices. In this, Israel held out hope and the promise of justice. Its founding narration, in short, is a complex of the history of struggles (Foucault uses the term 'race wars' but it is clear from the examples he cites that he really has in mind group, even class, struggles) in which Jews were invariably the quintessential pariah, they who did not belong, but mixed with the civilizing European imperative, the white man's burden, of what I have elsewhere characterized as 'racial historicism' (Goldberg 2002).

Moses Hess, important for introducing Engels to the socialist fold and one of the first to articulate the Zionist vision, implored 'the Jewish race' in 1862 to

> be the bearers of civilization to peoples who are still inexperienced and their teachers in the European sciences, to which your race has contributed so much. . . . [Jews are to be] mediators between Europe and far Asia, opening the roads that lead to India and China – those unknown regions which must ultimately be thrown open to civilization... [Jewish] labour and industry [in Palestine] will turn the ancient soil into fruitful valleys, reclaiming it from the encroaching sands of the desert (Hess 1995 [1862]).

Theodor Herzl, the father figure of the Zionist social movement, concurred: 'The immigration of Jews signifies an unhoped-for accession of strength for the land which is now so poor; in fact, for the whole Ottoman Empire' (1997 [1897]). The Zionist vision for Israel, as Ella Shohat has remarked (2003), represents the modernizing imperative in a region seen as still marked by the biblical backwardness of its Arab inhabitants.

Israel, it is accordingly apparent, has been thought of – has thought of itself in part precisely – from its initiating modern conception explicitly as racially configured, as racially representative. And those insistent racial traces persist despite the post-Holocaust European repression of the use of race as social self-reference or -representation. In this, as much as any other modernizing state, Israel has been caught in the race-making web of modernizing statehood. States assume their modernity, as I have argued in *The Racial State* (2002), through racial articulation. Israel is a modern racial state knotted with and in constitutive contrast to the pre-history of Palestinian antiquity, of its historicized racial immaturity. Israel represents modernization, progress, industry and industriousness, looking to the bright future, the civilizing mission of the best that has been thought and could be taught. Palestine represents the past, failed effort if effort at all, antique land still tilled by hand and the perennial failure of governance, a place constantly in the grip of its time past and passed. The larger relational condition, a state racially characterizing itself in its founding self-representation, is one in which the state of the latter, materially as much as metaphorically, is fuelled by the racially conceived, tinged (one might say singed) imposition of the former.

But this civilizing mission and self-determining drive thus initiated through Jews in the name of European civilization is one with a twist. Israel was forged, of course, in the fire and fury of all those migrations, the experiences of expulsions and exiles, arrivals and startings over, assimilations and abject evictions, wrongful convictions and threatened extinctions. The war of races in which the Jew is the hounded, the perennial foe and fugitive, becomes in Israel's founding a protracted conflict in which the Jewish state, Herzl's dream, is turned into oppressor, victimizer, and sovereign. Vulnerable, victim, and vanquished become pursuer, perpetrator, predator. The state is transformed, as Foucault says, into protector of the integrity, superiority, and more or less purity of the homogenizing group, what Foucault marks as 'the race'. State sovereignty defends itself above all else so as to secure the group, its ethnoraciality, to protect its purity, perpetuity, and power, for which it takes itself to exist and which it seeks to represent.

Despite debatable stories of early Zionist settlers driven by socialist ideals of peaceful coexistence with local Arabs on land commonly tilled and towns cohabited, by the early 1970s Golda Meir could claim rhetorically that the Palestinian people did not exist. Romantic coexistence in these parts has always gone arm in arm with assertive claims to territorial and political sovereignty, on both sides of the conflict. In Israel's triumphant War of Independence (what Palestinians characterize as *al-nakba*, their catastrophe), Israeli gains expanded the territory ceded it by the original 1947 UN Partition Resolution by almost one-third, widening its cartographic waistline, evicting 750,000 of the 850,000 or so Arabs living within enlarged Israel in order to ensure a Jewish majority. The moral qualms over eviction-driven expansion are well characterized in Israeli novelist Yizhar Smilansky's short story depicting the Sartrean dilemma faced by a young soldier caught between executing evicted Arab villagers and contributing to securing Israel's infant existence (1990). That dilemma seems now to have been resolved overwhelmingly in favour of the latter's national prerogative.

In short, since the earliest Zionist settlement, and intensifying with the declaration of Israeli independence in 1948, a dominant faction of the Israeli political establishment has been committed not simply to denying Palestinian existence, but to making the claim true, acting in its name and on its terms. An Israeli military planning document, known as Plan D (or Plan *Dalet*), formulated in the run-up to Israel's War of Independence in May–June 1948, sought 'destruction of [Arab] villages by fire explosives and mining' after the villages had been surrounded and searched, and resistance destroyed, and 'expelling the population beyond the boundaries of the State' (Benvenisti 2003; Pappe 2004; Pappe 2006).

Under Arafat, of course, Palestinians not only asserted a coherent identity, but sought to reciprocate that denial: the State of Israel does not, should not, exist. But however duplicitous and dirty-handed the Palestinian patriarch, and however rhetorically insistent concerning Israel's denial and demise, it is a whole lot more difficult, it would seem, to activate denial of the existence of one whose semi-automatic is at your nose than it is to insist that a stateless people, a nation of refugees on its own land, has no rights. It is not that might makes right in this case; it is that might manufactures the conditions and parameters, the terms, of political, and by extension historical and representational possibility.

Meron Benvenisti (2003) reports that something like 200 Arab villages were abandoned in May 1948, and another 60 in June. By the time the dust had settled, nearly half a million Palestinians had been reduced to refugees, fleeing expanded Israel, never to be allowed to return. Israel came into being, came to be, by virtue both of Jews staring at their own individual and collective extinction and of Palestine's constriction, if not cessation, at least of its realization, if not of its idea. The latter's deathly denial, rationalized in the name of the former, is as much a part of Israel's history as it is repressed, if not excised from, its official record. It is this tension between denial and repression that fuels Israel's sense of Palestine, and so, also, of itself.

There is a sharp distinction, often lost, between the notion of self-hating Jew and that of self-critical Jew. To criticize Israel as a state formation, and the Israeli state and governmental policies as enacting particularly vicious expressions of humiliation, dehumanization, and degradation, as Judith Butler has pointed out (2003), emphatically counts as the latter without amounting to the former. To criticize the government of Israel and its policies, even to criticize the partial grounds on which that state was founded, is not to criticize Jews as such, nor is it to place Jews anywhere and everywhere at risk, notwithstanding the spike in antisemitic attacks in the likes of France. It is not even to place Jews in Israel at risk. Quite the contrary; it is to point out the way in which such policies and governmentality manifest the very insecurity they claim to undo.

That there remains always the possibility of an Israeli government that does not discriminate against its own Arab citizens and Palestinian non-citizens, as numerous courageous groups and individuals within Israel itself are working under very trying conditions to secure, means that criticism of Israeli state policy and actions need not be – and often is not – antisemitic. Likewise, to make out an argument for one non-ethnoracially configured state incorporating Jews and Palestinians, among others, is not to call for the demise of Jews or the dissolution of Jewry. There are even some radical Jewish Old Testament literalists who call for ending Israel as we know it in favour of reinscribing some originary biblical formation; and while we might call them crazy, I have never heard them characterized as antisemitic.

To put it thus implicates Jews qua Jewishness as much in the necessity of critiquing the injustices in which the Israeli state engages as the refusal to criticize. More pressingly, the insistence that there be no such critique implicates silent and silenced Jews anywhere in that state's persistent injustices. This is a particularly knotted, if not inverted, expression of the traditional tensions between universalism and particularity, selfhood and alterity, strangeness and alienation.

As the self-anointed Chosen People, Jews are the objects at once of envy and scorn. Jews' 'right of return' is magically drawn into a landscape apparently never abandoned, while the Palestinian 'right of return' is buried in the rubble of a landscape to which they assertedly never laid claim and from which they have recently been exorcized, their homes bulldozed away, their right to live, to *be*, in either Palestine or Israel always in question, under threat, uncertain, no matter how deep any ancestral, familial claim.

The 'right of return' presupposes a belonging, a longing to be, a sense of security in a common place uniquely and always *ours*, a security coterminously common and false. For if all Jews were indeed to avail of 'return' it would be easier today to wipe Israel out with one blast, and with it all Jews, than it could have been under the Final Solution. The project of homogeneity, the artifice, the labour to realize in its name a state of homogenized commonality, of familiality and familiarity, constitute coterminously the ultimate threat to the group's existence.

Consequently, religious interest groups in Israel and other supporters elsewhere of a restrictively ethno-homogenous Israel are concerned to control the conception and administration of 'the true and pure Jew', a commitment logically not that far removed in the end from the likes of the De Rooij 'one drop rule.' *This* idea of Israel requires the 'Palestinian problem' to justify itself as the *Jewish* state, much as Germans required the racial logics of 'the Jewish problem' and America 'the Negro problem' to constitute themselves as self-projectedly homogeneous. In the face of its own increasingly radically Jewish heterogeneity – radically Jewish and radically heterogeneous – and so in the face of its own internal implosion, Israel seeks its familial artifice by projecting a threat within and purged to its shifting and shifted boundaries, at once within and without. From its earliest formative conception, a dominant order of Zionism articulated 'the Jewish race' as creating coherence, artificing initially discursive homogeneity of and for 'the Jewish people' in the face of a scattered and diffuse 'nation'. At the risk of dramatic over-generalization, if homogeneity tends to humiliate, heterogeneity tends to humble.

Israelis thus now require the Philistine, as Sartre (1948) once said about the Jew himself in France: if he didn't exist, he would have to be invented, as indeed he has been. *He* has been: for the figure of the Palestinian, of the threatening suicide bomber, of a refugee rabble reducible to rubble, is overwhelmingly male, supported by women considered, unlike their military-serving Israeli counterparts, too weak and too late to do anything about it. If men suffer for the state, or for the nationalist idea of one, women suffer more immediately for men martyred to the nationalist mandate or sacrificing and sacrificed to state security, and for the families they are left to feed, materially and spiritually. Few women walk the streets of the Territories, on either side of the catastrophe, of 'the Troubles', to borrow a telling phrase from another not so distant time and place.

The project of Israel accordingly became the materialization of this homogenizing fabric. Israel cannot live with the Palestinians, purging them persistently from green-line Israel, but cannot live without them, conceptually as much as materially, existentially as much as emotionally. No longer as dependent on Palestinian labour as a result of importing other others – Filipinos, Romanians, Thais – to do the dirty work for a pittance, the Israelis nevertheless need Palestinians to command militarization, American support and weaponry, even its own sense of victimized self. And the presence of Filipinos and Thais likewise makes it possible for Israelis to think of Israel as cosmopolitan, as an ethnically heterogeneous late modern state evidenced by the ready availability of Asian food. Middle Eastern cuisine no longer dominates Israeli eating culture as it once did, especially in the larger cities and hyper-modern commercial strips of the residential suburbs.

Israeli armed forces in the Territories have increasingly strangled the flow of Palestinian goods from one Palestinian town to another, and have decimated and confiscated Palestinian fields for the sake of erecting a security barrier and Separation Wall. The Palestinian Territories beneath Sharon's and his political offspring's boot and vision have suffered more than 50% unemployment, with 60% of the population living below the poverty line (a mere $2 per day). Health problems have spiraled, and securing health care is almost as hazardous as the health condition one might be seeking care to cure (Amnesty International 2003; De Rooij 2004).

Consequently, Israel's current crisis, like the Palestinian one, is as much economic as political, as much about the decimation of Palestinian survival and consumptive capacity as about Israeli self-security. It is a self-exacerbated crisis fed by a complex of factors. These include a contradictory collective egoism, exacerbated by perceived Palestinian intransigence and violence, and underpinned by a return to presumptions of racially conceived Palestinian in- or infra-humanity on one side and insistent Israeli assertiveness on the other. 'All Muslims are murderers,' Israel's deputy cabinet minister, Ze'ev Boim, declared knowingly in 2004 (see Ghanim in this volume). Well, what does that make all Israelis? Israel necessitates for itself the refusal of Palestine's realization, and as that necessity is insisted upon and enacted, it contradictorily fuels the separatist pipe-dream of Palestine, of an independent Palestinian state rather than mutually recognized respect and a common co-existence.

Here, then, is the knotty dilemma facing the region: Israel's sense of self, statehood, and security is predicated on restricting the scope of the same for those from whose landscape of life, loves, and longing the state of Israel was carved. And Palestinian possibilities, the very idea of a coherent Palestinian corpus, of Palestinian national aspirations, acquired a spirit, its very conception, as explicit resistance to and rejection of Israel's stake, at the extreme, of its being as such. They need each other, as perpetual grounds and justification for their own existence as much as they seek to undermine the possibility of the other. It's as though the existence of each is measured by the extent of the other's demise.

Israel is taken as an outpost of European civilization, a frontier of sorts, in an altogether hostile and alien environment. Brothers to Christians, keepers of the faith and holy sites, a flourishing democracy in the land of Christ and region of alien autocratic regimes, a defender against irrationality and irreverence of life surrounded by infidels, a tower of strength and stability fuelling American industry, readers of the same book(s) and lovers of the same culture. Israel is the only state outside of the European continental land mass to participate in the Eurovision Song Contest, for instance. In this scheme of things, it seems, Israel must be European, presumptively white. But in keeping with contemporary racial americanization, with born again racism, Israel's whiteness is transparent, virtual, invisible.

Israelis occupy the structural positions of whiteness in the racial hierarchy of the Middle East. Arabs, accordingly – most notably in the person of Palestinians – are the antithesis, a fact rendering the ambivalent situation of Arab Jews especially troubled, as Ella Shohat has demonstrated (2003). Historically, politically, religiously and culturally, Arabs are neither Jew nor (as such) white.

At the same time, the Arabness of Arab Jews is complexly undercut by their Jewishness. They are popularly referenced as *Mizrahim*, and Yehouda Shenhav (2006) makes evident just how racially indexed such a reference nevertheless remains by pointing out that it literally translates as De Rooij's 'Easterners', itself code for 'Orientals'. He cites Abba Eban, longtime foreign minister (1966–74), warning that 'One of the great apprehensions which afflict us is the danger of the immigrants of Oriental origin forcing Israel to equalize its cultural level with that of the neighbouring world'. In the complex codes of Israel's raceless racial history, *Mizrahim* occupy a status as white but not quite, more so than Palestinian citizens of Israel, but less so than the whiteness, the Europeanness, of Ashkenazis. *Mizrahim* are Israel's 'Coloureds'.

Prior to 1948, Jews living throughout what would become Arab states numbered fewer than one million. Today, that group collectively numbers just 8,000 people, a mere 1% of what it was prior to Israeli statehood. The Arab Jewish population of Israel, by contrast, has grown to almost 40%. They are in significant part de-Arabized (to riff on Shenhav's term) and de-nationalized, in order to be re-nationalized as they are re-oriented, to a degree Zionized, in their pan-ethnicity even as their different national histories disarticulate their respective experiences. But they continue to occupy ambivalent, even anxious status in Israeli socio-economic life – a 'necessary minority', given the country's broader demography, incorporated but significantly poorer and less powerful on every social index, a valuable intelligence commodity, given their ethno-linguistic backgrounds and cultural understandings, as Shenhav's account makes clear. The ambivalence nevertheless runs to the very early days of the state. 'We do not want Israel to become Arab,' declared Israel's first premier, David Ben Gurion. 'We are bound by duty to fight against the spirit of the Levant society' (quoted in Shenhav 2006: 140). Yet, because they are Jews, de-Arabized or not, they are better treated, considered to belong, with more access, rights, and acceptance than non-Jewish Arab Israelis.

Palestinians, by contrast, and especially in the Territories, not unlike Jews in Nazi Germany, have been evicted from what Immanuel Kant famously characterizes as the 'Kingdom of Ends', the moral realm, and so have lost any claim to moral protection. A senior Israeli military officer recently implored Israeli military personnel chillingly to be 'Judeo-Nazis' in order, somewhat ambiguously, 'to beat the Palestinians'. Another officer, even if self-consciously, opined uncannily in the daily press that 'If our job is to seize a densely packed refugee camp or take over the Nablus Casbah ... [we] must above all else analyze and bring together the lessons of past battles, even – shocking though this might appear – to analyze how the German Army operated in the Warsaw Ghetto' (quoted in Ahmad 2002). The term 'Judeo-Nazi,' now readily rhetorically circulated among Palestinian critics of Israel, was actually coined by the late Israeli orthodox philosopher, Yeshayahu Leibowitz, to refer to the behaviour of a group of Israeli soldiers in the wake of the 1967 War. Generally the association of Israel in any way with Nazi practices brings howls of protest, dismissing such references at best as insensitive, at worst as downright antisemitic. It is curious, as a consequence, that having been coined in a critical register initially, it has come, even if tentatively, to be modestly embraced by some as a term of the realm.

In August 2003, Israel introduced a disturbing new law: in the name of security, of not wanting to be overrun demographically, and so of the untouchable Jewish logic of survival, any Arab Israeli citizen marrying a Palestinian would be *required* to move to the Palestinian territories to live, or to leave the country altogether. Ethnoracial purging – deeply connected to but subtly differentiated from ethnic cleansing – is the process of removing, evicting (what Ghada Karmi [2004] calls 'vanishing') almost all Palestinians identified as such from green-line Israel. Since 1967, the Arab population of Jerusalem has declined from 72% to 28%. Palestinians born, bred and residing on property they have long owned within the boundaries of 'Jewish Jerusalem' are declared by the state residents of the West Bank. They may be registered accordingly as 'absentee landlords' in the very houses in which they (illegally) reside, their property subject to confiscation.

Where ethnic cleansing involves wiping a country 'clean' of an identifiable ethnic minority by wiping (many or most of) them out, ethnoracial purging involves forcing a considerable percentage of group members out of the national territory and so of the moral imaginary, moving them further away, outside of national boundaries, more and more into enclosed enclaves, even within what is regarded as their own territory. Radically minoritizing the remainder, ethnoracial purging lies between the national(ist) purification of ethnic cleansing, on one side, and bantu-stanization, on the other. Racial palestinianization provides the prototype – the rationales and representations, the logics and models, in short, the roadmap – for strategic ethnoracial eviction and ethnoracial culling.

Palestinianizing the racial

As Sartre (1948) remarks about antisemitism, so we can observe about palestinianization – that it is not simply an idea or set of ideas but as much a *passion*. Racial palestinianization turns on a revulsion and repulsion related to dispositions of abjection, horror, hatred, anger, inferiorization. The Palestinian's vulgarity and aggression are the source if not the totalization of Israel's woes. Were it not for the Palestinian there would be no terror, no threat, no insecurity, no challenge to Israel's very existence, no recession, no economic burden, no refugee problem, no insecurity regarding demographic swamping, no limit on Jewish settlements in Judea and Samaria. The Holy Land would be complete, unified, God's historical promise fulfilled. But perhaps too there would be no Israel (as we know it)!

Racial palestinianization is thus a conceit about contemporary conditions in terms of a projected past conceived in terms of the politics of the present. The Palestinians are philistines, with philistine values, interests and desires, primitive in the sense of never having evolved beyond ancient whims, drives, capriciousness, viciousness and the irresponsible impulses to which they give rise. The Palestinian is driven by nothing but unprovoked hate and anger, incapable of a higher order of values, of deeper causation, of responsibility as a product of free choice. Palestinianization, like the projection of 'Palestine', in short, is a state of passion, its only rationality purely instrumental, crudely calculated and cruelly calculating, consequential, awe-ful. It is a state in which justification, reasonableness, freedom, and justice are feared, from which they have been expunged.

Racial palestinianization is a projection, then, from arrogance and the racial labour of impotence. It is the disposition that arrogates to itself the source of universal and absolute judgement, ultimately over life and death, the quality of living and dying, over the state and civil society, the conditions of existence and civility. But it is a tenuous self-arrogation, one prompting death and destruction, on both sides, in the name of its execution that can never be satisfied or satiated. In creating the philistine, racial palestinianization licenses and unleashes the action-figure of its very invention. Samson, after all and altogether ironically, was the original suicide bomber.

By contrast, Arafat's interminable history, of course, was one of too often tragic and occasionally comic mistimings, miscues, and misdirections. The consequences were more than often bitter, even devastating, as much for his own people, whom he claimed to represent, as for the Israelis he clearly did resent. Orientalize the Palestinian, philistinize him, and he will act out accordingly. The Arab is a dog, Ariel Sharon had always said, the prototypical Judas; she a whore, the quintessential Delilah. He will howl, keeping you awake at night; she will infect you, blind you, sucking away your strength. Kill as many 'worms' as you can, the Sharonites have always implored, for fear they will otherwise overrun you. Take their land, for it is ours. Destroy their houses, villages, olive groves, for they do not belong. We should have done so long ago; let's finish it now.

Racial palestinianization accordingly is the prevailing response to a state of perpetual war. Indeed, it *is* a state of war declared perpetual, a war made the normal state of affairs. Permanent war enables a state of emergency suspending all rights for the target population. But suspension is tantamount to evisceration: rights continue to exist in name only, shadow conceptions of a world lost, never to be reinstated. But if sovereignty is defined in terms of the power to define the exception, then turning the exception into the norm effectively eviscerates the very grounds of sovereignty, as Wendy Brown has commented (2007). As norm, as given, as the naturalized state of being, the exceptional ceases to be, well, exceptional, the power to define exceptionality is rendered irrelevant, powerless. In making war permanent, the (once-)sovereign has made itself dependent – on the enemy, on maintaining the enemy as such. The ground on which the sovereign stands, makes its stand, has become quicksand.

Israel has perfected the bifurcated condition its principal patron now tries to emulate: a permanent war elsewhere – its horrors hidden from view, complaint or criticism cordoned off behind the Wall (or across the ocean), while the spectre of peace and prosperity is maintained at home. But such a state – or states, because the bifurcation necessitates always a doubling, two states of being, one here, the other there, one in peace but threatened always by the chaos beyond – requires, as Foucault says, that 'truth functions exclusively as a weapon' in the relationship of force. Perpetual war licenses 'a rationality of calculations, strategies and ruses' (2003).

Force enables one to speak, to interpret the truth, to elevate one's own proposals and claims to the status of truth while denouncing the other's as lies, illusions, errors, as deluded even. Racial palestinianization thus involves also transforming truth into a relationship of force, speaking truth in the name of power represented racially. A group is racially branded, as Mahmood Mamdani (2001) reveals, when it is set apart as racially distinct, thus rendering easier, and so more likely, its guiltless extinction, at least politically if not quite physically.

Since Sharon ascended to power in October 2000 by climbing the steps to Haram-al-Sharif in Jerusalem surrounded by surging rings of security guards, Israel has re-sought to dissolve, to destroy, the existence and self-determination of Palestinians as a people, politically, economically, socially and culturally in a deliberate and deliberative process Baruch Kimmerling (2003) has characterized as 'politicide'. This has culminated in almost complete social strangulation.

Targeted assassinations, effectively extrajudicial executions, while aimed rhetorically at all Palestinians, seek in their immediate destructiveness officially and officiously to kill the individual targeted. They do not look to obliterate the ethnoracially identified group, no matter how much Israelis desire Palestinians to disappear completely. And yet, in five years of the al-Aqsa Intifada more than three times as many Palestinians as Israeli Jews have been killed, 80% of whom were not involved in armed actions against Israel or Israelis and 20% of whom were children. The cycle of violent death, the performative aspects of mourning, resentment, bitterness and the resolution of revenge serve only to reinforce already hardened responses, on both sides.

Collateral damage, to paraphrase Mahmood Mamdani (2002), is not an exception in the war on terrorism but the exaggeration of its very point. It sends a message not just to the organizers of terrorist acts but to any passive supporters, any bystanders, anyone silently appreciating or vaguely sympathizing with the work of the branded terrorist. Racial branding makes it thinkable, targeted assassinations actualize its instrumentalization, disappearance its prevailing effect. Disappearance has collateral consequence not taken into account in the cost-benefit calculus of a governmentality as much about annexation as about occupation. Young teenagers are imprisoned by the Israeli authorities for as long as a year for stone-throwing, their parents uninformed even of their arrest by Israeli soldiers almost as youthful.

'A young man's war it is,' writes Eavan Boland in another context, 'a young man's war' –

Or so they say and so they go to wage
This struggle where, armored only in nightmare,
Every warrior is under age –
A son seeing each night leave, as father,
A man who may become the ancestor.
(Boland 1996)

These experiences are as likely to produce a seething disposition to suicide bombing upon release as a love of life, whether the occupiers' or their own.

The rationality of domination at the heart of racial palestinianization, then, is reckoned as the strategies of subjugation and techniques of terror, the calculation of insecurities, again political as much as physical, global as much as local. Benny Morris, Israel's best-known revisionist historian, captures this logic perfectly: 'When the choice is between destroying or being destroyed,' he insisted in clarification of his unstinting commitment to retaining Israeli domination, 'it's better to destroy' (Shavit 2004). As though these bifurcated choices are the only or best ones available!

This is a fragile rationality, indeed, as Foucault remarks more generally, one deeply insecure because always open to reversals, reprimands, recriminations, retaliations, revenge. The pathological insecurity at the heart of racial palestinianization, an insecurity that is simply the extreme embodiment of the characteristic insecurities of all racisms, calls forth the most pulverizing responses to any resistance as a way to cover over its own insecurities. 'Society must be defended', to use

Foucault's provocative phrasing, sealed from suicidal infiltration, configured against contamination, walled off from the weight of its own history, plastered against pollution.

The order of racial palestinianization

Racial palestinianization is today among the most repressive, the most subjugating and degrading, the most deadly forms of racial targeting, branding, and rationalization. It is, as Mandela has commented, a fate worse than apartheid. I have called it racial *palestinianization* rather than *israelification* (which would be more consistent with the other modes of racial regionalization, such as racial americanization) in order both to connect it to the representational and political histories of orientalism and to indicate its occupational singularities in the order of contemporary racial expressions and repressions. It may help to draw together its various instrumentalities elaborated above, not all of which need be implemented for the modality to persist or prevail.

First, and perhaps most basically, racial palestinianization is committed to land clearance underpinned by an accompanying, if not pre-dating, moral eviction. Territorial clearance in Israel's case has been prompted historically in terms of 'redemption of land'. This heartfelt historico-moral claim to land redemption, to retrieving territory always already biblically 'ours', distinguishes racial palestinianization from classic modes of settler colonialism. Reclamation through settlement is extended by renomination, the shrinkage of Palestinian proprietorship materialized in the disappearance of recognizable title. Dispossession of homes and groves, fields and terraces, through outright demolition, confiscation, or expropriation manifests homelessness in both the immediate and more nationalist senses of the term, and ultimately a virtually perpetual and perhaps permanent exilic refugeedom (one quarter of the world's refugees are Palestinian, according to the United Nations). This population expulsion and transfer, while in some ways not unlike 'forced removals' under apartheid, distinguishes racial palestinianization from that modality also.

In his characteristically blunt way, Benny Morris formulates the two options Israel has always posed for itself regarding Palestine and its people: create an apartheid-like state, a 'homeland', in which almost all Palestinians are located with radically reduced rights and power and excluded from property ownership, quality education, and economic opportunities, while their cheap labour is exploited to benefit the Jewish minority; or create a majority Jewish state in Israel by expelling all or the bulk of the Palestinian population preferably to Jordan, Egypt, and Syria, but more lately simply to the lock-up facility that today is Palestine itself (Shavit 2004). Israel has always vacillated between these two modalities, more recently opting to forgo exploitable Palestinian labour for its replacement by the likes of Filipinos, while transferring or displacing as many Palestinians as the world will tolerate from Israeli territory to imprisoned Palestine.

Israel has moved from a single apartheid state to establishing a state and a shadow state. The first, overwhelmingly for Jews, tolerates small Islamic, Christian, and Druze minorities. The shadow state for Palestinians, splintered into many non-continuous spaces by proliferating Jewish settlements, largely lacks self-determination, liberty, and any sort of security for its inhabitants. This is not so much the state form of apartheid as a distinct modality of the racial state in denial about its racial predication: racial palestinianization.

Racial palestinianization is likewise marked by the accompanying establishment and expansion of settlements outside the internationally recognized borders of Israel. A recent report based on Israeli administration figures by the Israeli anti-occupation group, Peace Now, on Israeli settlement patterns in the Occupied Territories reported that 40% of settlements are on land privately owned by Palestinians. Three settlements, two of which are suburban extensions of Jerusalem, Ma'ale Adumim and Givat Ze'ev, as well as Ariel, sit respectively on 85%, 44%, and 35% of private Palestinian property. Israel half-heartedly contests the figures, though not the fact of land expropriation, which has proceeded on classic Lockean principles.

These recognizably red-roofed hill-top settlements thus serve simultaneously as expanded Israeli residential terrain, offering a counter to the territorial claustrophobia of the homeland's narrow waistline, alongside pervasive 'eye-in-the sky' security oversight of palestinianized shantytowns, otherwise known as refugee camps. Holding the high ground has long been the logic of militarized dominance and domination. Settlement – the land of ancient debts reclaimed, calling in the historical chips – is accompanied by extended encirclement of Palestinian towns and villages deemed threatening to Israeli wellbeing and security, cutting Palestinians off from one another, effectively undermining any possibility of Palestinian coherence.

There are two further, complementary, foundational, and interactive features of racial palestinianization, namely, occupation and militarization. Occupation extends the possibility – the licence, the logic – of Israel's political economy as militaristically driven, as a war economy, as a military economic complex serviced by a state. The military orders Israel's regime of truth, as the late Tanya Reinhart (2006) made clear shortly before her untimely passing, shaping both how Israelis understand themselves and how the state structures conditions of life and death, the more so in the wake of Ariel Sharon's command. Occupation is both inevitable prompt and outcome of this militarily mobilized state self-conception, in a sense circular analytic implicatures of each other. Occupation is to Israel's military as blood is to the heart, lubricant to the pump. It not only primes the pump; it requires the switch to remain incessantly on, demanding that the pumping should not cease or slow down in a state geared to the exercise of its central instrumentality.

Occupation licenses every sort of invasive activity conceivable; but it likewise seeks to control the air above, the land, and the below-ground materialities, thus enabling the exploitation of all strategic resources of the territory occupied – land, water, labour, produce – with no commensurate respect for political, civil, environmental, or even the most basic of human rights.

People are killed, either as direct or indirect targets, without trial or trepidation, accidentally or collaterally. Curfews are imposed, randomly, 24/7. Schools are restricted, universities shut down, businesses shuttered. Palestinian life has no more value than an input in the geopolitical calculus of securities and losses, bits of manipulable data in the supreme (and extreme) militarization of expertise. Occupation encourages destruction of local, organic social institutions and infrastructure, making it impossible for Palestinians, for the local inhabitants, to govern themselves. Indeed, the point is not simply that they not be self-governing, but that they cease to be recognized as local, that they become alien, intruders in their own land. And that occupation be denied, legitimated as historical birthright, as rightful, self-righteous settlement, if one is to believe Israeli apologists like Ephraim Karsh (2004).

In short, this is a new modality of occupying state formation made possible conceptually by permanent infantilization and philistinianization. Palestine has been marked as the first 'permanently-temporary' state, to use Eyal Weizman's incisive characterization (2003). State boundaries are rendered impermanent, flexible according to the occupier's needs and whimsical determinations, visible only to the day's militarized cartographic dictates. Permanent impermanence is made the marker of the very ethnoracial condition of the Palestinian.

Palestinianization's temporary temporality is taken as ontological condition as much as political-military condition. The Palestinian is always between, always ill-at-ease, homeless at home if never at home in his homelessness, if anyone really could be, the explicit embodiment of Levinasian facelessness. Shifting, shiftless, unreliable, untrustworthy, nowhere to go, nowhere to be, the persona of negativity, of negation, of death's potential. He is the quintessential Nobody, as Memmi (2003) characterizes the figure of the colonized, the embodiment of enmity, almost already dead. The territory of the state is multiply divisible, broadly between three islands but more locally between multiplying settlements both overlooking and cutting off one local population from another. Indeed, the determination of the local, of who belongs and who does not, of the very meaning of occupier, is being rendered increasingly and deliberately, purposefully ambiguous, doubtful. Possession is nine-tenths of belonging, of being, to twist a cliché.

As Israel reinvaded Gaza in early July 2006, and enacted intensely hostile action in Lebanon to curtail the activities of Hizbullah, long a thorn in Israel's side, Prime Minister Olmert declared revealingly that 'the inevitable historical process of separation between Israelis and Palestinians cannot be stopped' (Wilson 2006). The declaration of historical inevitability, we know from long experience, must invariably be ensured by bombs, bullets, and boots on the ground. Ethnoracial separation can only be guaranteed with the alienating engagement of deathly weaponry.

Racial palestinianization

Finally, we need to say what it is that makes palestinianization racial. Palestinians are treated not *as if* a racial group, not simply *in the manner* of a racial group, but *as* a despised and demonic racial group. Struggling to maintain the semblance of a fair, judicious, and impartial governing overseer, Britain's Peel Commission, reporting to the League of Nations in 1937 on the Arab 'disorders' and disruptions' in Palestine of 1936, refers repeatedly to the '*racial* antagonism' between Jews and Arabs (Palestinians). The Commission characterizes Jews as 'a highly intelligent and enterprising *race* backed by large financial resources' in contrast to Palestinians as 'a comparatively poor, indigenous community, on a different cultural level' (1937, my emphases).

The Israeli state and its political and military representatives continue to devalue, debilitate, denigrate, humiliate, exclude, and evict Palestinians, morally, economically, legally, territorially. And it does so in the name of their ethno-naturalized or ethno-historicizing difference.

Palestinians, Lebanese, Arabs are all terrorists, hiding bombs under their beds to aim at Israel, lurking at the border ready to kidnap the stray Israeli soldier, scheming incessantly to obliterate the State of Israel (these are positions expressed to me, at various levels of volubility, by family long living in Israel). Palestinians in particular and Arabs more generally respond with equal contempt, and sometimes in explosive kind, each ratcheting up the anger and frustration of the other. But between the humiliations and devastations, there are daily examples of dignified resistance, from the facing down of bulldozers by courageous Palestinian and Israeli peace groups alike in order to hold onto private Palestinian land, to protests in villages and at border crossings, to making uncomfortable in their offices Israeli bureaucrats administering dehumanizing edicts committed to splitting married couples and families, and embarrassing young soldiers brutally enforcing border crossings. This is the fuel for coalitional antiracist social movements to emerge and enlarge, ultimately to flourish.

Palestinians in particular, and Arabs more generically, are treated directly as a subjugated race. Beaten in the name of devaluating stereotypes, concentrated in camps in the name of generalized security, displaced in the name of biblical right (effectively collapsing the historical into the transcendental, the naturalizing), killed in the name of retributive justice, Palestinians are ordered in the name of race rendered see-through, of a category in denial, of a conception unmarked because of a history cutting too close to the bone.

This critique of racial palestinianization is not to advocate nor self-loathingly to desire Israel's destruction, as so many bristlingly respond to any critical reflection on Israel's modus operandi. I am concerned here insistently to question *not* Israel's being, its right to exist, but rather its forms of expression and its modes of self-insistence and enforcement. I have been holding up to scrutiny, in short, the presumed singularity of Jewish ways of being on which the Israeli state has been predicated, a presumption that ironically reinscribes the restrictive, repulsive, even exterminating logic from which Jews historically have repeatedly fled. The (self) identification of Walter Benjamin's History's Angel necessarily makes for a cruel and violent demon bearing death and destruction.

I can only add, generalizing Gilad Atzmon's deep insight (as I listen to his lyrical music, *Exile*), that the sort of violent relationalities I have undertaken to excavate here are not simply cases of neighbours not loving neighbours. Those so ready to inflict so much pain on others cannot possibly 'like themselves either' (Atzmon 2006). The implication of becoming so unreservedly violent, with little restraint or self-consciousness, because, even while close, it is always placed at some psychic distance, can only be a mania of the most debilitating, distorting, self-destructive sort.

References

Ahmad, A. (2002) 'The Nazification of Israel', *Frontline*, Vol. 19, no. 8, April 13–26 « http://www.hinduonnet.com/fline/fl1908/19080100.htm »

Amnesty International (2003) *Israel and the Occupied Territories, Surviving under Siege: The Impact of Movement Restrictions on the Right to Work* « http://web.amnesty.org/library/Index/ENGMDE150012003 »

Atzmon, G. (2006) 'Israel's New Math: 2=500,000', *Counterpunch*, 22–3 July «http://www.counterpunch.org/Atzmon07222006.html»

Benvenisti, M. (2003) *Sacred Landscape: The Buried History of the Holy Land Since 1948*, University of California Press, Berkeley

Boland, E. (1996) 'A soldier's son', in *An Origin Like Water: Selected Poems 1967–1987*, Norton, New York

Brown, W. (2007) 'Porous sovereignty, walled democracy', lecture, Cultures of Violence Conference, UC Irvine, April 7

Butler, J. (2003) 'No, it's not anti-semitic', *London Review of Books*, Vol. 25, no. 16, August 21

De Rooij, P. (2004) 'The scale of carnage: Palestinian misery in perspective', *Counterpunch Online*, 3 June

Goldberg, D. T. (2002) *The Racial State*, Blackwell, Oxford

Goodenough, P. (2006) 'Members of UN body say Israel's military actions motivated by racism', *Crosswalk.com*, August 4 «http://www.crosswalk.com/news/1412594.html»

Hess, M. (1862 [1995]) *The Revival of Israel: Rome and Jerusalem, the Last National Question*, University of Nebraska Press, Lincoln

Herzl, T. (1997 [1897]) 'Address to the First Jewish Congress', in A. Hertzberg (ed) *The Zionist Idea: A Historical Analysis and Reader*, Jewish Publication Society, New York

Karmi, G. (2004) 'Vanishing the Palestinians', *CounterPunch*, July 17/18 «http://www.counterpunch.org/karmi07172004.html»

Karsh, E. (2004) 'What occupation?' *Aish.com* (reprinted from *Commentary Magazine*), http://www.israel-wat.com/h9_eng6.htm

Kimmerling, B. (2003) *Politicide: Ariel Sharon's War Against the Palestinians*, Verso, London

Mamdani, M. (2001) *When Victims Become Killers: Colonialism, Nativism, and the Genocide in Rwanda*, Princeton University Press, Princeton

Mamdani, M. (2002) 'Good Muslim, Bad Muslim: A political perspective on culture and terrorism', *American Anthropologist*, Vol. 104, no. 3, 766–75

Memmi, A. (2003) *The Colonizer and the Colonized*, Earthscan, London

Morris, B. (2001) 'Revisiting the Palestine Exodus of 1948', in E. Rogan and A. Shlaim (eds) *The War for Palestine*, Cambridge University Press, Cambridge

Pappe, I. (2004) *A History of Modern Palestine: One Land, Two Peoples*, Cambridge University Press, Cambridge

Pappe, I. (2006) *The Ethnic Cleansing of Palestine*, Oneworld Publications, Oxford

Peel Commission (1937) *Report of the Palestine Royal Commission*, League of Nations C.495.M.336.1937.VI, Geneva, 30 November, 1937 «http://domino.un.org/ UNISPAL.NSF/9a798adbf322aff38525617b006d88d7/08e38a718201458b052 565700072b358!OpenDocument»

Reinhart, T. (2006) *The Roadmap to Nowhere: Israel/Palestine Since 2003*, Verso, London

Sartre, J. P. (1948) *Anti-Semite and Jew*, Schocken Books, New York

Shavit, A. (2004) 'Survival of the fittest: An interview with Benny Morris', *Ha'aretz*, 9 January

Shenhav, Y. (2006) *The Arab Jews: A Postcolonial Reading of Nationalism, Religion, and Ethnicity*, Stanford University Press, Stanford

Shohat, E. (2003) ' "Rupture and Return": Zionist discourse and the study of Arab Jews', *Social Text*, no. 75, Summer, 49–74

Smilanski, Y. (S. Yizhar) (1990) 'Silence of the Villagers', in *Stories of the Plain*, Zmora Bitan, Tel Aviv

Tamari, Salim (1999) *Jerusalem 1948: The Arab Neighbourhoods and their Fate in the War*, Institute for Jerusalem Studies, Jerusalem

Weizman, E. (2003) 'Ariel Sharon and the Geometry of Occupation', *Open-Democracy*, 9 September

Wilson, S. (2006) 'Israeli leader defends incursion into Gaza', *Washington Post*, 11 July

Gargi Bhattacharyya

2 Globalizing Racism and Myths of the Other in the 'War on Terror'

This chapter considers the impact of Israeli representations of terrorism on the politics of 'race' in Britain and other places; the central role played by the figure of Palestinian terrorism in speeches and policy choices in the 'war on terror'; the transferral of palestinianized conceptions of minority communities into the racial politics of Britain and other European nations; and the convergence of renewed state racisms and participation in the 'war on terror'.

I am beginning from the view that support for Palestinian human rights and self-determination has become the emblematic solidarity movement of our time. Palestine has become our Spanish civil war, our Cuba, our Nicaragua – the young of the rich world yearn for the exoticism of a far-away battle. For defenders of Israel, this is yet another example of the world's failure to understand that the complexities of the conflict cannot be reduced to pleas for love not war.

The struggle for a free Palestine has been popularized, pop-culturalized, and added to the style pantheon of the global left. At the numerous anti-capitalist carnivals of resistance before the 'war on terror', it could seem that the whole world was on the street supporting the Palestinians. Paul Berman, who views this as a symptom of the wrong-headedness of the left, describes this moment as reaching a peak in 2002:

> In Washington, D.C., in April 2002 the anti-globalization movement staged a mass protest in which the new theme of Palestinian solidarity managed to overwhelm the old and traditional theme of protest against the plutocratic institutions of world finance (Berman 2003: 130).

Simultaneously, across so-called postcolonial nations, the Palestinian struggle is regarded as the unfinished business of a previous imperial era. Indian leftists remind a weapons-hungry government and military that Palestinians have been regarded as another colonized people seeking independence and self-determination, and that alliances with Israel disrespect and forget India's own nationalist struggles (Swamy 2006), and Brazilian landless workers reach out to Palestine as a symbol of the global struggle against injustice (MST 2007). These are the remaining traces of older anti-imperialist alliances, taken up with renewed vigour in this age of hyper-exploitative global relations.

Equally there is reinvigorated support through greater political consciousness among Muslim youth across the world, most of all among the youth of migrant communities who are reclaiming Islam as their response to local discrimination and global inequality.

This is the issue that links the secular left and young Muslim activists – a coupling enabled by a coming together of the anti-capitalist and anti-war movements and a reawakening of political Islam among minorities in the West. This unlikely alliance draws the wrath of commentators such as Nick Cohen, who argues that the left has forgotten its own values and vision by aligning itself with illiberal religious activists (Cohen 2007), and Melanie Phillips, who suggests that both the traditional left and Muslim activists are motivated by a desire to curtail everyday freedoms and a hatred of Israel and, by association, the Jews (Phillips 2007).

Undoubtedly, alliances thrown up by the campaigns against the wars in Afghanistan and Iraq, and against the wider conduct of the 'war on terror', are surprising. The European left has had an ambivalent relationship with religion and a chequered history of attempts to work with migrant and minority communities. Building alliances with Muslim activists has proved challenging, although some left groupings have thrown themselves enthusiastically into working with these new comrades. Now the public expression of a politicized Muslim identity as part of a larger claim for inclusion in mainstream politics has become part of the British landscape at least (Fulat 2005). Within these fragile and unfamiliar alliances the issue of Palestine holds a particular anchoring role, serving as a touchstone of shared objectives and values.

Of course this is to be welcomed – at long last Palestine has been receiving the international attention and popular support that is long overdue – but there is also the extra burden of being construed as the archetypal anti-imperialist movement of our time. The mobilization against interventions in Afghanistan and Iraq constantly referenced Palestine as key to understanding occupation politics. In western imaginations, the struggles of Palestine and Iraq were tightly tied together. An intensification of resistance in Palestine was regarded as a reason for the US and UK to postpone temporarily their planned attacks on Iraq.

There are both pros and cons to this taking on of iconic status. The interest and support is very welcome (after years of organizing solidarity events with handfuls of people) but this symbolic burden can obscure some of the issues at hand. If Palestine is understood as a cipher for, say, resistance to US-led imperialist globalization, or the struggle for Muslim pride and identity everywhere, or equally as the spectre of international antisemitism on the march again, in international parlance there can be a lot of talk about Palestine without much attention to the situation of Palestinians. Serving as a cipher for the aspirations and alliances of others brings greater attention to the Palestinian struggle, but this is achieved at the cost of bearing the symbolic burden of other struggles and issues.

In terms of the politics of 'race', the issue of Palestine serves as an indicator of integration/allegiance/adherence to western values and a model of how such conflicts can be represented and policed by racist states in various locations. The use of Palestine as cipher for a larger clash of civilizations seeps into more local politics of difference. Since the beginning of the 'war on terror', the distinction between local, national and global interactions has become blurred. In this context, the use of Palestine as shorthand for inter-ethnic conflict and seemingly intractable difference has taken on a new significance – with outcomes that are bad for Palestinians and for antiracism in many other places.

There are several components of this palestinianization of discourses of 'race' in other places. The most obvious is the identification of the issue of Palestine as the key to understanding the radicalization of Muslim communities and global divisions between Islam and the West. In recent years Palestine has been identified by all sides, including former British Prime Minister Tony Blair, as the issue that inflames public opinion and thus gives succour to 'extremists' (Wintour and Norton-Taylor 2006).

As a result the manner in which this conflict is narrated is important for racialized structures of governance within Britain and other western nations. Equally, if the 'war on terror' represents a racialized global conflict without end or limit, the racialized representation of the Israel/Palestine conflict enables Israel to present its interests as coterminous with others fighting the forces of international terrorism. The disputed issues of land, right of return, illegal detention and access to scarce resources become obscured by a narrative of inter-cultural misunderstanding, now reworked to show that 'they', barbaric Islamicized others, are not capable of mutual coexistence due to their dangerous culture.

Racialization and cohesion

I am proposing that a particular representation of the Palestinian struggle serves to transform political conflict into impassable cultural conflict, into a matter of 'race', not politics. At the point when western nations such as Britain are learning to erase the idea of racism by suggesting that the problem is really integration – meaning that minorities must learn how to get along, accept the will of the majority and not annoy or frighten people – Israel offers a model for transforming the justified demands of the racialized other into evidence that this otherness is innate, impassable and can only be contained and disciplined in the interests of the enlightened western state and its (full) citizens.

This is what I am describing as a taking up of palestinianized conceptions of 'race' for the purposes of local racist politics. Palestinianization here is a term to describe the transformation of racial or related categories into clashing cultural types destined to miscommunication and perhaps violence without end.

To take the example of Britain, recent years have seen a rapid retreat from the conclusions and recommendations of the Lawrence Inquiry. This report, the culmination of intensive campaigning from a wide alliance of actors, was regarded as a watershed in British race relations and resulted in legislation in 2000 that requires public institutions to challenge institutional racism in all their functions (MacPherson 1999). However, since then a series of government pronouncements and initiatives appear to retreat from this active commitment to the eradication of racism. Most importantly, the debate has shifted back to blaming minority ethnic groups for their alleged failure to progress, integrate and take a full part in the life of the society ('Community Cohesion' 2007).

Israel's rehabilitation through the 'war on terror'

Israel has, of course, needed no rehabilitation. There has been no break in the support that Israel enjoys and little threat that it will be called to account by the international community. However, the 'war on terror' has provided a context for Israel to reiterate longstanding claims about the alleged inadequacy of international law and the nature of terrorist enemies.

To illustrate, I want to use the speech given by former Israeli Prime Minister Benjamin Netanyahu in Washington on 20 September 2001 outlining the key points of Israel's insertion into the 'war on terror'. Many regard the doctrine described in this speech and the US take-up of this philosophy as a belated appreciation of Netanyahu's earlier conception of how to fight international terrorism, as expounded in his 1995 book *Fighting Terrorism: How Democracies Can Defeat Domestic and International Terrorism*. In this, champions of Israel are able to argue that the 9/11 attacks have brought the dangers of extremist terrorism home to western audiences and they are at last beginning to appreciate Israel's fears.

The speech outlines the five key aspects of Netanyahu's vision of global security. The framing of the argument is not new. Equally, this is not a vision limited to Netanyahu; its elements can be discerned in various neo-con pronouncements. I am arguing that this formulation of Israeli interests and actions is influencing not only the wider conduct of global politics but also the conceptualization of race and racism within nations. Netanyahu begins with the foundational claim that this is a struggle for survival:

> What is at stake today is nothing less than the survival of our civilization. There may be some who would have thought a week ago that to talk in these apocalyptic terms about the battle against international terrorism was to engage in reckless exaggeration. No longer. Each one of us today understands that we are all targets, that our cities are vulnerable, and that our values are hated with an unmatched fanaticism that seeks to destroy our societies and our way of life (Netanyahu 2001).

This is the first and foundational point in the argument. The 'West' is presented as a unified civilization under attack and defending itself against extinction. The acknowledgement of this new (to western nations other than Israel) threat of international terrorism slips into the assertion that this violence is motivated by an irrational hatred of the values, way of life and very being of 'our civilization'. This is a hatred that cannot be appeased and which seeks total destruction. Nothing other than total defence can answer this level of threat.

For Netanyahu, this is an opportunity to reiterate longstanding claims about the character of the threats facing Israel. As a result, his pledge of solidarity with America also serves as a demand for reciprocal support for Israel, not on the basis of special treatment, but because this reciprocity is described as in the interests of both parties.

Today, we are all Americans – in grief, as in defiance. In grief, because my people have faced the agonizing horrors of terror for many decades, and we feel an instant kinship with both the victims of this tragedy and the great nation that mourns its fallen brothers and sisters. In defiance, because just as my country continues to fight terrorism in our battle for survival, I know that America will not cower before this challenge (Netanyahu 2001).

The implication is clear. We may all be Americans, but in a context where Americans are learning what it is to be Israelis. This understanding is enabled by horrific events, but builds on the underlying 'kinship', the familial relations, that link America and Israel as victims of international terrorism and members of the same civilizational family, a family facing an attack on its very being. This is the second point in the argument. Other 'civilized' nations now know what Israel faces, and therefore understand the necessity of Israeli tactics.

The establishment of this empathetic kinship of shared experience forms the basis on which the remaining three components are built. Once the argument that 'we' are one, linked by culture, civilization, and perhaps even by stock, has been established, Netanyahu elaborates on what this commonality demands:

A simple rule prevails here: the success of terrorists in one part of the terror network emboldens terrorists throughout the network (Netanyahu 2001).

This is the third element of the framework. International terrorism represents a new level of threat both because it is committed to the destruction of western values and ways of life and because it operates through that mobile example of globalization in action, the network. The concept of the network intertwines the security concerns of the US and other western nations with that of Israel – one, albeit dispersed, enemy against the 'us' of western civilization. This enemy may be dispersed in geography and organization, but it is characterized by a unifying and pathological ideology.

Though its separate parts may have local objectives and take part in local conflicts, the main motivation driving the terror network is an anti-Western hostility that seeks to achieve nothing less than a reversal of history. It seeks to roll back the West and install an extremist form of Islam as the dominant power in the world. It seeks to do this not by means of its own advancement and progress, but by destroying the enemy. This hatred is the product of a seething resentment that has simmered for centuries in certain parts of the Arab and Islamic world (Netanyahu 2001).

This is the fourth point in the sequence. This enemy is essential, timeless, primeval, a mythic enemy that must be destroyed before it destroys us. There may be a comprehensible politics informing these movements. However, any such local concerns fade to insignificance against the larger motivation of defeating and destroying the West, a project which demands violence because it is unable to challenge the ideas that sustain western dominance. This, apparently, has been the 'seething resentment' of centuries. While the Arab and Islamic world may appear to have travelled the same unpredictable paths of history as other places – nationalist struggles, battles between the forces of secularism and religion, the building of economic alliances, political movements – we are told that all of these varied events are nothing against the underlying hatred of the West. It is this primal conflict that is seen to animate international terrorism. It is only by understanding this that the West can unite to defeat this relentless enemy.

If we begin to distinguish between acts of terror, justifying some and repudiating others based on sympathy with this or that cause, we will lose the moral clarity that is so essential for victory. This clarity is what enabled America and Britain to root out piracy in the nineteenth century. This is how the Allies rooted out Nazism in the twentieth century. They did not look for the 'root cause' of piracy or the 'root cause' of Nazism – because they knew that some acts are evil in and of themselves, and do not deserve any consideration or 'understanding' (Netanyahu 2001).

This is the final and concluding point. This is an enemy beyond reason or understanding and all attempts to understand the motivations or grievances of the other weaken our defences. Moral clarity here demands an absolute refusal of politics. There can be no consideration of competing claims, only an opposition to evil. In this account there is no context, no politics, no explanation and therefore no hope of an alternative to violent conflict. To accept the premises of this framework is to accept that negotiation and diplomacy are useless and only all-out warfare remains.

The framing of these ideas has seeped into the politics of 'race' and now the grievances of those who suffer racism within western nations are viewed through this distorting lens. Now, it seems, all criticism of western societies is viewed as evidence of deep-seated anti-westernism, and therefore part of the continuum of evil that must be resisted. These five points continue to inform the conduct of racialized politics within key western nations and globally through the conceptualization of the 'war on terror'.

Palestinianizing Iraq

Early reports on plans for the invasion of Iraq appeared to validate Israel's claim to be ahead of the curve on dealing with a threat to all 'western' nations. It is Israel who can train others in the dubious techniques of urban warfare in civilian areas (Borger 2003; JINSA 2004).

As a result the terms of this conflict become shaped by Israeli practices. How you fight is shaped by how you conceptualize your 'enemy', your own identity, your role and your legitimation. Palestinianizing the enemy creates a spectre of a people, desperate and beyond negotiation, inflamed by political and/or religious extremism, indifferent to human life including their own (a very important component in representations of the 'war on terror'), willing and able to employ the young, the old, women and children in 'battle' (in an echo of other imperial encounters with guerrilla resistance), motivated by mythical and/or religious goals and thus beyond reason or limit in their violence.

In response, Israel teaches occupying forces to view themselves as the embattled party under attack, forced to respond with excessive violence: due to facing an irrational enemy that seeks 'our' annihilation; as part of a moral crusade to defend 'our' values and way of life; and in order to beat back a new global threat ('Islamic fascism').

These associations transform the 'war on terror' into a version of World War Two fought on guerrilla terms; 'our' enemies are genocidal maniacs pursuing an absolutist and evil ideology. A dehumanized enemy associated with the epitome of human evil justifies any kind of violence in response. There is no limit to what can be done to fend off such creatures.

I don't think that popular opinion or even government opinion in a range of western nations accepts any more that Palestinians can be characterized in this manner, although little is done to address the military tactics employed by Israel as part of this mythology; but the portrayal of Iran in recent years demonstrates a shift and replaying of this same mythology and infects, for example, debates about Lebanon and Iraq (Lobe 2006).

Unintentional echoes of Intifada

In the northern British city of Bradford in the summer of 2001, before anyone knew of the term 'war on terror', there were disturbances on the streets when Asian communities feared that the racist British Nationalist Party (BNP) would be marching through their neighbourhoods.

In the aftermath of confrontations between Asian and white youths and the police, the iconic image of the stone-throwing youth relayed around the British media. As a result of a poster campaign publicizing mug-shots of young (Asian) men who were present, many families encouraged their sons to hand themselves in to the police, certain that this misunderstanding could be cleared up (Kundnani 2001).

In practice, hundreds of young men from this tight-knit community were sentenced to lengthy prison terms, because the Home Secretary, David Blunkett, used his authority to render this a 'riot' rather than a public disturbance. As a result, most Asian defendants were given long prison sentences and most white defendants were not (Fair Justice for All Campaign).

There are several UK-specific factors here. Blunkett was keen to show himself as a hard man of politics and to dispel any suggestions that the New Labour government could not be tough on crime and minorities. A number of British cities experienced disturbances that summer when young Asian men felt that their neighbourhoods were under threat from BNP activity. Asian/Muslim youth were in the process of becoming a new folk demon, in the manner of African-Caribbean youth before them – although the place of 'Islam' in this demonization was still unclear or undecided.

What had been decided was that New Labour's retreat from race equality and multiculturalism in favour of authoritarian versions of integration needed to be affirmed loudly and publicly. This was seen as the way to 'defeat' the BNP, by stealing their clothes, and to rebrand the Labour Party as a party of patriotic nationalism, not liberal accommodation of minorities and diversity. The process of establishing this shift, which predates 9/11, expanded on the cultural racism that had infected everyday life for some time (Blackledge 2005; Kundnani 2007).

Since then, other urban disturbances, such as in Paris, have echoed these themes, racism has been celebrated as a justified defence of 'liberal' values in the Netherlands, and the far right has gained a block of elected representatives in the European Parliament, indicating the political appeal of defending Europe and its values against the diffuse threats of immigration, terrorism and change.

The association of stone-throwing youths seems clear and I want to suggest that it is this association, even when unspoken, which enables the hyped-up state response. It is palestinianization that transforms street disturbance into a threat to 'our way of life' and the harbinger of future violence and destruction, because in the logic of the 'war on terror' expressing grievances in this way must lead to other acts.

Stuart Hall wrote long ago of the impact on British racism of African youth doing the 'Soweto shuffle' across TV screens (Hall 1981) and the synergy between this and the uprisings of urban black youth, for both participants and viewers. I suspect that Palestine serves as a similar touchstone for Muslim youth now and that these echoes of Intifada are policed as such.

Palestinianizing 'race'

Within Britain, the advent of the 'homegrown suicide bomber' has greatly energized this process and initiated a widespread condemnation of 'multiculturalism' as the allegedly failed policy that has led to this violence. However, even before the 7 July 2005 London bombs (7/7), recent processes of racialization have borrowed from the portrayal of Palestinians.

The concept of the 'Arab street' as indicator of popular opinion has influenced British governmental strategies of engagement (Foreign and Commonwealth Office 2007; Mark 2005). A chain of connection – from the Arab street to the Muslim street in the West – serves as barometer of opinion, but without the status of political interlocutor.

Instead, this is to be placated and contained and as such represents a move away from a 'rational' addressing of particular political issues to culturalist accounts of how to manage these inherently angry and irrational people.

There has been some recognition that Muslim and minority communities have legitimate grievances, but a failure to address these issues across generations has led to a retreat from active anti-racism within the Labour government. The debates about 'democratic deficit' and 'community cohesion' have shifted blame and responsibility away from the state and racist institutions, despite the still quite recent exhortations of the Lawrence Inquiry, to the failure of minority communities – who have creepingly come to be coded as Muslim – to participate in mainstream political life and integrate with their (racist) neighbours. Now, the state decries the methods of these communities, however mainstream the manner of protest involved, and blames their inability to challenge extremism for state inaction on all fronts. Now, longstanding grievances, previously recognized as legitimate by some government actors and mainstream political figures, are being diverted by the claim that 'these people' cannot engage in proper political debate. This mimics the Israeli example of how to demonize the racialized other in order to be absolved of the responsibility to engage in mutual resolution of problems, and mobilizes the backlash against multiculturalism that implies that people are so different that trying to get along or find mutual solutions is a waste of time.

Demography and clashing cultures

It is argued that Israel is founded on a majoritarian logic (Bishara 2001; Davis 2003). As a result, Israel has developed structures of racism that protect and elevate the (Jewish) majority and demonize the (Palestinian) minority as a threat to the very existence of the majority culture and way of life (Davis 2003). The lesson that Israel wishes to teach its allies is that the culture of these minorities is itself an attack on multicultural ideals. This is a culture that is absolute, deathly and genocidal. To allow it space and expression is to endanger 'our' way of life.

This implication is echoed in the allegation that minority communities have used the discourse of multiculturalism to exploit western liberal indulgence. Since 7/7, Britain has been engaged in a sporadic and highly charged debate about diversity, cultural expression and citizenship. Much of this discussion has rested on the question of whether political grievances can be negotiated or whether the world is divided into irreconcilable camps. The British government has transferred this question to both local and international settings and, as former Prime Minister Blair argued, the choice between dialogue and, in his terms, moderation and a hopeless clash of civilizations is a choice that Muslims must make. We, reasonable, secular and/or Judeo-Christian westerners of liberal conscience cannot engage with you, ungrateful Muslim minorities here and Muslim nations abroad, until you relinquish your violent and deadly culture that is founded on a genocidal hatred of us. In this portrayal, Palestine once again takes on a central emblematic status. For Blair, the representation of the issue of Palestine was the trope that illuminated the challenges facing the international community and at the same time that revealed the limitations of diplomacy and international law as previously conceived. The long quotation below, from Blair's famous speech in 2006 outlining the terms of a new approach to foreign policy, reveals the influence of the Netanyahu approach and Israeli depictions of terrorist threat.

...there was one cause which, the world over, unites Islam, one issue that even the most westernized Muslims find unjust and, perhaps worse, humiliating: Palestine. Here a moderate leadership was squeezed between its own inability to control the radical elements and the political stagnation of the peace process.

When Prime Minister Sharon took the brave step of disengagement from Gaza, it could have been and should have been the opportunity to re-start the process.

But the squeeze was too great and as ever because these processes never stay still, instead of moving forward, it fell back. Hamas won the election. Even then, had moderate elements in Hamas been able to show progress, the situation might have been saved. But they couldn't.

So the opportunity passed to Reactionary Islam and they seized it: first in Gaza, then in Lebanon. They knew what would happen. Their terrorism would provoke massive retaliation by Israel. Within days, the world would forget the original provocation and be shocked by the retaliation. They want to trap the Moderates between support for America and an Arab street furious at what they see nightly on their television. This is what has happened.

For them, what is vital is that the struggle is defined in their terms: Islam versus the West; that instead of Muslims seeing this as about democracy versus dictatorship, they see only the bombs and the brutality of war, and sent from Israel. In this way, they hope that the arc of extremism that now stretches across the region, will sweep away the fledgling but faltering steps Modern Islam wants to take into the future (Blair 2006).

Palestine becomes once again a synecdoche for this larger 'arc of extremism' and in the process the well-articulated demands of the Palestinian people that Israel abide by international law and respect Palestinian human rights are transformed into indications of a centuries-old hatred of the West, something beyond politics altogether.

Difference as irreconcilable and demanding containment

I want to argue that there has been a two-way reinforcement of racializing Palestinians and palestinianizing 'race' in recent years. As well as the world learning from Israel's representation of and response to the Palestinians, Israel has itself been influenced by the larger cultural shift across developed nations against so-called multiculturalism. The spectre of an alien other who hates the West and is characterized by an impassable cultural difference is floating around a range of domestic and international political debates.

The Blair government's embrace of the 'war on terror' and its exclusionary terms signalled a shift away from previous attempts to accommodate minority cultures. Now, we are pressed to believe, the game is up. Multiculturalism has not worked and, in fact, could never work. Instead we must learn the ugly lesson that 'our' culture and their 'culture' are absolutely incompatible – our ways of life cannot be reconciled and, more than this, the presence of this alien other is a direct threat to our own survival.

It is this account of the impossibility of coexistence – not because of 'us', but due to the murderous nature of 'them' – that echoes and reinforces Israel's portrayal of the Palestinians. Now nations that have addressed minorities in terms of training for majority cultural membership are seen to be vindicated. How foolish to think that they could keep their own ways: proving themselves to be capable of being like us is the minimum requirement for tolerance and freedom from persecution, that and the majoritarian logic that requires a strict cap on the numbers of such dangerous aliens.

Other countries are less entrenched in this US/Israeli view of the world, but even those who query the absolutist terms of the 'war on terror' appear willing to adapt the terms of a palestinianizing of 'race' for their internal state practice.

Although I am wary of implying that these narratives become powerful as a result of (another) Israeli conspiracy, I do think that the redeployment of a palestinianized concept of 'race' is seen to meet some of the various problems of globalization, from changing migration patterns to the challenge of coexistence and the establishment of recognizable minority communities, all against a backdrop of transnational networks of economic activity and state repression.

With Iraq there is a discernible shift that reduces all political conflicts to the impossibility of dialogue with fanatical Islam. However, it is Palestine that is the model of how well-articulated and internationally recognized political demands are reworked to be seen as expressions of incomprehensible violence by an absolute other.

Understandably, there has been a take-up by Palestinians and their supporters of racialized terms of reference, because this is an accurate account of Israel's discriminatory state institutions and is designed to snatch back association with the moral high ground and other recognized and respected global struggles. However, this take-up is made problematic by the widespread reinvigoration of racism as a necessary element for promoting superior values in the face of newly virulent and barbaric enemies. If racism is no longer a problem – and now it seems it was never a problem in the manner previously thought – then appeals to international antiracism are complicated by this backlash. Most of all, empire is back in fashion: as an unavoidable duty, as necessary for the survival of our way of life, and as the better route for the world (for a critique, see Mooers 2006).

This rehabilitation of empire includes acceptance of Israel's terms of reference – yes, what we do is very regrettable, but it is the least bad option. The 'war on terror' resurrects imperial ambition as a regrettable but necessary ideological project and this cultural and political shift among key western nations serves to further consolidate support for Israel and Israeli accounts of the necessity of violent occupation.

This represents an odd and shifting battle of ideas. Moving away from an earlier suggestion that Palestine is an issue that destabilizes the region and the world, the current attempts to palestinianize race argue that clashing civilizations are real and inevitable and instead of embodying a legitimate concern, the issue of Palestine represents the impassability of the divide between Islam and the West, and different ethnic cultures everywhere. Multiculturalism is dead (if it was ever alive); empire is back as an explicit and celebrated practice; and the powerful must use all the might at their disposal because this is better for civilization and the world. Palestinians are not Palestinians; they are pawns of Islamofascism. Racism is not racism; it is proof that minority communities hate the West. There is no politics for the losers of global battles, only an endless battle to the death between competing cultures.

References

Berman, P. (2003) *Terror and Liberalism*, W.W. Norton, London

Bishara, M. (2001) *Palestine/Israel: Peace or Apartheid*, Zed Books, London

Blackledge, A. (2005) 'The discursive construction of social contexts: The politics of multilingualism', National Association for Language Development in the Curriculum Annual Conference, University of Warwick, November

Blair, A. (2006) 'Speech to the Los Angeles World Affairs Council', 1 August

Borger, J. (2003) 'Israel trains US assassination squads in Iraq', *Guardian*, 9 December

Bridges, G. and R. Brunt (eds) (1981) *Silver Linings*, Lawrence and Wishart, London

Cohen, N. (2007) *What's Left? How Liberals Lost their Way*, Fourth Estate, London

'Community Cohesion' (2007) ‹http://www.idea.gov.uk/idk/core/page.do?page/d=5770022›

Davis, U. (2003) *Apartheid Israel: Possibilities for the Struggle Within*, Zed Books, London

Fair Justice for All Campaign ‹http://www.fairuk.org/docs/Fair%20Justice%20Campaign.pdf›

Foreign and Commonwealth Office (2007) 'Engaging with the Islamic World' ‹http://www.fco.gov.uk/servlet/Front?pagename=OpenMarket/Xcelerate/ShowPage&c=Page&cid=1133774698707›

Fulat, S. (2005) 'Recognise our role in society', *Guardian Unlimited* ‹http://www.guardian.co.uk/islam/story/0,,1395064,00.html›

Hall, S. (1981) 'The whites of their eyes: Racist ideologies and the media', in G. Bridges and R. Brunt (eds) *Silver Linings*, Lawrence and Wishart, London

JINSA (2004) 'Israel assists US forces, shares lessons-learned fighting terrorists', Jewish Institute for National Security Affairs, 27 December ‹http://www.jinsa.org/articles/articles.html/function/view/categoryid/1701/documen-tid/2774/history/3,2360,655,1701,2774›

Kundnani, A. (2001) 'From Oldham to Bradford: The violence of the violated', Institute of Race Relations, 1 October ‹http://www.irr.org.uk/2001/october/ak000003.html›

Kundnani, A. (2007) *The End of Tolerance: Racism in 21st Century Britain,* Pluto Press, London

Lobe, J. (2006) 'Yellow Journalism and Chicken Hawks', *Asia Times Online*, 25 May «http://www.atimes.com/atimes/Middle_East/HE24Ak03.html»

MacPherson, Sir W. of Cluny (1999) *The Stephen Lawrence Inquiry,* presented to Parliament by the Secretary of State for the Home Department, Stationery Office, London

Mark, D. (2005) 'Home Office to meet Muslims in Yorkshire', *Yorkshire Post*, 1 August

Mooers, C. (2006) *The New Imperialists, Ideologies of Empire,* Oneworld Publications, Oxford

MST (2007) *Movimento Dos Trabalhadores Rurais Sem Terra, Brazil's Landless Workers Movement* « http://www.mstbrazil.org/?q=history »

Netanyahu, B. (1995) *Fighting Terrorism: How Democracies Can Defeat Domestic and International Terrorists*, Farrar, Straus and Giroux, New York

Netanyahu, B. (2001) 'Statement before the Government Reform Committee, Washington DC', September 20

Phillips, M. (2007) 'The Jewish enemy within', *Jewish Chronicle,* 16 February

Swamy, R. (2006) 'The case against collaboration between India and Israel', *Z-Net* 31 August «http://www.zmag.org/content/showarticle.cfm?ItemD=10862»

Wintour, P. and R. Norton-Taylor (2006) 'Blair urges White House to shift focus to Israel-Palestine conflict', *Guardian*, 14 November

PART II
Palestine: Biopolitics and States of Exception

Honaida Ghanim

3 Thanatopolitics: The Case of the Colonial Occupation in Palestine

Introduction

On 23 March 2005, Amnesty International published a disturbing report about the social life of Palestinian women in the Occupied Territories, titled 'Conflict, occupation and patriarchy: Women carry the burden'. Although the report includes many dramatic stories and testimonies about Palestinian women, Rula's testimony especially shocks the reader.

> *Rula* We took a taxi and got off before the checkpoint because cars are not allowed near the checkpoint and we walked the rest of the way; I was in pain. At the checkpoint there were several soldiers; they were drinking coffee or tea and ignored us. Daoud approached to speak to the soldiers and one of them threatened him with his weapon. Daoud spoke to them in Hebrew; I was in pain and felt I was going to give birth there and then; I told Daoud who translated what I said to the soldiers but they did not let us pass. I was lying on the ground in the dust and I crawled behind a concrete block by the checkpoint to have some privacy and gave birth there, in the dust, like an animal. I held the baby in my arms and she moved a little but after a few minutes she died in my arms.

> *Daoud (Rula's Husband)* I pleaded with the soldiers to let us pass; I spoke to them in Hebrew; I know Hebrew because I used to work in Israel; they understood what I was saying but did not let us pass. After the baby was born Rula screamed, then after a while she screamed that the baby died. She was crying. I burst into tears and ran toward the cars on the

other side of the checkpoint, ignoring the soldiers; I brought a taxi and went back to Rula; I felt so bad to see her in such condition; she was holding the baby in her arms, covered in blood and the umbilical cord was on the ground, in the dust and still attached and I had to cut it with a stone; I didn't have anything else to cut it with. Then I picked up Rula in my arms and she was holding the baby and I carried her to the car and we went to the hospital (Amnesty International 2005).

I knew about Rula's story a few months before it was published in the Amnesty report. A close friend of mine who worked in a humanitarian organization told me that she had met Rula a few days after the event. She said that she was deeply depressed and was crying a lot. Hearing Rula's story left me shocked and mainly very scared.

I was pregnant at that time and lived in Dahiyat al-Barid, in Jerusalem, between two main checkpoints that were strictly controlled by the Israeli army: Qalandya checkpoint, which controls movement into and out of Ramallah, and al-Ram checkpoint, which controls Palestinians' movements in and out of Jerusalem. I could not help imagining myself experiencing the same fate. Nothing could guarantee a different outcome. We were already experiencing the arbitrary closures of the checkpoints; we knew about sick people who die while waiting for hours for the soldiers to open the checkpoint. The only thing that we were sure about in those days was the uncertainty of everything: we could not plan our day, every hour could lead to chaos. I could not imagine myself having a different fate from Rula's. I did not want to believe the story; I kept telling myself that this story could not be true! I kept thinking about international humanitarian laws, but eventually became more desperate and scared: these laws did not save Rula's baby.

According to the Fourth Geneva Convention (GCIV),[1] which relates to the protection of civilians during times of war, Rula represents precisely the 'civilian', the harmless and the unthreatening: she has the right gender (woman), carrying the archetypical motherhood signifier, pregnancy, in the precise physical status, woman in labour. Even her husband is the precise example of the harmless Palestinian man, who is begging the soldiers, in Hebrew, to let his wife cross the checkpoint. We also have all the dramatic marks of human weakness, the man who begs the soldiers, the woman who cries, the man who is asking for help, and in the end the tears, the blood, and the death. But under colonial occupation in Palestine this precise type of civilian, who should be protected during armed conflict, was constantly exposed to an ongoing disruption, which ended in the compression of the Palestinians into one homogenous total category of 'otherness' where every Palestinian is a potential terrorist. This process ultimately left no room for the category of civilian.

I argue that in order to understand population management under colonial occupation it is inadequate to use Foucault's analytical notions of biopower and biopolitics alone, concepts developed in the analysis of population management in the modern European nation-state. Instead, I suggest that biopower's opposite – thanatopower – is the appropriate conceptual frame for understanding the management of colonized occupied spaces and subjugated populations. Thanatopower is the management of death and destruction. Under colonial occupation, the lives of subjects are expropriated. They are exposed to the continual threat of death that becomes a permanent shadow accompanying them. Death is just on hold, again and again, from moment to moment. It's not because of the conscience of the sovereign or his sleepless nights that the subject's death is constantly delayed. On the contrary, the delay is clearly a product of economic calculation of cost and benefit, as well as an effort at making the system efficient. In fact, the delay is a moment when all power is drained: the power populates the moment of delay, with clear and disguised signs of death threats, like a permanent shadow. Because of this threat of death, granting life becomes a tremendous 'favour' (Ghanim 2005).

In the modern nation-state the organization of power over life deployed around the regulations of the body (disciplinary power) and the regulations of populations (biopower), is reflected through the inclusion of man's natural life in the mechanisms and calculations of power (Foucault 1978: 139; Agamben 1998: 119). From the seventeenth century, the 'old power' of death that symbolized sovereign power was gradually 'supplanted by the administration of bodies and the calculated management of life' (Foucault 1978: 140). According to Michel Foucault, in its old form, the power of the sovereign was the right to take life and let live, which meant the right of the sovereign to decide life and death (1978: 135–6). But since the classical age the West has undergone a very profound transformation of this mechanism of power; the death, that was based on the right of the 'sovereign is now manifested as simply the reverse of the right of the social body to ensure, maintain or develop its life' (136). What is at stake in the modern state is the 'biological existence of the population' where power 'is situated and exercised at the level of life, the species, the race and the large-scale phenomenon of population' (136–7).

I want to argue that along with the transformation of power, from its ancient form to its new modern form of 'biopower', a twofold process was initiated: on the one hand, power was localized in the domain of life, and directed towards the 'investment' in the 'good race', its public health and efficiency, in improving its life quality and social security. Therefore the war is no longer waged in the name of the sovereign who must be defended, but in the name of the society that must be defended (Foucault 1978: 2003). On the other hand and in 'the name of the society that must be defended', regimes initiate slaughters and massacres against their own populations 'who represent a kind of biological danger' (1978: 138). In this sense the concentration camps become, according to Agamben (1998: 117), the biopolitical paradigm of the modern.

The problem that resulted from the use of the biopolitical paradigm for understanding the regulation of the life of the 'wanted' and 'unwanted' races is that it dismisses the phenomenological experience of the destructive side of power from the viewpoint of its victims, and prevents an understanding of the experience of the power used on both sides by victims and oppressors.

From the viewpoint of power's victims, the moment that power is directed to destroying, eliminating and dismantling their group, the decision about their life becomes a decision about their death. In other words, this is the moment when (bio)power is transformed into (thanato)power. In this sense, thanatopower is not an independent or unique form of power, but is always already a supplement of biopower, which is called to action at those delicate moments of passage from calculating life to calculating death, from managing life to managing death, and from the politicization of life to the politicization of death. At this moment of transformation from the bio to the thanato, the old archetypal form of power to 'make die and let live' reappears under the new form of 'giving death and bargaining living', best reflected in our times in the new form of military occupation in Iraq, Afghanistan, Chechnya, and the colonial occupation of Palestine, the core of this chapter.

Under the colonial occupation of Palestine, the extreme form of thanatopower is reflected in the active putting to death of Palestinian activists and political leaders through targeted assassinations. But in its more subtle form it is reflected in exposing the Palestinians to the ongoing destructive power of the occupier through putting them under continual closures, ongoing curfews, arbitrary closing of main roads, the destruction of cultivated fields, the confiscation of agricultural land, bombing cities, using artillery fire in populated neighbourhoods, operating bypass roads and separating the spaces of the Palestinians and the Jewish settlers and, finally, conducting a siege policy that aims to 'put the Palestinians on a diet, but not make them die of hunger'.[2]

Moreover, historically and politically the notion of biopolitics has multiple positive meanings indicating qualified life as opposed to 'natural life'. Giorgio Agamben claims that the Greeks had no single term to express the modern meaning of life, using two terms: *zoē,* expressing the simple fact of living common to all living beings (animals, men, or gods), and *bios,* which indicated the form or way of living proper to an individual or a group (Agamben 1998: 1). What was at issue for Greek philosophers is not the mere fact of simple natural life but rather a qualified life, a particular way of life. According to Aristotle, 'this [life according to the good] is the greatest end shared both by all men and by each man separately' (Agamben 1998: 2).

Hannah Arendt (1998 [1958]: 24) notes: 'The good life can be practiced only through the mediation of the polis, which is placed in direct opposition to the natural association whose center is the home (*oikia*) and the family.' According to Arendt, being eligible for social access to the polis means that the person receives, 'beside his private life a sort of second life, his *bios politicos*'.

Eligibility to biopolitics was conditional on several variables, including gender, social status, age, and physical condition. Women, slaves and children were eligible to participate in the polis but could not gain the supplement of *bios politicos*. Aristotle's definition of the life of the citizen in the polis as 'the good life' was, according to Arendt (1998: 36), 'not a result of a merely better, more carefree life or one that is nobler than the ordinary life, but of an altogether different quality. It was "good" to the extent that by having mastered the necessities of sheer life, by being freed from labour and work, and by overcoming the innate urge of all living creatures for their own survival, it was no longer bound to the biological life process'.

In this context of conditioning eligibility for political life, the Greeks defined the social hierarchy of subjects according to their ability to distance themselves from the necessities of life, or according to their psycho-cultural state. In this context, neither women, who are bound to the state of their bodies, nor slaves, who are fully dependent on their masters, are able to gain full political existence, and thus full humanity (Schlaifer 1936: 168). The inability to gain political eligibility spread out from the internal community of the Greeks to the Barbarians, who, according to these definitions, were also unable to gain political eligibility, since they were enslaved to the monarch. There were different kinds of slavery, which included slavery as an imposition of fate, slavery as the justifiable position of inferiors, communal slavery and the slavery of men to their own evil selves and base desires (Cuffel 1966). Helen Kinsella (2006) clarifies that all those who were ineligible to enter the polis (including women, children and older people) were categorized in international humanitarian law as civilians who must be protected in war zones, while those who were eligible to gain access to the polis (men) were excluded from this category.

Therefore, says Kinsella,

> to be innocent in war, according to the terms set by the laws of war, is to be deficient or lacking in a multitude of ways that in the end, implicitly if not explicitly, cites an incapacity for politics… Equally significant, an incapacity for politics is also, at least for Aristotle, incapacity to become fully human. This is not benign, for it shows how the rights and protections of international humanitarian law are genealogically derived or grounded in what some might call 'subhumanity'. What this portends is that international humanitarian law requires and produces 'subhumanity' as the predicate for extending recognition of its rights or offering its protections (Kinsella 2006: 3).

Spatial and symbolic construction of the space of exception

The operation of thanatopower depends upon 'imaginative geographies' and imaginative others, who are defined/produced through the ongoing demarcation of spatial and symbolic boundaries that separate spaces of occupation as spaces of exception from spaces of rule and normality. This physical demarcation is the material instantiation of a symbolic/categorical separation between the 'legitimate political subject of the citizen' and the 'illegitimate political subject'.

According to Edward Said, 'imaginative geographies' fold 'distance into difference through a series of spatializations' (cited by Derek 2004: 17[3]). According to Said, imaginative geographies work by 'multiplying partitions and enclosures that serve to demarcate the "same" from the "other"', at once constructing and calibrating a gap between the two by designation in one's mind of a familiar space which is "ours" and an unfamiliar space which is "theirs"' (Derek 2004: 17). Derek claims that distance does not refer to a fixed, absolute and given fact, but is a concept and experience, a process, that is only made meaningful through cultural practice (2004: 18).

Following the second Intifada, the imaginative geography of 'the space of exception' was activated through the construction of a physical signalling system that includes the construction of the Separation Wall, the establishment of permanent checkpoints, temporary checkpoints, and other obstacles that mark the Occupied Territories as 'abnormal space', the antithesis of Israeli 'normal space'. The Separation Wall has become a master signifier, marking the difference between the two opposite spaces: the space of exception and the space of normality. 'Imaginative geographies' became meaningful through a symbolic process which marks moral and cultural boundaries as impermeable between the two populations, while also presenting the social, cultural and especially moral order of the people who live beyond the Wall as inferior to the moral and social order of 'here' (Israel). Constructing these physical and symbolic boundaries demarcates boundaries between one kind of people, who, due to their culture and values, can expand their biological existence into a political and social existence, and another kind of people, who, by their very essence and due to the barbarian position they continue to inhabit, cannot be eligible for a political supplement that will include them in the polis, thus expanding their existence beyond the biological.

Demarcating a space of exception: the Separation Wall as a master signifier

On 16 June 2002, Israel began constructing a massive Separation Wall between the West Bank and Israel. Israeli leaders see this wall as an answer to a pressing security need, supposedly blocking the entry of Palestinian suicide bombers into Israel and thus saving the lives of Israeli citizens. To Palestinians, these security reasons are an excuse for using the Wall to build facts on the ground, 'to confiscate more Palestinian lands. The rationale is not the security of Israeli citizens, as the Israeli government claims; rather, this is the result of long-term Israeli plans and land grab policies intended to control the Palestinian territories' (ARIJ 2003: 38).

Indeed, during 2002, military orders were issued to seize 224,000 dunams[4] in the northern areas of the West Bank, in order to construct the Separation Wall. According to these military orders, isolated Palestinian areas along the 1949 Armistice Line (the so-called 'Green Line') have been designated closed military areas, i.e., areas that no Palestinian is allowed to enter without a special permit issued by the Israeli authorities (ARIJ 2003: 31). During the same year, on 15 May 2002, Israel announced a policy of dividing the West Bank into eight siege areas, requiring Palestinians to obtain special permits from the Israeli authorities in order to move between these areas (ARIJ 2003: 35).

Beyond its effect of transforming many villages into de facto prisons,[5] the Wall has become a tool for demarcating clear boundaries between inside/outside, rule/exception, political life/bare life. The Wall became a physical and symbolic signifier separating the normal space of social and political life, which is populated by 'innocent citizens', from the space of exception and bare life populated by groups arguably contaminated by genetic terror and cultural disease, as described by former Israeli President Moshe Katzav:

> There is a huge gap between our enemies and us. Not just in ability, but also in morality, culture, sanctity of life and conscience. They are our neighbours here. But it seems to me that a few hundred meters away from us, there live a people who not only do not belong to our continent, not only do not belong to the planet, but actually belong to another galaxy (Shchori 2001).

This hierarchical moral categorization of 'us' against 'them' is exemplified in the inability of Israeli Deputy Defence Minister Ze'ev Boim to understand what he sees as the enigmatic, murderous culture of Islam in general and Palestinians in particular:

> What is it about Islam in general, and about the Palestinians in particular? Do they have a cultural deficit, a genetic defect? There is something incomprehensible in this ongoing murderousness (Barzily and Alon 2004).

Likud member of Knesset Yehiel Hazan expressed total support for Boim's statement:

> Boim is 100% right, given the fact that they [the Palestinians] have been slaughtering the Jews for decades. You must not believe the Arabs even if they have been dead and buried in their graves for forty years. It is in their blood. Murdering Jews comes naturally to them. This is where the

[popular] saying comes from, 'don't turn your back on them, because they will stab you' (Barzily and Alon 2004).

It was not an exceptional depiction of Palestinians as subhuman; a few months before the above statements, the same member claimed in the Knesset:

> In every place, they are worms underneath the earth, above the earth, and in every way... These worms have been harming the Jewish people for 100 years, while we have been stretching our hands out in peace. As long as we continue not to understand that we are dealing with a nation of murderous terrorists who do not want us here, we will have no quiet (Ynet, 13 December 2004).

These views, which assume an essential difference between Israelis and Palestinians, are not new. They have been deeply rooted in the imaginary Zionist conceptualization of the Palestinians since the beginning of the Zionist colonial enterprise. In 1914, Zionist leader Moshe Smilansky claimed:

> We must not forget that we are dealing here with a semi-savage people, who have extremely primitive concepts. This is their nature: if they sense power in you, they will surrender and will hide their hatred towards you. But if they sense weakness, they will dominate you... Moreover... owing to the many tourists and to urban Christians, there developed among the Arabs base values which are not common among other primitive people... lying, cheating, harboring grave [unfounded] suspicions and telling tales... and a hidden hatred for the Jews. These Semites – they are anti-Semites (Morris 1999: 43).

Marking Palestinians as genetically defective, morally inferior and socially impure has transformed them into a unique category: on the one hand, they live in a continual state of exception (the Israeli occupation); on the other hand, their very acts of resistance to this occupation, in order to gain political rights, become yet another indication of their 'inherent' ineligibility to these rights. To use Arendt's words, one may say that the Palestinian has become nothing but 'a man who has lost the very qualities that make it possible for other people to treat him as a man' (1976: 300), living as bare life, without right to access life within the state that offers qualified *bios* – the polis. Therefore, from the viewpoint of those who possess the power, Palestinians are living as biological subjects. It is impossible to understand the IOF's (Israeli Occupation Forces) mission, which is 'to defend the existence, territorial integrity and sovereignty of the State of Israel; to protect the inhabitants of Israel and to combat all forms of terrorism which threaten daily life',[6] without contextualizing it in the social imagery of the Palestinians as politically deficient.

Population management: death as a political tool

The ability to oppress the occupied, to rule them and to manage their existence is neither supported nor upheld by the principle of life. It is the perpetual threat of death and the transformation of death into a political collective experience.

Death becomes the field into which the power relations between occupier and occupied flow. When the State of Israel declares that its war is against terror and supporters of terror, we find ourselves facing a state that is 'targeting' the theoretical possibility of civilian existence in the Palestinian territories because this population is seen as supporting 'terror', articulating its support clearly by voting in the 'terrorist' Hamas to represent them.

On 18 February 2004, the Ynet[7] internet forum hosted Professor Assa Kasher, author of Israel's military ethics code and a well-known ethics philosopher, in an open discussion with surfers. Kasher talked about the Israeli war against Palestinian terror and proposed renewing and updating the Israeli army's ethical principles to suit the new kind of war that Israel is facing: 'We must understand that a new kind of war demands new principles of action. The old principle that distinguished between combatants and civilians is no longer relevant, now that we are fighting Palestinian terrorists who operate from within Palestinian populated areas.'

Two years later, in October 2006, Kasher gave an interview to a religious Jewish bulletin that is distributed in synagogues (*Yediot Aharonot*, 18 October 2006). Kasher argued that the Israeli army did not use sufficient power to end the Intifada, employing a medical metaphor to clarify his point: 'Using less than the required dosage of medicine may have detrimental effects on the patient.' Kasher also added that the Israeli army's attempts to avoid harming innocent people can be a mistake in some cases, because it may result in the death of innocent Israeli citizens. Following this statement, Kasher used the same medical vocabulary to clarify his statement to Ynet:

A doctor may give a patient too little or too much of a particular medicine. In both cases, this may result in tragedy. Therefore, one must give the exact dosage. In this case [that of the army], the exact dosage translates into striking terrorists with the least amount of injured civilians.[8]

It is important to juxtapose Kasher's argument with the reality of the Palestinian context. According to a report published by the Palestinian Central Bureau of Statistics on 26 December 2006,[8] the Palestinian population in the Occupied Territories would have reached a total of 3.9 million by the end of 2006, 2.5 million in the West Bank and East Jerusalem and 1.5 million in the Gaza Strip.

From the beginning of the second Intifada until December 2006, approximately 4,984 Palestinians were killed by Israeli forces or by settlers, while 49,377 were injured. The number of Palestinians to be arrested was 41,156, including approximately 5,200 aged under 18.[9] Of those arrested, 10,500 are still incarcerated in Israeli prisons and detention centres, including hundreds held under administrative detention, without charge or trial.

Among the fatalities, 810 were minors (under 18), 343 were killed during the course of targeted assassinations, and 208 were the object of targeted assassinations.[10] In a dramatic event that took place on 8 November 2006 (less than a month after Assa Kasher's statements), according to the Palestinian Centre for Human Rights,[11] 'the Israeli Occupation Forces shelled a residential area in the northern Gaza Strip town of Beit Hanoun, killing 18 Palestinians, among them 17 members of the al-'Athamna family (including 6 children and 7 women), and wounding 55 others. Most of the victims were sleeping in their homes when the attack took place. The IOF fired at least 10 artillery shells at the area.' A few months prior to that, on 9 June 2006, the Ghalia family was severely hit in an Israeli attack during a picnic on Gaza beach. The incident received worldwide attention, mostly due to the horrifying video footage taken minutes later of devastated 10-year-old Huda Ghalia running wildly along the Gaza beach crying 'father, father, father' and then falling weeping beside his body. This footage instantly turned the distraught girl into an icon of the Palestinian struggle, before she had fully grasped that most of her family were dead (McGreal 2006). In the attack, 7 family members were killed (Ali 43, his wife Raisa 36, their children: Haytham 8 months, Hanadi 2, Sabrin 7, Ilham 17, Alia 24) and seven more were injured (Hamida, Amane 22, Ayham 17, Adham 12, Huda 10, Hadil 6, Latifa 4). The family had already been hit in the past as a result of ongoing Israeli shelling into civilian neighbourhoods of the densely populated Gaza Strip. On 4 January 2005, an Israeli shell killed 8 and injured 5 in the family's strawberry field. Nine of the 13 hit were family members.

Two months earlier, 10 Palestinians were killed by Israeli artillery fire in the northern Gaza Strip: a little girl in one incident, 2 adolescents on their way to school in another, and youngsters playing soccer on yet another occasion. 'When thousands of artillery shells are fired into such a small area, the results are predictable', according to Ha'aretz (Harel and Issascharoff 2006). According to PCHR,[12] between 29 September 2001 and 29 September 2006, 10,000 Palestinians were wounded by the IOF in the Gaza Strip and 12,920 Palestinians were wounded in the West Bank.

Palestinians have been killed not only by direct fire. Casualties have also been caused as a result of delays at checkpoints or of being refused entry, thus preventing Palestinians from receiving suitable medical treatment.[13] Data show that, in May 2005, the IOF was operating 27 permanently staffed checkpoints in the West Bank, leading to most severe restrictions on the movement of Palestinians. The IOF checks every person who crosses the checkpoints, which frequently results in lengthy delays. The IOF also operates 26 additional checkpoints between the West Bank and the territory of the State of Israel. An additional 16 checkpoints are generally open for Palestinians to cross without being checked. Some have a watchtower. In Hebron alone there are 12 checkpoints, particularly where there is friction between settlers and Palestinians. These checkpoints are permanently staffed and all persons who cross are checked. The IOF has also erected hundreds of physical obstacles in the West Bank, in the form of concrete blocks, piles of dirt, or trenches, preventing access to and from towns and villages. Palestinian travel is restricted or entirely prohibited on 41 roads and sections of roads throughout the West Bank, including many of the main traffic arteries, covering over 700 kilometres of roadway. Israelis can travel freely on these roads without being stopped or checked (B'Tselem 2005).

In the Gaza Strip, the houses of 24,768 Palestinians have been totally demolished, and the houses of 25,211 partially demolished. In Rafah, in the south of Gaza, the houses of 15,427 Palestinians have been totally demolished and 13,457 houses have been partially demolished.

Despite all this, the very political act of electing Hamas in January 2006 led to Palestinians being portrayed as unable to practise mature politics, and generalized as one homogenous group of terror supporters. This logic leads to Israel's policy, described by a governmental spokesman as 'putting the Palestinians on a diet, but not making them die of hunger'.[14] The question is where one draws the line between diet and death. What does 'pressure' mean in a zone of exception? Indeed, according to UNRWA, every person in the Palestinian refugee camps has been issued a ration of 2,300 calories a day, dropping to 1,500 calories in the summer. This was calculated by the United Nations and UNRWA as the exact amount a human being needs in order to survive – no more and no less (Pilger 2006: 63). In the West Bank and Gaza, the poverty rate (a daily per capita income below $2.10) has dramatically risen from 13% in the West Bank and 32% in Gaza in 1999 to 47% in the West Bank and 64% in Gaza in 2003 (B'Tselem 2004).

Drawing the line between dieting and starvation becomes a political issue, making it crucial to understanding the delicate differences between dying and death. The distinctions between dying – a process – and death, which intervenes between dying and being dead – help us understand that the power used against the Palestinians is not about killing them, eliminating them or pushing them collectively into their graves. Rather, it is about managing them as biological subjects through localizing them in the liminal zone between life and death, between dieting and starvation – not really dying but being one step before that, where 'a decision on life becomes a decision on death. Biopolitics can turn into Thanatopolitics' (Agamben 1998: 222).

Conclusion: the political life of death

Turning decisions of life and death into political issues creates a deadly reality of action and reaction, best reflected in the phenomenon of suicide bombers. According to research conducted by the psychologist Fadal Abu-Hin in April 2001, over 40% of 1,000 young Gaza Strip Palestinians aged 9 to 16 said that they were actively involved in the Intifada. Over 70% said that they wanted to be martyrs. 'If I were to carry out the same study today', says Abu-Hin, 'I am sure the figures would be even higher,' adding that he believes that similar figures would be found in the West Bank (cited in Hage 2003).

When the Palestinian subject feels unable to control his/her life and his/her death, 'suicide' become an escape route from the total control of the occupation where s/he can liberate the sphere of death from the control of the occupier by deciding the time and the way of death. In so doing, s/he recharges the 'death act' with a symbolic political meaning, giving it a unique form of eternal life, which cannot be controlled by any outsider. One suicide bomber who was captured before the act explains his decision:

> Not a single living creature dared walk the streets. Soldiers fired at everyone, even at those who just stepped into their gardens. I peeked out through the window and suddenly I saw a dog wandering freely in the street. The soldiers didn't arrest it or shoot at it. At that moment I thought, either I live a life that is less than the life of this dog, or I die as a *shahid* (Hass 2003).

Here the threefold meaning of the term *shahid* in Islam is significant: 'witness', 'always alive', and as the one who 'killed in the name of God'.

According to Butrus al-Bustani, author of the Arabic lexicon *Muheit al-Muheit* (1870), originally the word *shahid* is one of God's names,[15] literally meaning 'witness'. According to this text, God is the first and archetypal witness, who by his divine ability to be present everywhere and anytime knows everything without any mediation. Later, with the beginning of Islam, the word *shahid* came to mean the one who 'killed in the name of God'. According to al-Bustani, the one who kills for the sake of God is considered a witness in two ways: first because God and the angels will 'witness' his entrance to paradise; second, because at the end of the world the *shahid,* along with the Prophet Muhammad, will bear witness to the deeds of 'others'. For this reason, the *shahid* is considered to have 'never died, but lives on', ready for his holy mission to provide his testimony. Therefore, unlike other dead, who must wait until the resurrection to reawake, the *shahid* passes directly from the secular world to the divine world without going through the liminal mediation of death.

Despite its religious origins, the term *shahid* has been secularized by many Palestinian organizations that use it to refer to anyone killed by the occupation, militant or civilian, directly or indirectly, without regard to his religion.

When Palestinians experience life as meaningless, less than that of a dog, and beyond individual control, the act of committing suicide could be a meaningless answer to a desperate life. But when suicide is resignified with religious and national meanings, it becomes an act of resistance, and can be viewed as a means of political salvation.

When the occupier reduces life to 'biological' fact and uses death as a tool of political subjugation, the *shahid* redraws the meaning of death, recovering it from subjugation and control, in the very act of deciding the time and place of his/her own death. By the act of *shahada* (testimony), death becomes an overdetermined political act: the *shahid* becomes the ideal witness and representative of his community, who, through his mere physical elimination, creates an alternative stage from which to judge and convict the oppressor, but also to justify the victims. Controlling death becomes a political option available not only to the occupier, but also to the subject of occupation. According to a former Palestinian political prisoner, Mahmoud Najar (2005):

> Yes, death is a choice. The death of my body is your highest possibility but it is my highest possibility too. The difference between both possibilities is life. To you, my death is the death of another Palestinian terrorist. To me, my death is the total defeat of a system, but when a man defeats a system of death, he is eternal.

In this deadly trap, the occupier can use the threat of death to oppress and control the Palestinians, but they can turn their own death into a way of gaining political meaning, as a way of compensating for a meaningless life. This is a deadly trap not only because of its fatal human results, but also because it turns the political into a state that can be gained only at the moment of its elimination.

Notes

1. The convention was published on 12 August 1949, at the end of a conference held in Geneva from 21 April to 12 August 1949. The convention entered into force on 21 October. Full text of the Geneva Convention at «http://www.icrc.org/ihl.nsf/CONVPRES?OpenView»

2. «http://news.independent.co.uk/world/middle_east/article348712.ece»

3. The British geographer, Gregory Derek (2006), adds that the use of the term 'civilian' as the opposite of 'military' emerged in the second half of the eighteenth century. It was closely tied to colonial military adventures and referred to European servants employed by the East India Company. It later became a commonplace during the course of the nineteenth century.

4. A dunam equals 1,000 square metres.

5. For further information about the effect of the Wall on Palestinians, see 'The Segregation Wall in the West Bank', ARIJ, Jerusalem, 2003.

6. «http://www1.idf.il/DOVER/site/mainpage.asp?sl=EN&id=31»

7. «http://www.ynet.co.il/articles/1,7340,L-3316557,00.html»

8. The website of *Yediot Aharonot*, one of Israel's leading newspapers.

9. Published in aljazeera net. See «http://www.aljazeeratalk.net/forum/show thread.php?p=82737»

10   DCI-Palestine, 2006. 'Palestinian child political prisoners 2006 report'. Ramallah. «http://www.dcipal.org/english/display.cfm?DocId=559& Category Id=2»

11   «http://www.btselem.org/English/Statistics/Casualties.asp» (viewed January 2007)

12   PCHR, 2006 'Statistics related to Al Aqsa Intifada: 29 September 2000-updated 28 September, 2006', «http://www.pchrgaza.org/Library/alaqsaintifada.htm»

13   PCHR (Palestinian Centre for Human Rights) press release, 8 November 2006, «http://www.pchr.org»

14   Accumulated reports by the Health Work Committees, the Palestinian Central Bureau of Statistics, the Palestinian Ministry of Health, and the Palestinian Red Crescent Society, which have documented the following: 'In the first year of the Intifada: 15 deaths due to inability to access medical care facilities. Births at checkpoints – 11 documented cases. Eight newborns died because of inadequate medical care. Inadequate vaccination programmes – one quarter of all children in Palestine have been prevented from receiving appropriate vaccinations. Prevention of patients from reaching health care facilities – tens of thousands of patients have been prevented from gaining access to medical facilities. 16,210 injury cases have been documented, 38% from live ammunition, 72% in the upper torso of the body. Of those injured, 2,151 are schoolchildren. Permanent disabilities – estimated at 2,500 people, among them 537 children.'

15   According to Islam, God (Allah) has 99 names that symbolize his divine power.

References

Agamben, G. (1995) 'We Refugees', *Symposium*, Vol. 49, no. 2, 114–19

Agamben, G. (1998) *Homo Sacer: Sovereign Power and Bare Life*, Stanford University Press, Stanford, CA

Amnesty International (2005) 'Conflict, occupation and patriarchy: Women carry the burden', 31 March 2005 «http://web.amnesty.org/library/index/engmde150162005 »

Arendt, H. (1976) *The Origins of Totalitarianism*, Harcourt, New York

Arendt, H. (1998 [1958]) *The Human Condition*, University of Chicago Press, Chicago and London

ARIJ (2003) 'Undermining peace: Israel's unilateral segregation plans in the Palestinian territories', Jerusalem «http://www.arij.org»

Barzily, A. and G. Alon (2004) 'Boim: Are the Palestinians killers because of a genetic defect?' *Ha'aretz*, 25 February 2004

B'Tselem (2004) 'Statistics in unemployment and poverty', «http://www.btselem. org/english/Freedom_of_Movement/Unemployment_statistics.asp»

B'Tselem (2005) 'Statistics on checkpoints and roadblocks', «http://www.btselem. org/english/Freedom_of_Movement/Statistics.asp»

Bustani, B. (1870) *Muheit al-Muheit, Arabic lexicon*, Lebanon

Cuffel, V. (1966) 'The classical Greek concept of slavery', *Journal of the History of Ideas*, Vol. 27, no. 3, 323–42

Derek, G. (2004) *The Colonial Present*, Blackwell, Oxford

Derek, G. (2006) 'The death of the civilian', *Environment and Planning D: Society and Space* «web.mac.com/derekgregory/iWeb/Site/Orientalism%20and%20occupation.html»

Foucault, M. (1978) *The History of Sexuality*, Vintage, New York

Foucault, M. (2003*) Society Must Be Defended: Lectures at the Collège de France, 1975–1976,* Penguin Books, London

Ghanim, H. (2005) 'Thanatopolitics: Dialectics of life and death under occupation', *Theory and Criticism*, Vol. 27, 181–6

Hage, G. (2003) '"Comes a time we are all enthusiasm": Understanding Palestinian suicide bombers in times of exighophobia', *Public Culture* Vol. 15, no. 1, 65–89

Harel, A. and A. Issascharoff (2006) 'So vicious, this cycle', *Ha'aretz*, 10 November 2006

Hass, A. (2003) 'Flying to Paradise', *Ha'aretz*, 4 April 2003

Kinsella, H. (2006) 'Gendering Grotius: Sex and sex difference in the laws of war', *Political Theory,* Vol. 34, no. 2, 161–91

McGreal, C. (2006) 'Who really killed Huda Ghalia's family?' *Guardian*, 16 June 2006

Morris, B. (1999) *Righteous Victims: A History of the Zionist–Arab Conflict, 1881–1999*, Alfred A. Knopf, New York

Najar, M. (2005) 'Prison: Analysis of the imprisonment of Palestinians'. Autonomy and Solidarity Website «http://auto_sol.tao.ca/node/view/1362»

PHRC (2006) 'Statistics related to the Al Aqsa *Intifada*: 29 September 2000 – updated 28 September 2006' «http://www.pchrgaza.org/Library/alaqsaintifada.htm»

Pilger, J. (2006) *Freedom Next Time*, Bantam, London

Schlaifer, R. (1936) 'Greek theories of slavery from Homer to Aristotle', *Harvard Studies in Classical Philology*, Vol. 47, 165–204

Shchori, D. (2001) 'Katzav on the Palestinians: "They belong to another galaxy" ', *Ha'aretz*, 2 May 2001

Sari Hanafi[1]

4 Palestinian Refugee Camps in Lebanon: Laboratories of State-in-the-Making, Discipline and Islamist Radicalism

Introduction[1]

The armed battle between the Lebanese army and Fatah al-Islam inside the Nahr al-Barid refugee camp, north of Tripoli, lasted forty days, resulting in the destruction of more than half of the camp's premises and the flight of around 30,000 persons to other camps. In Ein al-Hilweh camp, many arguments developed into clashes between armed young men. Some other camps were besieged by the Lebanese army in an attempt to control human and arms flows to the camps. Fatah-al-Islam (500–700 persons), Usbet al-Ansar (League of Partisans, 200–300 persons), Jund al-Sham (Army of Greater Syria, 100 persons), are the names of extremist Islamist organizations, franchises of al-Qaida, which invest progressively in the space of the camp. Fingers have been hypothetically pointed at Saudi Arabia, Syria, and al-Qaida as supporting these groups, but regardless of the authorities behind them, they all know very well that the camp is a space of exception, a space out of place.

How have we arrived at this point? Why has violence erupted in the Lebanese camps and not in the Jordanian or Syrian camps? This chapter argues that for sixty years, the space of the refugee camps in Lebanon was treated as a space of exception and an experimental laboratory for control and surveillance. Exception is not promulgated by one sovereign; many actors involved in the different modes of governance have been contributing to the suspension of this space under the cover of the law. These actors, involved in the politics of space, are mainly the host authorities, and to a lesser degree the Palestine Liberation Organization (PLO) and the United Nations Refugee and Works

Agency for Palestine Refugees in the Near East (UNRWA), but also Islamist groups and different local political commissars.

From the initial construction of the camp, it remains for these actors the most suitable spatial configuration for control and surveillance, as the refugees themselves resist their confinement to this kind of space. According to the UNHCR, in 2002 only 38% of the world's refugees were camp dwellers, while 20% were urban-zone dwellers. In the case of the Palestinians, 29% of the refugees live in camps, though in Gaza and Lebanon this rate rises to around 50%. What is the impact of living in such dwellings on the inhabitants' socio-economic situation and their political and national identities? Many studies I have conducted in the Palestinian diaspora demonstrate substantial differences in terms of socio-economic status, living conditions and identity formation between Palestinian camp dwellers and city dwellers (Hanafi 1997, 2001). This chapter develops this further. I start by presenting a comparative overview of the living conditions of Palestinian camp dwellers, arguing that there are major differences between closed and open refugee camps and that the camp setting as a closed space is not a 'natural' setting but rather has its *raison d'être* in terms of disciplinary power, control and surveillance, and of deploying the state of exception. Contrary to those who consider the absence of refugee camps as a determining factor in diluting the refugees' national identity with that of the host country, I argue that the relationship between national identity and residential setting is very weak and that the camps create a new, much more urban identity rather than a national one.

Palestinian refugee camps are highly problematic, given the gap between refugees' legitimate claims and rights with regard to UN Security Council resolutions and international law (Hanafi 2002), and the demographic expansion and structural changes that have taken place in the camps since their establishment. This brings them ever closer to being slum areas and underdeveloped urban sprawls.

This chapter is based on several years of fieldwork, including interviews with the population of the Palestinian refugee camps and those who lead the camps in Lebanon and the Palestinian Territory, but also in Syria and Jordan.

Palestinians in camps: closed versus open space

Although refugee camp dwellers generally enjoy adequate health and education services, they are disfavoured and overlooked in the socio-economic plans of the host country. While differences between camp dwellers and refugee urban dwellers in Syria and to a lesser extent in Jordan are minimal, the gap between camp and urban refugee dwellers in Lebanon is enormous. This can be explained by the fact that the camps in Jordan and Syria by and large constitute open spaces regulated by the host state, while in Lebanon they are set in a closed space. I define 'open space' as both urban and societal. Speaking of the urban, the space is regulated by the host country to look like any residential low-income neighbourhood, allowing it to be connected with the surrounding cities and villages. From the societal point of view, camp dwellers are relatively integrated socially and economically into the surrounding neighbourhood and labour market. A closed space does not meet any of these conditions, and is constituted of urban enclaves or satellites located at the urban periphery, lacking green spaces, with poor access and poor housing.

My previous studies (Hanafi 2006) of refugee camps show a correlation between the relative poverty rates of Palestinian refugees and discrimination in both housing and the labour market. The poverty rate is higher compared to the local population only in Lebanon and in the Palestinian Territory (mainly the West Bank), despite the fact that in the latter area there is no institutional discrimination in the labour market.[2] This demonstrates how salient such a space is, not only regarding refugees' living conditions, but also their urban identity and their relationship to Palestinian nationalism.

According to the Norwegian Institute for Applied Social Science (Fafo)'s various surveys in Jordan and Syria, the living conditions of Palestinian refugees outside the camps are not much different to that of the general population of the host country (Khawaja and Tiltnes 2002; Ugland 2003). Although the situation for refugees living in camps in all countries is worse than for other segments, the camp populations do not face homogeneously poor living conditions, nor do they constitute the main poverty problem of the host countries. An exception is Lebanon, where all the indicators of Fafo's survey illustrate poorer living conditions than in other areas (Hanssen-Bauer and Jacobsen 2003).

Even though education levels are generally good, thanks to UNRWA, in Lebanon 60% of Palestinian youngsters aged 18–29 do not complete their basic education. In the Palestinian Territory, girls tend not to finish high school because of early marriage, and there are higher illiteracy rates for females than for males. The incompatibility between the relatively high level of education and the low socio-economic status of camp dwellers arises from the fact that people whose economic status improves usually leave the camps for the cities, where work is more readily available.

Over 60% of homes in the Lebanese and Jordanian refugee camps lack proper sanitary installations for drinking water. Yet the most serious problem concerns the population density inside the camp: 30% to 40% of the homes have a density of three to eleven people or more, causing huge environmental problems. The buildings are often squashed tightly together in narrow alleys, with no natural light, exposed to hazardous building materials, inadequate temperature control and poor ventilation. Infant mortality rates in the camps in Lebanon stand at 239 deaths per 100,000 births, and the rates of chronic infant illnesses are two or three times the national average.

Palestinians in Lebanon

The story of the Palestinian presence in Lebanon is one of deep ethno-national divisions, political confrontation and, in the post-civil war years, ideological controversy. During the Israeli-Arab war in 1948 100,000 people fled to Lebanon. My interviews with many refugees attest to the brutality and oppressive nature of the control over the camps by the police, army and Deuxième Bureau – the feared Lebanese internal security apparatus. While some of the camps (in the south), according to Jihane Sfeir-Khayat (2001), acted as transit camps, they later became permanent.

Palestinian nationalism grew quickly from 1965 onwards. After the PLO in Jordan was crushed in 1970 and its leadership relocated to Beirut, the Lebanon camps became the centre of the Palestinian resistance against the Israeli state. While UNRWA had already been set up to provide the Palestinian refugees with education, health and social services, following the arrival of the Palestinian leadership, a sizeable number of Palestinian institutions, including nurseries, vocational training centres, health clinics and various industries (textile, leather goods, ironwork, furniture, handicrafts) were also established in the 1970s (Farsoun and Zacharia 1997; Peteet 2005). This allowed for the establishment of camp committees and a number of other organizations engaged in health, education, culture, and sports in and around the refugee camps. At one point up to two-thirds of the Palestinian labour force was employed by the PLO and the resistance movement, including in political offices and armed units (Sayigh 1994; Hanafi and Tiltnes forthcoming).

The Palestinian community in Lebanon took shape not only economically but also politically and spatially. The re-emergence of distinctly Palestinian nationalist politics in the mid-1960s followed the progress made by the scattered Palestinians in rebuilding their socio-political space. Progress enhanced by the Palestine Resistance Movement and the PLO played a key role in promoting a collective political and national identity among the exiled Palestinians, who, until then, had seen themselves merely as refugees. The camps played an important role, as the 1969 Cairo Agreement between the Lebanese government and the Palestinians secured the Palestinians full control over the camps, which virtually became a state-within-a-state. To this day the camps make up enclaves out of reach of Lebanese law.

The 1982 Israeli invasion, however, forced the PLO to leave Beirut, and with the Palestinian leadership gone, scores of social and economic institutions disappeared, and with them employment and income. The expulsion of the PLO coincided with falling remittances in the 1980s, particularly from the Gulf states. In the wake of the Oslo Accords, the diversion of foreign aid from Palestinians in Lebanon to the Palestinian Territory made the situation worse. After 1982, with the exception of a few organizations such as the Palestinian Red Crescent, almost all PLO-created organizations collapsed and, as a result, the Palestinian refugees residing in the camps had only UNRWA to cater for their needs. Despite UNRWA's efforts, the conditions of the Palestinian refugees have gone from bad to worse. Housing problems became more acute, the economy deteriorated, and the social environment reached an alarmingly unhealthy level.

Although at present there are in excess of 400,000 Palestinian refugees registered with UNRWA,[3] only about 200,000–250,000 refugees are actually residing in Lebanon (Pedersen 2003). Of these, up to two-thirds live in refugee camps served by UNRWA, or in small communities adjacent to the camps where people have access to the services of UNRWA and Palestinian and other NGOs. The remaining third reside elsewhere in Lebanon and are generally thought to be better off than the camp population, although there are no statistics to support such a claim. Some of them are 'naturalized' and have been granted

Lebanese citizenship.[4] Some 100,000 Palestinian refugees have left Lebanon, many to Europe and particularly the Scandinavian countries and Germany (Doraï 2006), especially after the Israeli invasion and the war against the camps, fleeing the conflict, but also social exclusion.

Distrust between population groups appears to be a significant trait of the current Lebanese psyche, extending to the attitude of Lebanese citizens, especially among the Christians, vis-à-vis Palestinian refugees, held responsible for the civil war. The majority of the Lebanese vehemently oppose the permanent resettlement of Palestinians in the country. Curiously, such *towteen* (implantation) is also strongly rejected by the Palestinians, who insist on the 'right of return' to Palestine (Nasrallah 1997; Haddad 2000; Sayigh 2001; Khalili 2005). The Lebanese position on resettlement also translates to discriminatory policies with regards to the social, economic and civil rights of the Palestinians.

Palestinian camp dwellers refer to themselves as the 'forgotten people'. They feel that they live in a hostile environment without basic human rights, including the right to work, and with no effective means of representation or protection.

According to the Danish Refugee Council (2005), Palestinian refugees in Lebanon can be categorized into three groups. The majority (400,582) are 'registered' refugees by both UNRWA and the Lebanese authorities, and benefit from the services offered by UNRWA. They constitute approximately 10% of the population of Lebanon. The second category (35,000) is 'non-registered' refugees (NGO estimate 2004). These refugees fall outside the UNRWA mandate because they left Palestine after 1948, and took refuge outside UNRWA's areas of operation; they were registered only by the Lebanese government. Not until January 2004 did UNRWA start to serve the non-registered population. The third category (3,000) is that of the 'non-identified' refugees, who are not registered with any agency in Lebanon or internationally and thus possess no valid documents. They do not have access to UNRWA's assistance. They endure difficult socio-economic conditions as they lack stable income due to their ineligibility for work. They do not have access to health care, educational facilities or other forms of humanitarian assistance. Other local organizations, such as the Palestinian Red Crescent Society, provide health facilities to non-ID refugees. However, in most cases they have to pay for these services (Danish Refugee Council 2005).

Camps as humanitarian space

The biopower (Foucault 1994) exercised by humanitarian organizations has created categories for those in need with the effect of depoliticizing them. Refugees are transformed into bodies to be fed and sheltered. The accounts of many refugees attest to having been treated like animals by the international community (Romig 2006). Humanitarian law used to talk about 'protected people', but current humanitarian practice focuses mainly on 'victims'. By classifying people as victims, the basis of humanitarian action shifts from rights to welfare. In disaster areas – the space of exception – values of generosity and pragmatism obscure any references to the rights and responsibilities of the people concerned (refugees, humanitarian organizations, international community, etc.).

However, the activities of refugee organizations, according to their statutes, have only a 'humanitarian and social', but not a political character (Agamben 1997). Despite the fact that the majority of cases that refugee organizations deal with are of a mass nature, refugees' political identity and existence are submerged by their status as individuals in need of shelter and food. In this way, the task of providing for Palestinian refugees was transferred into the hands of the police and military forces, and of service organizations like UNRWA.

Returning to my initial problematic of the emergence of the camp's urban identity, the camp as closed space forms the very conditions for facilitating the use of biopolitics by the host countries and UNRWA, as refugees are gathered in a centralized and controlled place where they can be under constant surveillance. This 'care, cure and control' system has transformed refugee camps into disciplinary spaces (Zureik 2003: 165; Peteet 2005: 45). Under the pretext of facilitating service provision, the camp is conceived as the only possible space (Romig 2006). The question, however, is not only the form of the space but also the nature of the UNRWA mandate.

UNRWA has been conceived as a service provider organization since its creation in 1950 as a specific body for Palestinian refugees, and was given a specific mandate by the UN which did not encompass protection or return. Despite its very strict mandate, there have been some transgressions during the past fifteen years, including 'passive protection' for Palestinian refugees during the first Intifada. Since its 2004 Geneva donor meeting, UNRWA has been linking service provision to advocacy. However, taking into account housing, children's and

women's rights and other rights does not mean that the right of return
has become part of UNRWA's advocacy strategy. The USA and some
of UNRWA's European donors consider that if UNRWA goes in the
direction of looking for a durable solution (like settlement and return),
it will mean a dangerous politicization (Takkenberg 2007).

UNRWA has played a very important role in empowering Palestinian
refugees by providing education, health and sometimes work. However,
this has not been sufficient to get the Palestinians integrated into the host
society. UNRWA has sometimes submitted to the will of the host
authority in maintaining the camps as temporary spaces. While the tents
disappeared from refugee camps in Syria after one year, in Lebanon they
lasted ten years (Doraï 2006). One of the indirect consequences was emigration: while the first wave of emigrants to the Gulf area in the 1960s
and 1970s was economically successful, the second wave of emigration to
Europe in the 1980s and 1990s was not (Hanafi 2005). The result of maintaining refugees in camps so as to keep the camps operational for the return
of the refugees relocated them farther from their place of origin, keeping
them in a state of double alienation, both from their place of origin and
from the urban and social domains in the host society.

This double alienation is related to both spatial and temporal suspension. These refugee camps, characterized by what the French anthropologist Michel Agier calls 'frozen transience', are an ongoing lasting
state of temporariness. As in the prisons and 'hyperghettos' scrutinized
by Loïc Wacquant (1999), camp dwellers 'learn to live, or rather
survive, in the here-and-now, bathed in the concentrate of violence
and hopelessness brewing within its walls' (Agier 2002: 318).

Finally, it is interesting to note that the discipline of 'Refugee Studies'
is mainly the study of the humanitarian condition of refugees rather than
their political condition (Malkki 1995: 599). The discipline is functional-
ist and the questions it studies are shaped by the international organizations that fund it, while issues such as protection are still very loosely
articulated with the political rights of the refugees as human beings.

Closed camps: between space of exception and space of void

The closed camps in Lebanon have become a space of exception. They
are subjected to biopower and the use of the state of exception, put into
play by different actors, including the Lebanese authorities, the PLO
and UNRWA, among other emerging actors, constituting different

sovereigns over the camp. The sovereign, according to the German philosopher Carl Schmitt, is the one who may proclaim the state of exception. He is not characterized by the order that he institutes through the constitution but by the suspension of that order (Agamben 1998). My argument is that the politics of exception has been exercised in these urban places since the establishment of these camps. But exactly how?

While the Lebanese state is present in the public space by the rule of urban laws, it has abandoned the camps and allowed them to become spaces devoid of laws and regulations. The urbanization process takes on a wild nature, stemming from the absence of planning policies and, in particular, the non-enforcement of construction laws. Everyone builds as s/he sees fit, and the result is hundreds of illegal buildings spreading in all directions. The urbanization process of the unregulated camps resulted in a large population suffering from poverty, living in slum areas surrounding the cities.

In this situation nothing is legally defined. Everything is suspended, yet upheld without any written documents relating to this suspension. Camps had been under the PLO authority since the 1969 Cairo Agreement, but the expulsion of the PLO in 1982 led to their being governed by a web of complex power structures composed of two popular committees (one pro-Syrian and the other pro-PLO), a security committee, a committee of camp notables, a local committee, political factions, Islamist non-Palestinian groups, imams, PLO popular organizations (workers, women, engineers, etc.), NGOs,[5] and UNRWA directors[6] (Kortam 2007). The interviews I conducted in different camps showed how camp populations have lived with the disarray caused by this state of exception. According to an elderly female refugee expressing her anger: 'Who can I complain to when my neighbour builds a second and third floor without leaving any proper space for my apartment?' Many interviewees used the word 'chaos' to describe the situation in the camps.

Chaos, however, is not based on the absence of law but on the exclusion by the sovereign(s) of the population from the space where the law is operated (see Romig 2006): 'Camps are not under the responsibility of the Lebanese state,' says a senior officer in the Lebanese security forces. This means camp dwellers are excluded from the spheres of work and civil rights but at the same time included when it is a question of security and paying taxes. This subtle use of law and its suspension justifies the use of the space of exception to understand the relationship between the camp and the Lebanese space. At times, however, the situation comes closer to a state of void, filled in a very ad hoc way as the result of the architecture of power structure. The state of exception, according to Agamben, is the suspension of law whenever possible by one sovereign. However, in the case of the Lebanese Palestinian refugee camps, we have a tapestry of multiple partial sovereignties: real sovereigns like the Lebanese government or the PLO, but also phantom sovereigns like UNRWA, in addition to a web of actors who contribute to the state of exception and the suspension of laws.

At this point it is important to understand UNRWA as a phantom sovereign. While UNRWA was not intended, nor does it pretend to govern the camps, it has the status as such, and interviewed camp dwellers consider it responsible for the disorder in the camps. UNRWA calls its representatives in the camps 'camp directors', an appellation definitely carrying symbolic violence, the violence of occupying a ruling position without acting accordingly. This confusion is not due to the refugees' cognitive disorder but rather to the historical role played by UNRWA directors in not merely service providing but rather in organizing the refugees' lives.

Due to the sovereign exercising the state of exception, the camps became the symbol of territorial illegitimacy. However, this state of exception is exercised not only by the sovereign, but also by the actors themselves. Agamben falls short of addressing the agency of the actor resisting the 'total institution'. He perceives the camp as a paradigmatic place of modernity and modern politics, using concentration camps such as Auschwitz as examples (Agamben 1998). As zone of indistinction between public and private, Agamben's theorization of the camp lacks agency, and all is submitted to the sovereign's subjectivation. However, the Palestinian refugee camps are spaces of resistance and transgression, where agency expresses itself not only through resistance, but also through the use of the same process of power: the state of exception. Discursively, many actors, often the political commissars of these camps, and what I call the local sovereign, insist on the exceptional status of the camps while refusing to submit them to Lebanon's urban and tax regulations. This is a power strategy used by political commissars to keep their authoritative power without elections. This refusal results from the need to keep the status quo where the majority of the camps' popular committees are nominated by the various

Palestinian factions. However, does the position of the political commissar reflect the position of the whole camp population? Many interviews we conducted in the Badawi and Burj Barajneh camps show the growth of a pervasive, often angry disillusionment with any kind of politics, secular or mainstream religious, especially with the onset of factional strife in Gaza and the destruction of Nahr al-Barid.

Before 1970, the camps had been governed by the state of emergency where security forces (Darak and Deuxième Bureau) had suspended the laws. However, since 1970 the police have not been able to penetrate the camps without negotiating with the powerful actors, who decide, on a case by case basis, whether to cooperate. In any quarrels or problems the camp population would resort to imams and local notables, as well as local security leaders, before going to the police. While such conflict resolution methods have been rather successfully used in the Palestinian Territory throughout the Israeli occupation, refugee camps no longer enjoy harmonious communitarian structures headed by local notables (*mukhtars*). For quite some time we have witnessed the emergence of a new elite whose legitimacy is based on the Palestinian national struggle. Nowadays, however, to become a powerbroker, this struggle alone is no longer sufficient.

Many stories we have recently collected show the problem of this multiplicity of actors governing the camp. In one of the camps in the South, a girl was raped in 2007 by two young men belonging to an influential Fatah family. When the girl's parents reported the rape to the Fatah leader, he interrogated the perpetrators until they admitted the crime and were imprisoned. Two weeks later, they were released. The victim's family addressed Fatah, who controls the camp, threatening to sue the boys under Lebanese law, but Fatah warned the family against doing so. In this case, the class conflict was obscured by the informal justice system provided by the Palestinian factions. Another example occurred in 2005 at the Badawi camp. An alleged spy for the Lebanese Deuxième Bureau, his wife and one of his children were shot dead by armed members of a Palestinian military faction. While Hamas denounced the action, other factions kept silent. Our interviewees criticized the silence of some of the factions and reported a growing feeling of insecurity in the camp.

Living in a space of exception proclaimed by either the real, phantom or local sovereigns has serious consequences for the urbaniza-tion of the camp and its relation to the surrounding urban or rural environment. The most salient example is that of Ein al-Hilweh camp in Sidon (South of Lebanon). Operated by different Palestinian factions as well as Islamist non-Palestinian groups, this combat zone and forbidden place is spatially and administratively modelled on prisons as its entry is guarded by Lebanese army checkpoints. Four checkpoints serve 45,967 camp inhabitants (UNRWA 2007). Severely over-crowded, this camp has become a fertile recruiting ground for jihadists and for the evolvement of radical Islamist movements and conservative religious forces. It is a conflict zone on the verge of spilling over into the neighbouring Lebanese city of Sidon, as radical jihadists return from wars in Afghanistan, Chechnya, and Iraq, imbued with Islamist extremism that is drawing more recruits and changing the complexion of the once secular Palestinian movement in the camp (Prothero 2006).

With the acquiescence of the Lebanese authorities, Nahr al-Barid, already partially destroyed, and Ein al-Hilweh project the image of Agamben's concept of *homo sacer* (1998). These camps have become a 'sacred' space or *space sacer* in the sense of spaces that can be 'eliminated' by anyone without being punished, without proper attention from the Lebanese public sphere.

Conclusion: camps as laboratories

The camps have four principal spatial functions: a place of habitat, economic space, a space of memory and identity affirmation, and a space for exercising power, including its function as a type of military base (Doraï 2006). These functions render the camp a laboratory of Palestinian society/state-in-making, but also an experimental laboratory for control and surveillance, and a technical model of repression developed by its sovereigns' know-how, implemented and deployed in other parts of the world that do not 'behave'. But beyond this, as for-mulated by Bernard Rougier (2007), the camp has emerged as a sort of laboratory or microcosm for the vast range of thought relating to politi-cized Islamism. However, compared with other Islamist groups, the question is not the emergence of a new al-Qaida ideology, but a new mode of action. My interviews with Syrian Palestinian refugee camp dwellers who have gone to fight with al-Qaida in Iraq show clearly that they are fighting against the American project in the region and not against Western values.

The portrait I paint, though seemingly dark and threatening, does not concern all the refugee camps in Lebanon. However, it is time to ring serious alarm bells about what is going on in the specific space of the refugee camps, as exemplifying the state of exception and the politics of void.

For Mohamed Kamel Doraï (2006), the different functions create a Palestinian socio-spatial dynamics based on three aspects: territorial permanence (a place of stability and continuity), communitarian space, and space of contact with Lebanese society. However, stressing this last point, Dorai illustrates that while the al-Buss camp is integrated into the urban fabric, the other camps are very different. This is why camp dwellers in Lebanon are very communitarian compared to other Palestinian camp-dweller communities in the diaspora.

While I look at the refugee camps as an extreme case and on the legal edge, epitomizing sometimes the state of exception and at other times the state of void, I do so by applying a typology of camps as open or closed. The closed camp is subject to the state of exception, albeit in different modalities ordered by various types of sovereignty: real, phantom or local. While Palestinian refugees are examples of *bare life*, subjected to extreme legal conditions, by revolting and resisting they are expressing human subjectivity.

The dominant Palestinian and humanitarian organizations' imaginary discourses have narrated the conflict in terms of human suffering and victimhood. Such narratives are enabled by portraying closed camps as museums. Moreover, these spaces are considered the primary units for maintaining the refugees' Palestinian identities in Arab host countries. As a result, the camp as a quasi-political entity has been investigated by social scientists, journalists and experts and shown to reproduce the structure of pre-1948 Palestinian society, including the reproduction of the place of origin inside the camps, as if Lobieh, Safad, etc. could be reproduced in the Ein al-Hilweh or Yarmouk camps. In most ethnographic studies this ethnicization of the refugees' history overlooks the importance of the economic, social, and cultural relationships with the host countries (Zureik 2003: 159).

The image of a refugee in the Arab region is thus confined to those who dwell in miserable camps and not necessarily those who dwell outside. The assumption, both in popular thought and within the scholarly community, was that the more miserable the camp, the less people would want to settle in the host countries and the more they would ultimately return home. The discourse of misery revolves around stagnation, control, and the muzzling of camp dwellers. However, the relationship between Palestinian national identity/ belonging and the type of residential area is very loose. There is no relationship between place of residence and support for the right of return. The right of return movement has emerged in Europe and North America rather than in the Arab world. We therefore do not need to be members of a closed refugee camp to maintain a belief in the right of return or in Palestinian identity. Contrary to the popular belief that the camp nurtures Palestinian national identity, my argument is that the camps, where radical national movements mingle with religious conservatism, have produced a new un-docile urban identity rather than a national one. Ein al-Hilweh, which has a long history of resistance to the Israeli colonial system, has today become disconnected from the Palestinian–Israeli conflict and from Palestinian nationalism, reaching out to a broader world of Islamicist activism, with frightening consequences for the camp dwellers, the Lebanese population and perhaps the whole region (Rougier 2007). We may be witnessing a definitive rupture between the camp and its roots in Israel/Palestine, while camps remain ideologically and financially connected to a network of Salafi or Wahhabi support for the camps, carried through specific clerical figures from Saudi Arabia and sometimes Iran.

While the PLO is currently pushing for cooperation between the Lebanese and Palestinian authorities in governing the camp, as has been clear from the declarations of the Palestinian ambassador in Lebanon, Abbas Zaki, on many occasions during 2007, many local pro-Syrian and Islamist actors have rejected this and pressed to keep the status quo of the state of exception. Many scholars, in the name of supporting the Palestinian national movement, are unaware of the form of totalitarian nationalism being cultivated in the camps. In addition, our observations of female school pupils a decade ago showed that fewer than a third wore the Islamic foulard (a veil that covers the hair but not the face); today, virtually all do so, some covering the face too. Emerging scholars, such as Khaled Hroub (2007) and Oraib Rantawi, oppose the right of return in favour of the 'right of survival', alluding to a form of camp nationalism based on an abstract discourse of the right of return which is threatening the survival of the Palestinian national movement and even the Palestinians as a nation.

We must re-think the refugee camps as a space of radicalism and a space that contributes to perpetuating the Palestinian–Israeli conflict rather than resolving it. There is a real need to empower camp dwellers by giving them civil and economic rights, recognizing the transnational character of their identity, and radically improving the urban conditions of their space. This will not be possible without connecting these spaces to the urban tissue of the neighbouring cities and creating a transparent mode of governance based on local elections.

I am not advocating a *tabula rasa* approach, but rather the rehabilitation of the refugee camps and their design as an urban space, not only with reference to their political and social status, but also to becoming part of the city and not opposing it, as in the Yarmok refugee camp in Damascus. An urban master plan based on rehabilitation should take into account the physical, socio-economic, and cultural fabric of the concerned spaces. A bottom-up participatory approach should be used to outline the differentiated needs of the Palestinian refugee population: women, men, children, working class and middle class, etc. A solution grounded in the right of choice (between return, settling in the host land, Palestinian Territory or in other countries), and close cooperation (not competition) between the PLO, the Palestinian National Authority, UNRWA and the host country, is the first step in alleviating the problems of the refugees. Alleviation would form the basis for empowering the refugees as transnational subjects. Some efforts are being made in Jordan and to a lesser extent in Syria to include the camps in the state's urban infrastructure but nothing has yet been initiated by the Lebanese authority (Hanafi 2005).

Towteen (implantation) is the scarecrow that can release a public phobia against the basic rights of the Palestinians. Any debate about civil and economic rights starts by affirming that the objective should not be *towteen* and ends by substituting rights with fast humanitarian or security solutions. The only common ground between the various Lebanese political parties is the use of *towteen* as taboo. Others (including religious authorities) consider mere talk about the Palestinians' right to work the first step towards *towteen*.

Throughout this debate the individual Palestinian is invisible. The deployment of biopolitics by humanitarian organizations (regarding Palestinians as bodies to be fed and sheltered, *bare life* without political existence) is one end of the spectrum, the *towteen* discourse the other end. For those conducting this debate, the Palestinians are mere figures, demographic artefacts and a transient political mass waiting for return. Between the humanitarian discourse in the zones of emergency on the one hand, and the *towteen* discourse on the other, the rights-based approach for the Palestinians as individuals and collectives, as refugees but also as citizen-refugees with civil and economic rights, including the right to the city, is lost.

Palestinians play a minor part in the 'new' Lebanon. Politically, economically and socially marginalized, they constitute a minority sect without a recognized place in a sectarian system, no longer vanguard of the revolution (Mattar 2004). However, to cite Alessandro Petti (2007), the problem of this sect is that it is almost spatially enclaved. We live in a world where enclaving undesirable, risky groups and confining them in the space of exception is seen as the very condition for the 'free' circulation of 'civilized' people in the global archipelago.

Notes

1   I would like to thank those who contributed to enriching the first version of this chapter, especially Michal Givoni, Yael Barda, Marwan Khawaja, Aage Titles and Rima Rassi. A special thanks to Ronit Lentin for her thorough reading and editing of this chapter.

2   What I am describing here is true on one level, but not on another. It holds when comparing the camp populations in Jordan and Palestine to the country average. But in both places there are large population groups with much poorer living conditions.

3   «http://www.un.org/unrwa/publications/index.html» (figures as of 31 March 2006).

4   There were supposedly at least 25,000 Palestinians, the majority Christian, among those who received Lebanese citizenship in 1994 (Haddad 2000: 85).

5   In many camps, the social role of the NGOs is much more important than that of the political factions. However, some of these NGOs are connected to the political factions. Interviewees reported a climate of mistrust against the NGOs. Recently a rap song has compared NGO leaders to thieves. In the meantime, Hamas is increasingly playing a social role in the camps.

6   I am grateful to Manal Kortam for the fieldwork she undertook in January and February 2007 in Burj al-Barajneh and al-Badawi camps dealing with modes of governance.

References

Agamben, G. (1997) 'We refugees', «http://www.egs.edu/faculty/agamben/agamben-we-refugees.html»

Agamben, G. (1998) *Homo Sacer: Sovereign Power and Bare Life*, Stanford University Press, Stanford

Agier, M. (2002) 'Between war and city: Towards an urban anthropology of refugee camps', *Ethnography*, Vol. 3, no. 2, 317–66, London

Ajial (2001) 'Palestinian non-government organizations in Lebanon', unpublished report, Ajial Centre, Beirut

Danish Refugee Council (2005) 'Non-ID Palestinian refugees in Lebanon' «http://www.drc.dk/fileadmin/uploads/pdf/English_site/Lebanon/Non-ID_Refugee»

Doraï, M. K. (2003) 'Les réfugiés palestiniens en Europe et en Suède. Complexité des parcours et des espaces migratoires', in M. Guillon, L. Legoux, E. Ma Mung (eds) *L'asile politique entre deux chaises. Droits de l'Homme et gestion des flux migratoires*, l'Harmattan, Paris

Doraï, M. K. (2006) *Les Réfugiés Palestiniens au Liban. Une géographie de l'exil.* CNRS Editions, Paris

Farsoun, S. K. and C. Zacharia (1997) *Palestine and the Palestinians*, Westview Press, Boulder

Foucault, M. (1994) *The Essential Works of Foucault, 1954–1984*, New Press, New York

Haddad, S. (2000) 'Sectarian attitudes as a function of the Palestinian presence in Lebanon', *Arab Studies Quarterly*, Vol. 22, no. 3, 81–100

Hanafi, S. (1997) *Entre deux mondes. Les hommes d'affaires palestiniens de la diaspora et la construction de l'entité palestinienne*, CEDEJ, Cairo

Hanafi, S. (2001) *Hona wa honaq: nahwa tahlil lil 'alaqa bin al-shatat al-falastini wa al markaz* ('Here and there: Towards an analysis of the relationship between the Palestinian diaspora and the centre'), Muwatin, Ramallah; Institute of Jerusalem Studies, Jerusalem

Hanafi, S. (2002) 'Opening the debate on the right of return', *Middle East Report*, no. 222

Hanafi, S. (2005) 'Reshaping geography: Palestinian community networks in Europe and the new media', *Journal of Ethnic and Migration Studies*, Vol. 31, no. 3

Hanafi, S. (2006) 'Vivre dans le camp, vivre ailleurs: Les Palestiniens réfugiés en Egypte et dans les Territoires palestiniens', *GEOGRAPHIES. Bulletin de l'Association des Géographes Français*, Association de Géographes Français, Paris

Hanafi, S. (2007) 'Palestinian refugees, citizenship and the nation-state', in Françoise De Bel-Air (ed.) *Migration et politique au Moyen-Orient*, IFPO, Amman

Hanafi, S. and Å. A. Tiltnes (forthcoming) 'The employability of Palestinian professionals in Lebanon', *Knowledge, Work and Society*, Vol. II, l'Harmattan, Beirut

Hanssen-Bauer, J. and L. B. Jacobsen (2003) 'Living in provisional normality – The living conditions of Palestinian refugees in the host countries of the Middle East', paper presented to the Stocking II Conference on Palestinian Refugee Research, IDRC, Ottawa

Hroub, K. (2007) 'Between Right of Return and "Right to Survive"!', *al-Ayyam*, 8 June

Khalili, L. (2005) 'A landscape of uncertainty: Palestinians in Lebanon', *Middle East Report*, no. 236, 34–39

Khawaja, M. and Å. A. Tiltnes (eds) (2002) *On the Margins: Migration and Living Conditions of Palestinian Camp Refugees in Jordan*, Fafo, Oslo

Kortam, M. (2007) 'Le rôle des acteurs locaux dans le processus d'incorporation des Palestiniens du Liban', unpublished MA thesis, University of Saint Josef, Beirut

Malkki, L. (1997) 'Speechless emissaries: Refugees, humanitarianism, and dehistoricization', in Karen Fog Olwig and Kirsten Hastrup (eds) *Sitting Culture. The Shifting Anthropological Object*, Routledge, London and New York

Mattar, D. (2004) 'Containment and exclusion: A comparison of Jordanian and Lebanese conflict–regulating state strategies towards the Palestinians between 1948 and 1988/89', unpublished thesis

Nasrallah, F. (1997) 'Lebanese perceptions of the Palestinians in Lebanon: Case studies', *Journal of Refugee Studies*, Vol. 10, no. 3, 349–59

Pedersen, J. (2003) 'Population forecast of Palestinian refugees 2000–2020', in L. Blome Jacobsen (ed.) *Finding Means, UNRWA's Financial Crisis and Refugee Living Conditions: Socio-economic Situation of Palestinian Refugees in Jordan, Lebanon, Syria, and the West Bank and Gaza Strip*, Fafo Report 427, Vol. I, Fafo, Oslo

Peteet, J. (2005) *Landscape of Hope and Despair: Place and Identity in Palestinian Refugee Camps*, University of Pennsylvania Press, Philadelphia

Petti, A. (2007) *Arcipelaghi e enclave. Architettura dell'ordinamento spaziale contemporaneo*, Bruno Mordadori, Rome

Prothero, M. (2006) 'A wellspring of anger: The meanest Palestinian camp in Lebanon is a recruiting ground for jihadists', 26 June «http://www.usnews.com/usnews/news/articles/060626/26beirut_2.htm»

Al-Rimmawi, H. and H. Bukhari (2002) *Population Characteristics of the Palestinian Refugee Camps, Ramallah: PCBS and Dissemination and Analysis of Census Findings*, Analytical Report Series no. 3

Romig, M. (2006) 'The consolidation of impermanence. The establishment of Nahr el-Bared Palestinian refugee camp' (November 1947–May 1950), unpublished Independent History Study Project, University of Geneva

Rougier, B. (2007) *Everyday Jihad: The Rise of Militant Islam among Palestinians in Lebanon*, Barnes and Noble, New York

Sayigh, R. (1995) 'Palestinians in Lebanon: Harsh present, uncertain future', *Journal of Palestine Studies*, no. 97, 37–54

Sayigh, R. (2001) 'Palestinian refugees in Lebanon: Implantation, transfer or return?' *Midde East Policy*, Vol. 8, no. 1, 94–105

Sfeir-Khayat, J. (2001) 'Du provisoire au permanent: Les debuts de l'installation des refugiés au Liban, 1948–1951', *MIT Electronic Journal of Middle East Studies*, no. 5, 30–42

Takkenberg, L. (2006) 'The search for durable solutions for Palestinian refugees: A role for UNRWA?' in S. Hanafi, E. Benvenisti, C. Gans (eds) *Palestinian Refugees and Israel*, Max Planck Institute for Comparative Public and International Law, Heidelberg

Ugland, O. (ed.) (2003) *Difficult Past, Uncertain Future. Living Conditions Among Palestinian Refugees in Camps and Gatherings in Lebanon*, Fafo Report 409 «http://www.fafo.no»

UNRWA (2005) 'UNRWA in figures' «http://www.unrwa.org»
UNRWA (2007) 'UNRWA in figures', «http://www.unrwa.org»
Wacquant, L. (1999) *Les prisons de la misère*, Éditions Raisons d'Agir, Paris
Zureik, E. (2003) 'Theoretical and methodological considerations for the study of Palestinian society', *Comparative Studies of South Asia, Africa and the Middle East*, Vol. 23, no.1–2, 152–62

Laleh Khalili

5 Incarceration and the State of Exception: Al-Ansar Mass Detention Camp in Lebanon

Introduction

Between June 1982 and May 1985, 12–15,000 Lebanese and Palestinian men and women were held in a massive camp near the village of Ansar between Saida and Nabatiyya in southern Lebanon. The camp was built to take in prisoners who had already gone through extensive interrogations and 'screenings' throughout southern Lebanon. In the early days of the Israeli invasion, several large buildings in Sour and Saida were expropriated for use as detention and interrogation centres. The most infamous of these were the Safa citrus factory and the St Joseph nunnery in Saida, shortly thereafter to become the Command Headquarters of the Israeli military (IDF). Prior to the invasion, General Ariel Sharon, then Israeli defence minister, had voiced his desire to evict the Palestine Liberation Organization (PLO) from Lebanon, obliterate the Palestinian refugee camps in Lebanon, and expel all 200,000 refugees (Schiff and Ya'ari 1984: 211). In the first days of the war, as Palestinian refugee camps were being laid to waste from land, sea and air, men, women and children were concentrated in the two sites. 'The Israelis announced that they would pursue a policy of "le-taher", purifying the zone it occupied in southern Lebanon' (Gabriel 1984: 105). This meant that they would 'cleanse the area of any remaining PLO and destroy their infrastructure. Searches for arms caches began, as well as systematic roundups of PLO suspects, who were arrested, screened, and [eventually] taken to the Ansar detention camp' (Gabriel 1984: 107).

By 10 June 1982, only four days after the start of the war, 50,000 people had been gathered at Safa and the nunnery. As IDF Lieutenant Colonel Dov Yermiya describes in his diaries, no provisions for food or water were made for this vast crowd which included substantial numbers of civilians, babies, and the elderly (Yermiya 1983: 15). The early stages of detention included identification of political officials and militants by hooded collaborators (Yermiya 1983: 28; personal interviews with Abu Khaled and Abu Wael, Burj al-Shamali camp, 9 November 2006). Even after it became known that the collaborators were implicating innocent people, the process was not halted. Yermiya writes (1983: 15): 'This too serves a purpose: "let them know what waits for terrorists, and let this be a warning about the future." ' The process went on for days, during which the prisoners were forced to stand in the sun and were denied food and water. One prisoner recalled: 'for food, they brought pieces of old bread and some tomatoes. A soldier stood on top of a tank and threw it at us, as you would throw it at dogs, and the men tried to catch it with their mouths' (PHRC 1986: 9). The detainees were subjected to beatings and – as Yermiya (1983: 28) describes it – 'torture and degradation'.   One former prisoner testified,

> They accused us of acts that we had not committed and of belonging to a political party or the Palestinian resistance. Those who denied these allegations were taken to the basement of the factory and beaten with large sticks of wood or pieces of electrical cable… After the interrogation, they blindfolded us, tied our hands and ordered us to sleep out in the open without covers. If one of us moved while sleeping, they would wake him without taking into account that when sleeping, one does not really know if one stirs or not (PHRC 1986: 1).

The beatings were systematic:

> I move along and see two husky soldiers passing among the rows, carrying thick meter-and-a-half long boards that are about 10 cm. wide. They are swinging them around, striking right and left, clubbing heads, shoulders, backs, and hands… The prisoners are ordered to sit with their backs bent forward and their heads between their knees. The air is filled with the stink of piss and shit. Not all of them get permission to get up in order to go to the outhouses. Some of the prisoners are sitting there in a state of shock, as if they were unconscious; some are choking and crying silently, out of pain and fear. There are those who are begging for a drop of water. The wounded are pleading to be bandaged. The soldiers on guard, except for the violent ones, look indifferent and

bored. Some of them seem to be enjoying themselves, and they make open comments of support for the work being done by those who are beating and torturing the prisoners (Yermiya 1983: 32–3).

Among the intimidation methods used in interrogation was 'the inciting of leashed dogs' against the detainees (Yermiya 1983: 111), an image that has now become familiar from the photographs taken at Abu Ghraib prison in Iraq. The conditions in Safa and the nunnery were degraded to such an extent that the military police feared losing control over them. There was little ability to feed the tens of thousands of detainees, and 'hundreds, perhaps thousands of women and children... stormed the gates at all hours demanding to see their loved ones' (Barnea and Barnea 1988: 139). Despite the fact that the transfer of prisoners of war to Israel contravened international law, the large Israeli prison and interrogation centre 'at Meggido, near Afula, was also full and a steady stream of new prisoners was arriving daily' on buses from Lebanon (Barnea and Barnea 1988: 139). To maintain control over prisoners and to allow for interrogations to proceed more smoothly at the already operational interrogation centres in Lebanon, a decision was made to establish a more permanent prison camp in a different locale. Colonel Meir Rosenfeld, who headed the department for POWs in the military police, was charged with finding the prison site. On 12 June, Rosenfeld expropriated a wheat field from a local farmer to become the camp and evicted the owner in order to use the farmhouse as the Ansar camp headquarters.

By 14 July, an area the size of a football field (*Ha'aretz*, 5 November 1982) was transformed into a massive detention camp enclosed in barbed wire and surrounded by watch-towers. Barbed wire, this most flexible 'and essential element in the frontier between life and death' (Razak 2002: 79) separated various sub-sections of the camp from one another. The camp was divided into two sections, Ansar I and Ansar II. Each section contained fifteen pens and each barbed-wire-enclosed pen had 250–300 detainees in some twelve tents watched over by a sentry tower. Each tent held twenty-five prisoners. This sub-division of the various sections of the camp and the strict control over interaction between different camp sections has been an important characteristic of detention camps throughout their history (Gregory 2005, 2006a, 2006b; Kreps 1992; Neal 2006; Razak 2002). The combination of the sentry tower and barbed wire acted not only instrumentally, as a method of surveillance and capture (Razak 2002), but also as a visible symbol of power and control. Large sand embankments around Ansar provided another layer of optical control. All roads around Ansar were blocked 'to prevent people from even glimpsing the detention camp' (*Toronto Globe and Mail*, 21 December 1982). On the one hand, the camp was made 'invisible' to those outside; on the other hand, the prisoners were made supremely visible to their guards. In addition to the 'pens' within Ansar, solitary confinement and interrogation rooms constructed from concrete prefabricated materials stood adjacent to the guard housing.

As the Israeli military considered the International Committee of the Red Cross (ICRC) a 'hostile organization' (Yermiya 1983: 69), its representatives and monitors were not allowed access to the camp detainees until months after the camp had opened (Yermiya 1983: 112). The degree of control in the camp was extraordinary. The military commander of the camp had chosen a *mukhtar* (village head) and a *shawish* (sergeant) for each pen and tent respectively, who were to represent the prisoners and keep discipline within their area of control. The prisoners were not allowed to protest the work of either (Husayn 1983: 37). The *shawish* was expected to organize meals, supervise the cleaning of the tents, and mediate and resolve disputes (Sayigh 1985: 28).

The prisoners were also severely limited in their ability to do much else (at least until the ICRC finally appeared in the camp). The detainees were not allowed to move when they were being counted, were not allowed to use the toilet at night, were not allowed to use the toilet without permission during the day, were not allowed to eat except at times dictated by the guards, and were not allowed to sleep as they were awakened arbitrarily and randomly at very odd hours in order to be counted (Husayn 1983: 36–7). The process of head counting every morning was particularly traumatic. In the early months of imprisonment (and until collective action put paid to it), the prisoners were forced to '[sit] down in two rows, oriental fashion [*sic*], their backs to the tent opening, and, with their hands on the back of their necks, [they were expected to drop] their heads between their knees' (Barnea and Barnea 1988: 144). No one was supposed to move and, if they did, they were hit on the back or on the head (Husayn 1983: 36). Prisoners were sometimes taken away for interrogation before or after the counting:

This was not done at random. They knew who they wanted. They called the numbers. Before they left the sections, the prisoners were handcuffed, chained and blindfolded. Then they were taken to the interrogation section. Each prisoner would ask himself, 'Whose turn is it today?' This was the first thing he would think of early in the morning.

There wasn't any way of knowing who would be taken next. The aim of interrogation was not always to obtain information; it was to terrorize, to demoralize, and to recruit, that is, to force the prisoners to collaborate.

'Troublemakers' were dealt with on a daily basis. They'd be put in solitary either in Ansar or in the occupied territories [i.e. Israel]. The interrogation place was called 'the hole' (al-jora) of interrogation, where prisoners could be exposed to all sorts of bad treatment; prisoners taken for interrogation would sometimes spend a few hours, or a few days or a few weeks chained and blindfolded (Tamari 1984: 57).

Intimidation and humiliation were also exercised in symbolic ways. The guards had forced the prisoners to build a mosaic of Jewish symbols that they associated with Israel (Barnea and Barnea 1988: 146).

The massive regime of control in Ansar was enforced at the lowest level by guards who were mostly − at least at the beginning − army reservists (Barnea and Barnea 1988: 144). Furthermore, a particular form of racial difference was reinforced in the ranks of the prison officers. Alongside the reserve soldiers, the guards were mostly Mizrahi, or Druze, but camp officers, and especially the interrogators, were senior Ashkenazi men (Barnea and Barnea 1988: passim; Sayigh 1985). Many guards 'got rid of their aggressions easily by cursing the prisoners or throwing stones at them' (Barnea and Barnea 1988: 152). In a few other instances, soldiers opened fire without provocation, killing several prisoners at a time and injuring dozens of people (Barnea and Barnea 1988: 153; Tamari 1984: 52).

The camp was a cornerstone of the Israeli security regime in southern Lebanon, and an important strategic asset for the Israeli military's counterinsurgency operations. It was used to conduct wide population sweeps and concentrate all who might be sympathetic to the PLO and nationalist Lebanese forces in order to cut off support for the insurgents. As an analyst sympathetic to the Israeli invasion of Lebanon writes, 'by far the most important factor in destroying the infrastructure of the PLO was the roundup of almost ten thousand PLO suspects at the conclusion of hostilities; they were sent to the detention camp at Ansar'

(Gabriel 1984: 114). By September 1982, around fifty people per day were being arrested in Sour alone (Merip, September/October 1982). In some villages, the entire male population was gathered in public squares, mosques and *husainiyya*s and arrested (*al-Safir*, 1 November 1982). Anyone wishing to travel from one point to another in southern Lebanon had to be screened to ensure no Palestinian could get through (Merip, September/October 1982). Previously collected intelligence provided the screeners with long lists of PLO fighters and officials who were especially wanted. But ordinary Palestinians were not spared either. Even after their release, Palestinians were kept under surveillance. As Israeli Minister of Economics Yaakov Meridor maintained, '[After their release] they can go back [to the refugee camps], but if they're Palestinians we will be keeping an eye on them' (*New York Times*, 28 August 1982: 4). Over the coming years, and with the evacuation of the PLO from Lebanon, the detainee profile at Ansar changed and large numbers of Shi'a southerners came to be imprisoned there. Some of these Lebanese detainees were affiliated with Amal and nationalist Lebanese groups, and later with Hizbullah; but large numbers of unaffiliated villagers were kept at Ansar as 'hostages'. This was particularly true of women related to activists or militant men (Sayigh 1985).

Micro-practices of incarceration

The particular micro-practices of incarceration used in al-Ansar are familiar from other contexts. Throughout the existence of al-Ansar detention camp, collaborators in hoods were continuously used to screen people. The camp did not have any hot water, even in the cold of winter. Securing camp beds during the winter – in order not to sleep in a sea of mud – only happened through prisoner collective action and the leadership of a Fatah officer, Salah Tamari (Barnea and Barnea 1988: 150). Access to food, healthcare, and medicine was used to control the camp populations. Food control was utilized to punish and discipline the detainees in the various secret detention centres throughout the south, before they were transferred to Ansar. In these secret detention centres, which were off-limits to journalists or the ICRC (even after the ICRC was allowed access to Ansar), every meal consisted of one piece of bread and one tomato (*al-Safir*, 1 November 1982; personal interview with Muhammad Safa, Beirut, 6 November 2006). No protein except one egg per week was provided; and the prisoners received half a cup of tea per day and half a cup of coffee per month (Tamari 1984: 53). Beatings and torture were common in the intensive detentions that the Israeli General Security (Shabak) conducted in these interrogation centres (personal interview with Muhammad Safa, as before; with Abu Ali, Beirut, 9 November 2006). Particularly coveted prisoners, if they were PLO officers or known mid-level to senior cadres, were transferred to Israel for special interrogations. There, the military gave certain approved journalists access to the prisoners for propaganda purposes (Barnea and Barnea 1988), in direct contravention of the Geneva Conventions.

Ansar continued to be the terminus for the detainees, although coveted prisoners were frequently taken away for interrogations in Lebanon or Israel. In November 1982, five months after the establishment of the prison, the first large-scale instance of violence against the prisoners occurred. When several women, whose kinfolk were detainees in the camp, came to the perimeter of the camp, the prisoners began chanting '*allahu-akbar*'. Angered by the prisoners' chanting, the guards opened fire, injuring some twenty-eight people and killing three. In June 1983, a year after the opening of the camp, an uprising by the camp residents, who were demanding their rights, resulted in the burning down of the camp. On 8 August, 1983, and after several failed attempts, the 'great escape' took place from pen number eight. After several days of digging, dozens of prisoners escaped; twelve were recaptured; two were killed (*al-Safir*, 30 October 1983). In response, ten days after the 'great escape,' a significant number of prisoners were transferred to a nearby narrow valley called Wadi Jahannam (literally, the Valley of Hell). The wadi is a limestone quarry measuring 400 by 400 metres, and it was divided into four equal 'pens' partitioned from one another, in which 2,000 prisoners were to reside. Food, water, and medical support were further circumscribed in the camp. The prisoners were denied tents in Wadi Jahannam and had to use their blankets for shade and shelter. The walls and floor of the wadi were of stone and hard clay respectively, and prisoners would be 'ankle-deep in shit and piss when it rained and the whole place flooded' (personal interview with Abu Wael, Burj al-Shamali, 9 November 2006; *al-Safir*, 30 October 1983).

The conditions in Wadi Jahannam were so unsanitary and difficult that large numbers of prisoners were taken severely ill. When the prisoners were rotated back to the main Ansar camp, it had been reconstructed, fortified, and made 'escape-proof.' Furthermore, instead of reserve soldiers, the camp was now to be guarded by 'fresh regular forces' (Barnea and Barnea 1988: 185). During the evacuation of prisoners from Wadi Jahannam back to Ansar, four prisoners who had hoped to hide in the wadi dug a bunker in which to remain. When the Israeli military forces conducted a final 'cleanup' of the wadi by spraying 'it with machine-gun fire from all sides and in all directions' (Barnea and Barnea 1988: 186), the four prisoners came out to surrender, 'with their hands above their heads'. However, the driver of the bulldozer brought to flatten what remained of Wadi Jahannam did not stop his vehicle, rolled over the prisoners and killed them all (Junaydi 1984: 144). In the re-fortified main camp, a 'new regime' of harsh measures led to a dozen prisoners being shot (one of whom was killed) for matters as trivial as throwing a ball beyond a designated 'white line' (Barnea and Barnea 1988: 187–8).

In November 1983, thousands of Palestinian and Lebanese prisoners held in Ansar and inside Israel were released in return for six Israeli soldiers held by PFLP-GC in Lebanon. Ansar was nearly emptied; but by then, the Shi'a population of southern Lebanon was becoming increasingly radicalized by the force and brutality of the occupation (see Hamzeh 2004; Norton 1987, 2000). Ansar soon filled with Lebanese prisoners and it was only closed down in 1985 when the Israeli military withdrew to the 'security zone' on the border between Israel and Lebanon. During the withdrawal, some 1,200 prisoners were transferred to Atlit prison inside Israel, and a number of them were later released through negotiations. Others remained in Israel for years, even decades more (for more on Ansar see al-Hurr 1985; Husayn 1984; Junaydi 1984; Sayigh 1985; Ta'amari 1994; Tucker 1982).

The familiarity of micro-practices at Ansar

What makes the Ansar detention camp a relevant subject of study is not its uniqueness as a concretization of the state of emergency (or exception), but rather its very familiar ordinariness as an instrument of control. The wide array of the practices used at Ansar was perfected in past colonial settings. In a sense, Ansar was the historic outcome of a whole series of strategies of counterinsurgency, institutions of domination, and technologies of control perfected through decades of colonial rule, beginning in the late nineteenth century. Mobilization of fear and generation of terror were as central to the crafting of the prison regimes as were the more pedestrian aims of extracting information.

For example, the process of screening has been so deeply seared in the minds of the colonized that in her extraordinary account of British prison camps in Kenya, Caroline Elkins (2005: 62) writes, '*screening* is the one word in Kikuyuland that is synonymous with British colonial rule during the Mau Mau' insurgency. Massive population sweeps which caught numerous non-combatants in their dragnet, the use of hooded informants, endless interrogations and brutal torture were significant elements of these screening processes. British colonial officer Frank Kitson had been very successful in 'turning' prisoners into 'pseudogangs' of collaborators in Malaya and later in Kenya, and the lessons he – and his prime operative in the field in Kenya, Ian Henderson – had learned were used in other colonial and 'security' contexts such as Zimbabwe (Cilliers 1984; Henderson 1958; Kitson 1960; Reid-Daly and Stiff 1982; Stiff 1982). Indeed, again and again, prison memoirs and interviewed prisoners point to this very fact: more often than not, the security men of Shabak already knew who the prisoners were; they already had long lists provided to them by existing collaborators. The intent of the screenings was therefore either intimidation or recruitment of new collaborators (Tamari 1990). Methods of recruitment have varied over time: black-mailing people who consider themselves to have sexually dishonoured their families or community is only one of the most recent techniques (Haj-Yahia 1999). Tamari describes a prison recruitment routine called '*asafir*' (sparrows) whereby a harshly interrogated prisoner is greeted in a communal cell by warm 'comrades' who entrap the prisoner through various means (Tamari 1990: 41).

In Kenya, as in many other colonial settings later, distinction was made between interrogation centres and prison camps. Although life in the prison camps was not comfortable, the interrogation centres that acted as way-stations to the prison camps were far more horrendous. Inaccessible to journalists, the Red Cross, and human rights NGOs, these centres became infamous as loci of information collection and of extraordinary violence. The British had set up such interrogation centres in all their counterinsurgency efforts and, for example, during the Aden insurgency, the Joint Interrogation Centre was the first stop where randomly arrested persons were taken before being sent to al-Mansoura prison (Halliday 1974: 203). The torture in these places consisted not only of massive physical beatings, but also of more 'scientific' methods such as the use of electrodes and injection of drugs, as well as psychological disorientation techniques such as sleep deprivation, food control, the use of noise, sensory deprivation, intimidation by dogs, etc. When such interrogation techniques were used in Northern Ireland, an official British investigation confirmed that these had been employed in 'counterinsurgency operations in Palestine, Malaya, Kenya, and Cyprus, and more recently in the British Cameroons (1960–1), Brunei (1963), British Guiana (1964), Aden (1964–7), Borneo/Malaysia (1965–6), the Persian Gulf (1970–1) and in Northern Ireland (1971)' (quoted in Halliday 1974: 206). Nor did these strategies, institutions and technologies necessarily culminate in Ansar; rather they have been continuously in use, most recently at Guantánamo, Bagram Airforce Base in Afghanistan and in Abu Ghraib (Cole 2003; Cook 2003; Council of Europe 2006; Danner 2004; European Parliament 2006; Greenberg and Dratel 2005; Gregory 2005; 2006a; 2006b; Grey 2006; Hooks 2005; MacMaster 2004; McClintock 2004; McCoy 2006; Neal 2006).

Methods of interrogation and torture used in various prisons have also travelled across time and place. The Public Committee against Torture in Israel delineated the forms of torture used frequently and fairly openly before the 1999 Israeli Supreme Court ruling which banned torture: 'tying up detainee in painful positions for hours or days on end; solitary confinement; confinement in tiny cubicles; beatings; violent "shaking"; deprivation of sleep and food; exposure to cold or heat; verbal, sexual and psychological abuse; threats against the individual or the individual's family; and lack of adequate clothing or hygiene' (PCATI nd). All these were familiar methods used when Ansar prisoners were taken away for interrogation, or placed in solitary confinement at Ansar (Barnea and Barnea 1988; Junaydi 1984; Tamari 1984; personal interviews with several prisoners). In recounting their experience of interrogation Ansar detainees also frequently mentioned the use of loud noise, being threatened with aggressive dogs, and sexual humiliation (PHRC 1986).

In addition to the micro-practices of incarceration, a specific legal and macro-political setting for 'war prisons' (Gregory 2006a) has to be crafted in order to allow their daily operation without intervention or monitoring. The legal manoeuvres which allowed the creation of Ansar detention camp were complex and drew a veil over the extraordinariness and brutality of the regime of incarceration used by the Israeli occupying forces. These mechanisms included: (a) stripping persons of their juridical rights (creation of 'exceptional' bodies or 'enemy aliens' who are not eligible for Geneva Convention protection); (b) extraterritoriality (and related processes, such as production of *terra nullius*); and (c) differential definitions of sovereignty (where, although all states are allegedly sovereign, some states are more sovereign than others).

The 12,000–15,000 prisoners at Ansar detention camp were held as administrative detainees under the Defence (Emergency) Regulations of 1945 drawn up by the British Mandate authorities in Palestine and later incorporated into Israeli law. These Defence (Emergency) Regulations were written to give the Mandate authorities (and the subsequent Israeli state) the ability to 'amend any law, suspend the operation of any law, and apply any law with or without modification' (quoted in Rudolph 1984: 61). Administrative detentions 'empower any officer with the rank of brigadier or above to authorize an arrest. Detainees can be held without trial [renewable every six months]... interrogated, and prosecuted, but no provisions are made for legal counsel or informing families' (Tucker 1982: 56). Salah Tamari (1984: 52) recounts,

> Whenever we asked the Israelis that Geneva Conventions be applied, the answer was, 'We treat you according to Geneva Convention Number 5.' At that time we didn't know what it was all about. When the Red Cross delegate came in, we rushed and asked him, 'Please, what is Geneva Convention Number 5; we want a copy of that convention.' He smiled and said such a thing didn't exist. That was a bitter joke.
>
> Then at a later stage, the Israeli Supreme Court issued a ruling that prisoners of Ansar should be treated according to Geneva Convention Number 4, that means as civilian detainees. But that was *never* implemented. The Israeli commander of the camp at that time responded to this by saying, 'I have never heard of an Israeli Supreme Court. Does it exist?' No lawyers were allowed in Ansar, not even Israeli lawyers. So we were given the status of 'Brought-ins.' We were called the 'Brought-ins,' that's all. The only law we knew was the whim of the commander and the soldiers.

Conclusion

The spatial placement of prisons is also significant. Ansar was established in a no-man's-land of war and occupation, ostensibly recognized as part of Lebanese territory, but claimed as 'Independent Free Lebanon' by the Israeli proxy South Lebanon Army, as well as commandeered as yet another 'security zone' that Israel seems in the habit of expropriating from the territories of various neighbouring countries. The area's indeterminate status, its inaccessibility to outside visitors and observers, and the palimpsest of territorial claims to it, all allowed for the placing of the particular territory outside all laws. Such claims were made as easily with colonial possessions. In fact, the very emergence of the state as the basic *nomos* of the earth or a 'concrete territorial and political organization of the world order, invested with symbolic meaning' (Cohen 2004: 2) is tied to colonization, and the sovereignty of powerful states cannot be understood without simultaneously comprehending the manner in which these powerful states declare certain places 'less' sovereign or 'outside' (Schmitt 2003 [1950]).

In some senses, the security zones with all the work that goes into instantiations of power within them serve exactly this function. Prisons on the one hand hold, discipline, and terrorize into submission whole populations, and on the other hand allow the gathering of information. If human bodies are to be subjected to violence in order to extract from them information or submission, they have to be shielded from the opprobrium of public, or local laws, or international sanctions. Placing such prisoners in massive numbers *inside* Israel rather than in a zone of exception would in fact make them more eligible for the application of laws. Thus, pushing potential conflict and violence to 'outside the normal penal system' (Arendt 1976) into the zone of security allows for a politics of invisibility that unties the hands of violence workers and the military.

To allow for certain people to be enclosed within such zones of exception, they have to be stripped of their status as persons to whom rights or laws apply. Hannah Arendt considers just such a move when she writes about 'kill[ing] the juridical person in man... by putting certain categories of people outside the protection of law' (Arendt 1976: 147). This juridical stripping is combined with the much more complex process of dehumanization perfected through racialized discourses and euphemized language. As the Israeli chief of staff, Rafael Eitan, had said in 1982, Palestinians were not human, but 'drugged cockroaches'; and former Prime Minister Menachem Begin called them 'two-legged beasts'. More insidiously, 'PLO infrastructure' often meant the homes and refugee camps housing Palestinians; 'terrorists' was any Arab fighting the Israelis, but particularly Palestinians. Dov Yermiya

(1983: 14) writes about the Israeli soldiers who could not imagine the Arabs they encountered as anything but 'terrorists' and for them, 'their entire world is filled with terrorists'.

In the end, to imagine that sovereignty is defined through law, or that international norms are the overarching basis of international politics, is to ignore the extraordinary sophistication that can be employed by dominant powers in placing the law at the service of the sovereign, or, if necessary, ignoring the law altogether. Philosophical discussions that see sovereign power – or the power over life and death – replaced gradually by disciplinary power often ignore that relocating the locus of exercise of power beyond a state's own borders – if one has the means, resources, and power to do so – ultimately gives the state the ability to exercise power however it pleases in that 'open space', to designate people outside law, and to effectively appropriate liminal territories through complex re-definitions of sovereignty. Such re-definitions in effect – if not *de jure* – give agency and the ability to act to more powerful – and, very often, colonial/imperial – actors. Ansar prison was one such zone of exception.

References

Arendt, H. (1976) *The Origins of Totalitarianism*, Harvest Books, Harcourt, San Diego

Barkat, S. M. (2005) *Le corps d'exception: Les artifices du pouvoir colonial et la destruction de la vie,* Éditions Amsterdam, Paris

Barnea, A. and A. B. Barnea (1988) *Mine Enemy,* trans. Chaya Amir, Halban, London

Cilliers, J. K. (1984) *Counter-Insurgency in Rhodesia,* Croom Helm Inc., London

Cohen, J. (2004) 'Whose sovereignty? Empire vs. international law', *Ethics and International Affairs*, Vol. 18, no. 3

Cole, D. (2003) *Enemy Alien: Double Standards and Constitutional Freedoms in the War on Terrorism,* New Press, New York

Cook, J. (2003) 'Facility 1391: Israel's Guantanamo', *Le Monde Diplomatique,* November

Council of Europe (2006) *Alleged Secret Detentions and Unlawful Inter-state Transfers Involving Council of Europe Member States,* CEP, Strasbourg

Danner, M. (2004) 'Torture and Truth: America, Abu Ghraib, and the War on Terror', *New York Review of Books*, New York

Elkins, C. (2005) *Britain's Gulag: The Brutal End of Empire in Kenya,* Pimlico, London

European Parliament (2006) *Interim Report on the Alleged Use of European Countries by the CIA for the Transportation and Illegal Detention of Prisoners,* Brussels

Gabriel, R. A. (1984) *Operation Peace for Galilee: The Israeli–PLO War in Lebanon*, Hill and Wang, New York

Greenberg, K., J. Dratel and A. Lewis (2005) *The Torture Papers: The Road to Abu Ghraib*, Cambridge University Press, Cambridge

Gregory, D. (2005) 'Vanishing points: Law, violence and exception in the global war prison', in D. Gregory and A. Pred (eds), *Violent Geographies: Fear, Terror and Political Violence*, Routledge, New York

Gregory, D. (2006a) 'The black flag: Guantánamo Bay and the space of exception', *Geografiska Annaler: Series B, Human Geography*, Vol. 88, no. 4

Gregory, D. (2006b) 'The death of the civilian?' *Environment and Planning D: Society & Space*, Vol. 24, no. 5

Grey, S. (2006) *Ghost Plane: The True Story of the CIA Torture Program*, St Martin's Press, New York

Haj-Yahia, Y. M. (1999) *Alleged Palestinian Collaborators with Israel and Their Families: A Study of Victims of Internal Political Violence*, Harry S. Truman Research Institute for the Advancement of Peace, Jerusalem

Halliday, F. (1974) *Arabia Without Sultans*, Penguin Books, London

Hamzeh, A. N. (2004) *In the Path of Hizbullah*, Syracuse University Press, Syracuse

Henderson, I. (1958) *Man Hunt in Kenya*, Doubleday, New York

Hooks, G. (2005) 'Outrages against personal dignity: Rationalizing abuse and torture in the war on terror', *Social Forces*, Vol. 83, no. 4

al-Hurr, L. (1985) *Mahajir ila Ansar*, Dar al-Bahith, Beirut

Husayn, S. (1983) *100 Yawman fi Mu'taqal Ansar*, al-Mu'assassa al-Rawa, Beirut

Husayn, S. (1984) *Ansar 33*, al-Mu'assassa al-Rawa, Beirut

Al-Junaydi, S. (1984) *Mu'taqal al-Ansar wa Sira' al-Iradat*, Dar al-Jalil, Amman

Kitson, F. (1960) *Gangs and Counter-Gangs*, Barrie and Rockliff, London

Krebs, P. M. (1992) '"The last of gentlemen's wars": Women in the Boer War concentration camp controversy', *History Workshop Journal*, no. 33

Lajna al-Mutabi'a Li Da'm al-Mu'atqilin al-Lubnaniyyin fi Sujun al-'Adw al-Sahyuni (Committee of Support for Lebanese Prisoners in the Israeli Enemy's Prisons, shortened to Lajna al-Mutabi'a) (1996) *Al-Khiyam: Mu'taqil al-Mawt al-Israili: Wathiqa 'an Awda' al-Rahain al-Lubnaniyyin fi al-Sujun al-Israiliyya*, Lajna al-Mutabi'a, Beirut

Lajna al-Mutabi'a (1998) *14 Tammuz: Yawm al-Asir al-Lubnani*, Lajna al-Mutabi'a, Beirut

Majlis al-Junub (the Republic of Lebanon) (2004) *Shumu' al-Hurriyya*, Office of the Head of the Parliament, Beirut

McClintock, S. (2004) 'The penal colony: The inscription of the subject in literature and law and detainees as legal non-persons at Camp X-Ray', *Comparative Literature Studies*, Vol. 41, no. 1

McCoy, A. W. (2006) *A Question of Torture: CIA Interrogations, from the Cold War to the War on Terror*, Metropolitan Books, New York

MacMaster, N. (2004) 'Torture: From Algiers to Abu Ghraib', *Race and Class*, Vol. 46, no. 2

Mirmil, 'A. and M. 'Asi, (eds) (2000) *Kam Murr min al-Waqt: 17 Asiran Lubnaniyyan Yaktubun Tajaribihim fi al-Mu'taqilat al-Israiliyya*, al-Masar, Beirut

Neal, A. (2006) 'Foucault in Guantánamo: Towards an archaeology of the exception', *Security Dialogue*, Vol. 37, no. 1

Norton, A. R. (1987) *Amal and the Shi'a: Struggle for the Soul of Lebanon*, University of Texas Press, Austin

Norton, A. R. (2000) 'Hizballah and the Israeli Withdrawal from Southern Lebanon', *Journal of Palestine Studies*, Vol. 30, no. 1

Palestine Human Rights Campaign (PHRC) and Ansar Resource Center (1986) *Ansar Prison Camp: The Testimony of Two Palestinian Prisoners*, Beirut

Public Committee against Torture in Israel. (n.d.) *Torture in Israel: 1990–September 1999*. «http://www.stoptorture.org.il/eng/background.asp?menu=3&submenu =1» (8 January 2007)

Razak, O. (2002) *Barbed Wire: A History*, Profile Books, London

Reid-Daly, R. and P. Stiff (1982) *Selous Scouts – Top Secret War*, Galago Publishing, Cape Town

Rudolph, H. (1984) *Security, Terrorism and Torture: Detainees' Rights in South Africa and Israel: A Comparative Study*, Juta and Co. Ltd, Cape Town

al-Sa'di, G. (1985) *Al-Usara al-Yahud wa safaqat al-Mubadala*, Dar al-Jalil, Amman

Sayigh, R. (1985) 'The Mukhabirat state: A Palestinian woman's testimony', *Journal of Palestine Studies*, Vol. 14, no. 3

Schiff, Z. and E. Ya'ari (1984) *Israel's Lebanon War*, Simon and Schuster, New York

Schmitt, C. (2003 [1950]) *The* Nomos *of the Earth in the International Law of* Jus Publicum Europaeum, trans. G.L. Ulmen, Telos Press, New York

Shu'ayb, H. (1984) *Jumhuriyya Ansar al-Arabiyya: Fasl min 'Azab al-Ahrar*, Dar al-'Alimiyya, Beirut.

Stiff, P. (1984) *Selous Scout: Rhodesian War, A Pictorial History*, Galago Publishing, Cape Town

Tamari, S. (1984) 'Salah Tamari', *Journal of Palestine Studies*, Vol. 13, no. 4

Tamari, S. (1990) 'Eyeless in Judea: Israel's strategy of collaborators and forgeries', *Middle East Report*, no. 164/5

Tamari, S. (1994) 'Memoirs', in S. Lynd, S. Bahour and A. Lynd (eds), *Homeland: Oral Histories of Palestine and Palestinians*, Olive Branch Press, New York

Tucker, J. (1982) 'The prisoners of Israel', *Merip Reports*, no. 108/109

Yermiya, D. (1984) *My War Diary: Israel in Lebanon*, trans. Hillel Schenker, Pluto Press, London

Alina Korn

6 The Ghettoization of the Palestinians

Introduction

The occupation of Palestine as a means of denial of freedoms can be usefully theorized using prison images. To understand the dynamic process by which control is exercised over the Palestinian people in the Occupied Territories, I propose to examine the relations between imprisonment and ghettoization, drawing on Wacquant's analysis of the relationship between ghetto and prison (Wacquant 2001). I argue that the Oslo process was a turning point: from then onward a dominant form of control has emerged, which includes ghettoization, spatial confinement and restriction of Palestinians to their villages and towns.[1] This process must be understood against a backdrop of the decrease in the use of Israeli prisons and the weakness of mass incarceration to assure efficient control.

The Occupied Territories as a prison

The Occupied Territories increasingly resemble a prison or a network of prisons. The Gaza Strip is sealed off and surrounded by a fence, and Israel controls movement to and from Gaza via land crossings. Despite the withdrawal of settlements and permanent Israeli military ground installations from the Gaza Strip (the disengagement plan), Israel retains control over borders, airspace, territorial waters, the population registry, the tax system, the supply of goods and services. In the first year following the completion of the disengagement programme, Gaza was cut off from the outside world 42% of the time. Regular planned

116

movement by traders, workers, students and others is impossible.[2] The crossings between the West Bank and Israel were closed at the end of 2000. A severe regime of movement restrictions was imposed on Palestinians, and hundreds of checkpoints, roadblocks and physical obstacles of various kinds were erected in order to restrict the movement of vehicles inside the West Bank. Movement restrictions include 75 manned checkpoints, approximately 150 mobile checkpoints a week, about 446 obstacles placed between roads and villages, including concrete cubes, earth ramparts, 88 iron gates and 74 kilometres of fences along main roads (Amira Hass, *Ha'aretz*, 19 January 2007). More than 2 million people are forced to go about their daily life mainly on foot, making their way between one obstruction and another.

The exits of hundreds of Palestinian towns and villages to main and regional roads are blocked. Transportation is routed to secondary roads and a small number of main roadways which pass through bottlenecks under Israeli military control. Palestinians are forbidden to enter the Jordan Valley and East Jerusalem. They are also forbidden to enter villages, land plots, towns and neighbourhoods along the 'seam zone' between the separation fence and the Green Line.[3] Private cars are not allowed to pass the Swahara-Abu Dis checkpoint, which lies on the divide between the north and south of the West Bank. Passage by car through the Qalandya checkpoint north of Jerusalem is limited to those who carry a Jerusalem ID, in cars with Israeli licence plates. Entering Nablus by vehicle is also forbidden. Jericho is blocked off by a ditch, and going out to the north requires a permit.

The Israeli Defence Force (IDF) imposes, intermittently and for varying lengths of time, a ban on movements from the north of the West Bank to any other part. In IDF jargon, this policy is called 'dissoci-ation': about 800,000 people, residents of the districts of Tulkarm, Nablus and Jenin, are forbidden from travelling towards Ramallah and further south. In addition to trisecting the West Bank, direct transporta-tion links are cut off and main roads are closed to Palestinian traffic. Villages along roads connecting Jewish settlements are barred by fences which prevent exit even through orchards. The exits to roads which are forbidden to Palestinians are blocked by concrete cubes, earth ramparts and iron gates. Palestinians who live near such roads are not allowed to use them. They are allowed only to cross them, climb over the rocks, slide through the wadis, go around the forbidden route and reach the nearby village (Amira Hass, *Ha'aretz*, 13 January 2006).

The so-called Separation Wall has been built since August 2003, designed to surround the entire West Bank. By mid-May 2006, 42% of the Separation Wall had been constructed – 336 km out of a planned total 790 km – and a further 102 km of the fence are under construction. According to a ministry of defence estimate, 95% of the entire Separation Wall was to be completed by early 2007 (Amos Harel, *Ha'aretz*, 17 May 2006). There are 83 iron gates along the Separation Wall, dividing lands from their owners, of which only 25 open occasionally. Special permits are required for farming along the 'seam zone'. Those with permits must enter and leave via the same crossing even if it is far away or closing early. The 'seam zone' surrounding the Separation Wall route – most of which lies within the West Bank and annexes 10% of its lands to Israel – severely interferes with the lives of half a million Palestinians. It creates twenty-one enclaves inhabited by some 250,000 Palestinians and divides the West Bank into at least three distinct enclosures. Other obstacles and secondary blocs surrounding Palestinian settlements confine some of them to inner enclaves separated from one another. However, describing the Territories as one vast or several incarceration facilities fails to provide a sufficiently dynamic description, yet there is a dynamics at work in the Territories.

Between prison and ghetto

According to the sociologist Loïc Wacquant, much can be learned from a historical comparison between ghetto and prison, because both belong to the same class of institution of forced confinement: the ghetto can be theorized as a 'social prison', while the prison functions as a 'judicial ghetto'. Both are entrusted with enclosing a stigmatized population so as to neutralize the material and/or symbolic threat it poses for the broader society (Wacquant 2000: 378). Wacquant's analysis of the Jewish ghetto in medieval Europe, the Black American ghetto in the Fordist metropolis during most of the twentieth century and the ghettos of ethnic outcasts in East Asia sheds light on the structural and functional homologies with the prison (Wacquant 2004).

Analysing the workings of the ghetto as a mechanism of ethnoracial closure and control and the kinship with the prison can be useful when discussing patterns of ethnic domination in Israel. For over two decades, until the early 1990s, the Israeli prison system underwent a steady growth. Prisons played an extra-penological role as instruments for the management and control of the Palestinian population. Thousands of Palestinians were tried and jailed every year for violating military regulations that restricted their movement and many aspects of their lives. Many Palestinian men in the Occupied Territories were veterans of Israeli prisons. From the beginning of the 1970s until the beginning of the 1990s, some 2,500 to 4,000 Palestinians were imprisoned in Israeli prisons (about 45% of the total prison population). During this period, the rate of Palestinian prisoners exceeded 250 per 100,000 Palestinian residents – two to three times the rate of incarceration for Israeli Jews (Korn 2003: 44).

The present dynamics began together with the Oslo process. Since the early 1990s there has been a change in the patterns of control. The number of Palestinian prisoners held in Israel declined sharply. In January 2000, the Palestinian rate of incarceration dropped to about 68 per 100,000 – the lowest rate ever recorded for Palestinians, and slightly more than half the incarceration rate for Israelis. However, after the outbreak of the al-Aqsa Intifada, the Palestinian prison population grew again.[4] The decline in the use of imprisonment during the 1990s was accompanied by the restriction of Palestinians to their dwelling places and a gradual transformation of the Palestinian territories into fragmented population reserves. Ghettoization (in Palestine) has replaced imprisonment (in Israel).

Following the 1967 War, and even more so since 1977, Israel has exercised a 'double policy' in the Occupied Territories, combining territorial integration with demographic separation. Emergency legislation enabled the military government in the West Bank and the Gaza Strip to confiscate Palestinian lands and transfer them to Jewish settlers. All aspects of Palestinian life were controlled by military regulations, which choked the Palestinian economy and increased its dependence on and incorporation into the Israeli economy. The institution of a 'permit system' and a regime of restrictions on movement allowed the Israeli economy to exploit Palestinian labour for the benefit of Israeli society, keeping the physical presence of the Palestinians at a safe distance, within the Territories, outside the State of Israel. Between 1967 and 1990 the borders between Israel and the Territories remained relatively open. During those years more than one-third of the Palestinian workforce was employed in Israel, generating over a quarter of the Gross Domestic Product (GDP) of the Territories. This form of colonization came to an end at the beginning of the 1990s.

The Oslo process was a turning point. The significant change in policy began at that point (and not, as some might think, with the construction of the Separation Wall and the unilateral moves led by Prime Minister Sharon attempting to set 'permanent borders'). Israel sought to neutralize the 'demographic threat' by separating itself from the Palestinians. In Oslo, Israel was determined to part with the Palestinians but not to partition the territory. Israel renounced its responsibility for the fate of more than three million people and withdrew from its duties as an occupying power. The Oslo Accords, although led by the Zionist left, did not attempt to reconstruct the ruined Palestinian economy, nor did they provide any substitute for its total dependence on Israel or any compensation for decades of exploitation. Worse: Israel had no intention of giving the Palestinians the right or the possibility of establishing an independent state. On the other hand, at no point was there any serious consideration of giving Palestinians civil rights and risking turning Israel into a bi-national state.

In fact, the Oslo Accords became a gradual process whereby Israel was to evacuate areas in which it has no interest and transfer them to the Palestinian Authority. In the first stage, the Palestinian Authority, denied full state authority, had to take charge of territories without sovereignty. Later on it was to become a government, exercising sovereignty over the liberated territories of the Palestinian 'nation-state' – those territories Israel was kind enough to withdraw from. The Oslo Accords assumed that 4% of the West Bank would be 'liberated' in the first stage, and the rest would follow. In reality, Israel took advantage of this opportunity to set the borders of the Palestinian 'cantons' by confiscating land, expanding Israeli settlements and constructing bypass roads. Successive Israeli governments, from Rabin's and through Sharon's and Olmert's, used this step-by-step process as a ruse to perfect the means of controlling the Palestinians by worsening the restrictions on their movement, with the aim of guaranteeing control over as much Arab-free land as possible.

The Oslo process as a means for the dispossession of lands

The Oslo process charted the path for the fragmentation of the Territories into autonomous-like enclaves, leading to the disintegration of the West Bank and the Gaza Strip, by splitting the Territories into separate territorial entities, unable to sustain themselves economically, and with no sense of political sovereignty. The Jewish settlements were the pivotal instrument for the territorial fragmentation of both the Gaza Strip and the West Bank. Through a system of bypass roads and four main blocs of settlements, the West Bank was divided into three parts and splintered into smaller population reserves, whereas the Gaza Strip was completely encircled and divided by fences and military paths. The introduction in 1990 of a stringent regime of closures and permits and the replacement of the Palestinian workforce by foreign workers made it possible to control Palestinian movement according to the exclusive needs and considerations of the settlers and the security forces. Through this geo-political ghettoization, Israel decomposed the West Bank into suffocated enclaves surrounded by a Jewish territorial continuum, disintegrating the Palestinian people into isolated communities.

The events of the al-Aqsa Intifada carried great weight in speeding up and tightening the siege of the Palestinians, while greatly minimizing debate in Israeli society and criticism from the international community. Thus, since 2001, under the auspices of the 'war on terror', the freedom of movement of the Palestinians in the West Bank was severely limited by a combination of dozens of checkpoints, closed roads, hundreds of roadblocks and locked gates dividing the West Bank into what the military jargon calls 'territorial cells'. In many cases, entering these territorial cells is forbidden to non-residents. The IDF makes sure that there are only one or two entries to each territorial cell, according to its size and the number of Jewish settlements and outposts in its proximity. At each entrance, there is a checkpoint of some kind, where troops may stop people for unlimited duration. The territorial cells are surrounded by 'Areas C' where, according to the 1995 Taba Accord, (part of the Oslo process), Israel maintains full civil and military control. In September 2000, on the eve of the outbreak of the al-Aqsa Intifada, approximately 60% of the West Bank was defined as 'Areas C'. By May 1999, Areas C, except for the built-up area in the settlements, were supposed to become 'Areas A' – i.e., territories under full Palestinian control. By means of this process of ghettoization, Israel takes over more and more Palestinian lands, condensing Palestinians within smaller territorial cells. Unregistered land over which Palestinians fail to prove their ownership is transferred to the state or to settlers. Nearly 40% of the land held by Israeli settlements in the West Bank (around 60,000 dunams) is privately owned by Palestinians (Peace Now 2006). In addition, thousands of acres of olive trees and orchards are locked up behind fences, walls and buffer zones erected around Jewish settlements. During most of the year, their owners are prohibited from entering their property. They can only watch from afar the neglect of their produce.

Bantustans and ghettos

As the closure of the West Bank and Gaza intensified, researchers and political writers from the Israeli left used the term 'bantustanization' to describe the process that the Territories have undergone. However, it should be stressed that the difference between ghettoization and bantustanization is not merely semantic. Unlike Bantustans, developed by the Apartheid regime in South Africa in order to segregate the indigenous population while better exploiting its labour force, the Palestinian enclaves seem to resemble the classic ghetto. They are smaller, splintered, and they serve as containers for storing unnecessary population. Their inhabitants are trapped behind barbed wire, fences, ditches and walls. They are impoverished, lacking infrastructure, cut off from public services and vital resources like agricultural land, water, workplaces and medical centres. The Palestinian ghettos are designed to preserve the Territories under Israeli control without providing for the existence of the non-Jewish population. Unlike the Bantustans, which enabled the white settlers to dominate the local population while keeping it segregated, the Israeli permit regime was introduced when Israel turned its back on cheap Palestinian labour. Unlike Apartheid South Africa, Israel does not need Palestinian labour anymore, having replaced it since the early 1990s, first by new immigrants from the former Soviet Union, and later by 250,000 migrant workers from Asia, Africa, Eastern Europe and Latin America.

The ghetto, in its full-fledged form, writes Wacquant, is a double-edged socio-spatial formation: it operates as an instrument of exclusion and ethnoracial discrimination from the standpoint of the dominant group. At the same time it also offers the subordinate group partial protection and a platform for succour and solidarity (Wacquant 2001: 102). This is how the black ghetto granted African Americans some organizational autonomy, which enabled them to develop their own social and symbolic forms, and thereby accumulate the capacities needed for escalating the struggle against their continued subordination.

By contrast, the process of ghettoization in the Occupied Territories did not lead to the construction of autonomous institutions capable of protecting the population. Rather, it led to the destruction of political and civic organization and to the dismantling of the natural and national fabric of Palestinian society. As Palestinians lost their economic value and as their labour was no longer indispensable, the trajectory of their containment escalated to the point of mere ostracism, seclusion, and dissolution. The enclosure of the Palestinians does not represent their separation from the Jewish population or their encasement in a ghetto within a Jewish urban space, but rather their separation from other Palestinians. It separates districts from other districts, suburbs from cities, and villages from urban centres and agricultural land. It splits populations, detaches people from their familiar environment, and prevents communities connected in every aspect of their lives from maintaining these connections. The natural development of large regions is delayed and they are condemned to ruin and depletion.

Ghettoization aims to change the organization of space and dictate new spatial relations. It fragments the physical and symbolic space of Palestinian society, enabling Israel to control it by creating new relations between 'inside' and 'outside'. Palestinians are often 'inside', trapped in their enclaves and separated from other areas or from their lands. Sometimes they are 'outside', west of the enclosed area, while their land is trapped within it. Yet at other times they are confined in an isolated territory, surrounded by fences on three sides – a space which is neither 'outside' nor 'inside'.[5] The ghettoization of the Occupied Territories is a mode of controlling the Palestinian space by weakening the mobility of the population. It operates as a mechanism of deterrence, dissuading Palestinians from leaving their areas of residence and reducing to the necessary minimum their attempts to travel through the arbitrary and humiliating system of checkpoints and roadblocks.

State of emergency and the suspension of law

Human rights violations in the Occupied Territories are often depicted as part of the deterioration in the rule of law or a state of anarchy prevailing in these areas. This view includes, for example, criticisms of the helplessness of law enforcement agencies in the face of continued attacks by settlers against Palestinians and their property. However, it is important to recall that the situation prevailing in the Territories is by no means anarchy. Rather it is closer to the opposite end of the continuum, namely the exercise of limitless state power. Very clear rules operate in the

Territories as almost every aspect of Palestinian life is regulated through permits and licences. As a matter of fact, Palestinians know very well what is allowed and what is forbidden. For example, Palestinians registered in the West Bank who without a permit 'infiltrate' East Jerusalem – up until the Oslo process the heart of Palestinian cultural and economic life – are very careful not to be arrested at a checkpoint and, of course, make it a habit to hide. Residents of East Jerusalem would not risk employing or driving them. Drivers of minibuses – the main means of public transport in the West Bank – are arrested and their vehicles confiscated if caught driving a West Bank Palestinian who does not possess a permit. Drivers of private cars are also careful not to get caught giving a ride to West Bank residents without permits, even siblings or relatives.

Indeed, Palestinians in the Occupied Territories are not protected by Israeli law. Their life and death are decided by the military. On the other hand, the Israeli legal and judicial systems have never ceased to operate in these territories. A very disturbing example of that contradiction culminated during the military operation in the Rafah Refugee Camp, between 13 and 24 May 2004. During the IDF incursion to Rafah, 58 Palestinians were killed, including at least 8 minors, 183 houses were destroyed, and more than 1,000 people were made homeless. Israel's Supreme Court ruled that houses could not be demolished except during a military operation and as part of ongoing fighting. This led to the continuation and expansion of military activity, with the demolition of houses declared part of the 'war on terror'. Subsequently, when the military operation was in progress and while hundreds of homes were being demolished and razed and massive damage was being caused to the civilian population, the Supreme Court passed a 'liberal-activist' ruling, to the great satisfaction of supporters of the Supreme Court of Justice and democratic Israel. The ruling required the IDF to care not only for the welfare of the troops, but also for the needs of the population: to ensure the supply of humanitarian aid, to enable the evacuation of the injured and a dignified burial of the dead.

Giorgio Agamben writes that the voluntary creation of a permanent state of emergency has become an essential practice of contemporary democracies. It allows the institution of a no-man's-land between the political and the legal (Agamben 2003: 10–11). He explains that a state of emergency or a state of exception is different from a state of chaos or anarchy because, juridically, it does keep a certain order, even if it is not a juridical order (Agamben 2003: 58). Agamben argues that a state of exception is not exterior, nor is it interior to the juridical order, insisting that the suspension of the law is taking place within a legal framework.

In her superb 'Indefinite Detention', relating to the detainees at Guantánamo Bay, Judith Butler has elaborated on the suspension of law in the name of security (Butler 2004). The 'indefinite' detention of the prisoners at Camp Delta is justified as part of a state of national emergency, a state understood as being out of the ordinary, not limited in time and space. However, Judith Butler writes, 'indefinite detention' does not signify exceptional circumstances, but rather the means by which the exceptional becomes established as a naturalized norm. It is the occasion and the means by which the extra-legal exercise of state power justifies itself, installing itself as a potentially permanent feature of political life (Butler 2004: 67).

The 'war on terror'

The IDF's actions in the Territories are justified as necessary, arising from the need to fight terrorism. But the 'war on terror' provides the smokescreen behind which something else is taking place, something that is supported by the conflict and indeed nourishes it. Since the beginning of the al-Aqsa Intifada in September 2000, the IDF initiated an escalation in the violence and spurred the militarization of the conflict. The political and military leadership in Israel had foreseen the outbreak of a new Intifada, prepared for it, and when it indeed occurred, reacted fiercely (Reinhart 2002). The IDF's policy of assassinating Palestinians suspected of involvement in terrorist activities, chosen as the primary strategy for suppressing the uprising, fanned the flames and provoked the harshest escalation of the conflict. Thus, for example, the assassination of Raed Karmi, commander of Tanzim-Fatah, in Tulkarm in January 2002 led to a renewed escalation in violence and bloodshed, culminating in March–April 2002 in the Park Hotel suicide attack in Netanya and the IDF's invasion of the West Bank (operation 'Defensive Shield'). Since then, Israel has bombed and destroyed all the facilities and institutions of the Palestinian Authority, demolished government compounds in Palestinian cities, and hit (and continues to hit) anyone who bears arms or wears a uniform.[6]

The escalation in the level of violence serves the Israeli agenda. Palestinian terrorist attacks provide the IDF with a legitimization of its policy, enabling it to implement a tighter schedule of 'exceptional measures'. The 'war on terror' justifies Israel acting in self-defence without legal restraints. The ghettoization of the Palestinians provides the conditions for the exercise of extra-legal state power. It is part of a broader tactic aimed at neutralizing the rule of law in the Territories in the name of security. Thus, for example, during 2004, before the withdrawal of its troops, the IDF invaded the Gaza Strip, causing massive destruction to houses and roads, and razing vast areas in Beit Hanoun (in the north of the Strip), in parts of Khan Younes and along the Philadelphi route in Rafah. In turn, military activity initiated by the IDF provokes the continued firing of rockets on the Israeli town of Sderot. Pictures of blood and 'public outrage' (in Israel) are needed to enlist public and legal support for the imposition of harsh collective means of punishment and inflicting further destruction and death all over Palestine. During 2004, 812 Palestinians were killed by the Israeli security forces in the Occupied Territories. Between September 2005 and the end of June 2006 – after the 'pullout' from Gaza in August 2005 – 239 Palestinians were killed throughout the Territories.[7]

The 'war on terror' assures a permanent tension of killing and exceptional activity. It is a means of guaranteeing further lists of terrorists deserving of execution, further lists of suspects planning terrorist acts, and further lists of individuals wanted for interrogation. The 'war on terror' necessitates the continued pursuit of terrorists even in the ghettos of Palestine: arresting more wanted men, killing more terrorists, erecting more buffer zones, bombing more areas from which Qassam rockets are fired, uncovering more tunnels used to smuggle arms, and destroying more homes. These actions guarantee a steady flow of terrorist attacks, revenge for revenge, and the crossing of further red lines in future actions. Following the abduction of the Israeli soldier Gilad Shalit, between 25 June 2006 and the end of November 2006 over 400 Palestinians were killed and some 1,500 injured. More than half of those killed and wounded were civilians. Of those killed some 90 were children. During the same period 3 Israeli soldiers were killed and 18 wounded, and 2 Israeli civilians were killed and some 30 injured in Sderot and its precincts by Qassam rockets fired by Palestinians from Gaza (Dugard 2007).

The occupation and humanitarian aid

It is worthwhile thinking of the ghettoization of Palestine within the broader context of large-scale segregations and the emerging paradigm of refugee camps. Zygmaunt Bauman writes of the in-built transience of refugee camps, conceived and planned as a hole in time and space, and organized to contain undesirable populations in isolated and remote spaces (Bauman 2002: 345). Agier argues that the massive use of the camp formula in the most dispossessed regions of the world suggests the formation of a global space for the 'humanitarian' management of the most unthinkable and undesirable populations of the planet. The camps, he writes, are both the emblem of the social conditions created by the coupling of war with humanitarian action, and the site where it is constructed in the most elaborate manner, as a life kept at a distance from the ordinary social and political world (Agier 2002: 320).

Because of the brutalization, disintegration and fragmentation of Palestinian life, the biological existence and the basic needs of the population become the main concern of control agencies as well as aid organizations. The treatment of 'humanitarian cases' becomes an inseparable part of the misery and inhumane life behind fences and checkpoints. Thus, for example, foreign and Palestinian field workers of international aid agencies, such as Médecins Sans Frontières, the Red Cross and OCHA (UN Office for the Coordination of Humanitarian Affairs), are allowed to pass through the iron gates, and the Red Cross coordinates the entry of Palestinian ambulances in and out of the closed areas. The Red Cross phones the Israeli Civil Administration, which gives instructions to the brigade's headquarters, which then directs the troops at the checkpoint to allow an ambulance with such and such a licence plate number and a specific driver to pass through the iron gate, drive about a kilometre, and pick up the patient (Amira Hass, *Ha'aretz*: 13 January 2006).

The involvement of international aid organizations in the conflict is inherent: Israel dictates the disastrous moves and the international community funds and provides the accompanying humanitarian aid. In order to prevent the total impoverishment of the population and delay the predicted 'humanitarian catastrophe', the international community, through the budgets of the donor states, continues to assist the Palestinians. Thus, through this aid, the concerned international community continues to fund, directly and indirectly, the Israeli occupation. European Union officials in Jerusalem estimated that institutions, organizations and persons in the Palestinian Authority received 500 million dollars in aid from Arab countries in 2006. International organizations, the UN and western nations transferred another 700 million euros to the Authority in 2006. According to estimates, a humanitarian support mechanism designed by the EU to circumvent Hamas has so far transferred 180 to 190 million euros to Palestinians in welfare payments and civil service salaries. The moneys have benefited about one million Palestinians, or a quarter of the population (Avi Issacharoff and Amiram Barkat, *Ha'aretz*, 27 March 2007).

The grotesque expression of the merger between these two functions, between the destruction and brutalization of Palestinians' lives and the humanitarian aid given to them, can be illustrated by the following story. During the IDF's raid in Jenin refugee camp in spring 2002, 530 residences were completely demolished. UNRWA, which is rebuilding the camp, decreased the space of the original residences by approximately 15%, and about 100 families were sent to a new neighbourhood constructed on the outskirts of the camp. Instead of the narrow alleys, broad streets between eight and ten metres wide are being paved, specially fitted to the size of Israeli tanks.

What is that place called, beyond ghettoization?

The Israeli occupation of Palestine is the longest military occupation in modern history. Beyond theoretical conceptualizations lies the danger of a major human disaster which words cannot describe. Israel is *de facto* annexing over half the West Bank and is not obligated by any accord. The colonization is intensifying, and Jewish settlers, defended by the army, behave in the West Bank as if it were their own country. They work and travel where they choose. Their roads – for Jews only – are better, and they are allocated more water than the native population. Palestinians are denied even their old roads. They are deprived of vital services and freedom of movement between parts of their own country.

Carrying on with the policy of ghettoization enables Israel to regulate the amount of food, medicines and raw materials entering the Territories and determine the level of shortages among the Palestinians. The Territories are thus held on the brink of starvation, forcing the international community and the donor states to continue to transfer emergency aid. Poverty in the Occupied Territories means that 80% of the population lives below the official poverty line. More than one million Gazans out of a population of 1.4 million receive food assistance from the United Nations Relief and Works Agency for Palestinian Refugees in the Near East and the World Food Programme. Recipients of food aid receive flour, rice, sugar, sunflower oil, powdered milk and lentils. Few can afford meat, fish – virtually unobtainable anyway as a result of the ban on fishing – vegetables and fruit (Dugard 2007).

The continued boycott imposed on the elected Hamas government (while equipping the Fatah security groups affiliated with Mahmud Abbas), the increasingly heavy siege waged against the Palestinians and the worsening of the conflict between Hamas and Fatah might accelerate the collapse of the Palestinian Authority and speed up the disintegration of Palestinian society. Such a process could bring about the transition of the Territories into international custody status or a UN protectorate, compelling the majority of Palestinian people to a daily struggle for existence.

Notes

1 The Oslo Accords are a set of agreements between Israel and the Palestinians laying down a timetable and rules for the progressive implementation of autonomy on the West Bank and in the Gaza Strip, and defining the conditions for the final negotiations on outstanding issues. Mutual recognition was declared by Yasser Arafat and Yitzhak Rabin on 9 and 10 September 1993. Since then a number of treaties have been concluded between the two parties, but in all cases their application has been considerably delayed (*Le Monde Diplomatique*, «http://mondediplo.com/focus/mideast/r1279»).

2 For a detailed discussion of the ways in which Israel continues to control Gaza, see Bashi and Mann (2007).

3 The term Green Line refers to the 1949 Armistice lines established before the occupation of the West Bank and Gaza in 1967.

4 As of November 2005, 6,530 Palestinians were held in Israeli prisons. At the beginning of 2007 more than 9,000 Palestinians were being held in Israel, the vast majority by the Israel Prisons Service (IPS), and a small number by the IDF. See B'TSELEM: the Israeli Information Center for Human Rights in the Occupied Territories «http://www.btselem.org» (10 April 2007).

5 For a discussion of the consequences for the daily life of tens of thousands of Palestinians trapped within the enclaves, see BIMKOM Report (2006).

6 For a discussion of the coverage in the Israeli press of the IDF's 'assassination policy', see Korn (2006).

7 For full data, see B'Tselem «http://www.btselem.org»

References

Agamben, G. (2003) *Etat d'exception*, Editions du Seuil, Paris

Agier, M. (2002) 'Between war and city: Towards an urban anthropology of refugee camps', *Ethnography*, Vol. 3, no. 3

Bashi, S. and K. Mann (2007) *Disengaged Occupiers: The Legal Status of Gaza*, Gisha: Legal Center for Freedom of Movement. «http://www.gisha.org»

Bauman, Z. (2002) 'In the lowly nowherevilles of liquid modernity: Comments on and around Agier', *Ethnography*, Vol. 3, no. 3

BIMKOM (2006) *Between Fences: The Enclaves Created by the Separation Barrier*, The New Israel Fund and the British Embassy, Tel Aviv «http://www.bimkom.org»

Butler, J. (2004) *Precarious Life*, Verso, London

Dugard, J. (2007) *Report of the Special Rapporteur on the Situation of Human Rights in the Palestinian Territories*, UN, Human Rights Council

Korn, A. (2003) 'Rates of incarceration and main trends in Israeli prisons', *Criminal Justice*, Vol. 3, no. 1

Korn, A. (2005) 'Joined forces: The IDF and the Israeli press reporting of the *Intifada*', in E. Poole and J.E. Richardson (eds.), *Muslims and the News Media*, I.B. Tauris, London

Peace Now (2006) *Breaking the Law in the West Bank – One Violation Leads to Another: Israeli Settlement Building on Private Palestinian Property* «http://www.peacenow.org.il»

Reinhart, T. (2002) *Israel/Palestine: How to End the War of 1948*, Seven Stories Press, New York

Wacquant, L. (2000) 'The new "peculiar institution": On the prison as surrogate ghetto', *Theoretical Criminology*, Vol. 4, no. 3, August

Wacquant, L. (2001) 'Deadly symbiosis: When ghetto and prison meet and mesh', in E. Garland (ed.) *Mass Imprisonment: Social Causes and Consequence*, Sage, London

Wacquant, L. (2004) 'Ghetto', in J. N. Smelser and P. B. Baltes (eds), *International Encyclopedia of the Social and Behavioral Sciences*, (revised edition), Pergamon Press, London

Raef Zreik

7 The Persistence of the Exception: Some Remarks on the Story of Israeli Constitutionalism

Introduction

This chapter aims to bring different discourses into a conversation – surrounding the question of sovereignty in general, and the 'state of exception' in particular (Agamben 1998; 2005). First is the discourse in constitutional theory regarding the relation between constituent power and constituted power (Preuss 1994; Negri 1999), and second is that related to a particular debate in Israel over the 'Jewish and democratic' nature of the state (Smooha 1990; Yakobson and Rubinstein 2003; Yiftachel 1999; 2006).

The chapter moves in two directions. The first move aims to shed new light on the nature of Israeli constitutionalism by introducing into the debate the model of the 'state of exception', and the ongoing tension between constituent power on the one hand and constituted power on the other, thereby hoping to propose a new way of viewing the drama of Israeli constitutionalism. The second move works backward. Thus, rather than reading the debates over Israeli constitutionalism in light of theory, I aim – by contemplating the Israeli case – to revisit and shed some light on constitutional theory itself.

Israel is in many ways extremely relevant to recent debates about the immanence of the 'state of exception'. In this state constituent power never disappears from the scene but insists on being present, lying latent within the system and raising its head from time to time to remind the institution of the state that the revolution is never completed. There is a permanent revolution, and underneath the demos lies the ethnos, and in moments of crisis – and Israel is almost constantly in a situation of crisis/emergency – the ethnos has the final word in the process of decision-making. However, the tension between the State of Israel's 'Jewish' and 'democratic' constituents, between the rule and the exception, or between the constituent and the constituted power is not formal or a mere façade; rather the tension is real, but that is the problem not the solution.

By contemplating the case of Israel I also want to say something about the theoretical debates on the matter. While the State of Israel is doubtless an extreme case, it nevertheless reveals major problems and weaknesses in liberal legality in general; in many ways the case of Israel exposes the Achilles' heel of liberal political and legal theory. Debating the case of Israel and the insistence of many Israeli scholars on viewing Israel as a liberal democratic state reveals certain aspects of liberalism that ordinarily remain hidden, as do tragic events such as the 9/11 attacks and the extreme legal measures adopted by the government of the United States, such as the Patriot Act, that remind us of the dark side of liberal legality and of the immanence of the state of exception.

Although Israel is an extreme case, it does nevertheless fall within a certain paradigm, and this chapter aims both to read the case of Israel in light of the paradigm and to read the paradigm in light of the case of Israel.

The chapter begins with a genealogy of the concept of the 'exception', connecting it to the concept of 'decisionism' and 'homogeneity'. In this section I will juxtapose two traditions in ethics and law: one that emanates from Grotius, Locke, and Kant, and understands law as the voice of reason; and a second that originates from Ockham, Hobbes, Hegel (?), Kierkegaard, Weber and – mainly – Schmitt, that understands law mainly as the will of the sovereign.

In tracing the second genealogy of the relation of rule and exception, fact and norm, chaos and order, I aim to draw attention to the dark side of the modern liberal constitutional state, and I believe that this genealogy assists us in accomplishing that task. After elaborating this theoretical background I move to the story of Israeli constitutionalism, to the debates on the 'exception' and the relation of constituent/constituted power. I end by evaluating the case of Israel in the light of the nature of the 'state of exception'.

Norm and exception

A main strand in liberal morality/legality is rules and rule-following.

When we encounter a case, crisis or conflict, we come equipped with rules that cover the situation at hand. These rules are the expression of right reason that stands above the conflict and allows us to adjudicate it. Rules are not arbitrary or the expression of a mere whim or caprice; rather, they express an immanent rationality. We adjudicate cases in light of the reasonable rule.

This ideal has always been under attack, or at least interrogation. In each and every generation there are scholars who support it and scholars who challenge it and wonder whether it is achievable.

According to the counter-tradition (Ockham, Hobbes, Kierkegaard and Schmitt), rules always 'run out' and reason can never support us with a moment of closure. The moment of closure comes not from reason but elsewhere. First came the exception, not the rule; the action, not the word.

The discussions regarding the priority of the will started as a theological debate. One of the most pressing questions that faced theologians was the nature of the relation between God and divine law, between God – the author or creator of the law – and his creation – the law. For example, what is the nature of the relation between God and the Ten Commandments? What lies at the basis of these commandments? Is it the voice of reason or the voice of God? That is to say, were there any constraints on God when he proclaimed his divine law? Do God's laws have to conform to a certain criterion of reasonability, or is the fact that they are the laws of God sufficient to ensure their justness and validity (Taylor 1989: 253–5)?

The problem is clear: to claim that God's laws must conform to a certain standard of reasonability would amount to heresy. The idea that there is an immanent rationality within the rules, a law-like structure to morality, would impose limits on almighty God's powers. This dilemma was exacerbated by the religious texts, mainly the Old Testament, in which God clearly abandons his own rules. The Old Testament is full of examples where the rule is suspended and God commands his subjects to act contrary to his previous command. How, then, can one make sense of these cases of exception in which God himself is not willing to follow his own rules and suspends the Ten Commandments?

Grotius and Ockham express two different ways of tackling this question, and introduce different paradigms for dealing with it. For Ockham,[1] what lies beneath the moral law is God's will, not reason or any built-in rationality. Ockham is representative of a voluntaristic tradition in legal and political theory that locates law in the will of God, not accepting the possibility of God's self-limitation. When God acts or legislates he does so *ex nihilo* and does not work under constraints. The secularization of this position in the hands of writers like Hobbes and Pufendorff generated the modern basis of secular law: this basis lies in the will of the sovereign (instead of God), who does not accept any limitations on his powers. The sovereign is conceptualized/understood/created in the image of God: God started *ex nihilo* – in the beginning there was nothing – and the will of God acts within a normative vacuum. This is the image of the modern sovereign.

Grotius introduced an alternative paradigm that creates more space for the possibility of self-limitation:

> Now the Law of Nature is so unalterable, that it cannot be changed even by God himself ... Thus two and two must make four, nor is it possible to be otherwise; therefore God himself suffers his actions to be judged by his rule (Grotius 1901: 22).

When this argument is secularized one receives the elementary idea of the rule of law: he who makes the laws is also subject to them. If God himself is subject to his own laws, then the sovereign, too, might be subject to his own rules. Grotius introduced the idea of self-limitation that lies at the heart of modern constitutionalism. The image in Ockham is one in which the rule always runs out or is suspended, and there is a will to decide when it does so. The essence of law does not lie in these regular cases of rule-following, but rather in deciding those cases that lie outside the rule.

This dualism has always been with us. At times, law appears as the voice of reason that manifests itself in rules, not in arbitrary power, and is synonymous with right. At other times law is an expression of might or power. When it is an expression of power it is arbitrary, and, as such, impossible to subsume under any rule. When law is the voice of reason it expresses itself as rules that aim to curb and restrain the arbitrariness of power; thus on the one hand it is rule and on the other the moment of exception is dominant.

In many ways liberal legal theory tries to marginalize the exceptional, hiding power, judgement and violence as exceptions. Modern democracy – so its proponents claim – exists wherever the rule of law and not the rule of men applies, where the sovereign himself is subject to the law, where there is no arbitrary power, and where the law is the voice of reason and not simply the whim of the powerful over the powerless, the rich over the poor, or the colonialist over the native.

However, a whole tradition, from Hobbes to Schmitt, draws our attention to the hidden exception. First came revolution, violence, lawlessness and formlessness, and thereafter came the norm, the constitution.

The norm, the rule, the normal, tries to blot out the exception, the violence, both historically and geographically. In terms of time it excludes the moment of its inception – the revolution and its violence. In terms of space it wants us to forget those who are geographically excluded from the system, those who are not citizens and therefore do not enjoy the rights enjoyed by the insiders. While the constitutional state is surrounded in time and space by violence, the modern state is based on the possibility of amnesia, of forgetting both what existed before there were laws and norms, and non-citizens, who are beyond the protection of law and norms.

Kierkegaard does not write as a political philosopher and does not address the question of the sovereign, and yet in his theological writings he takes up the concept of decision:

> A decision joins us to the eternal. It brings what is eternal into time. A decision raises us with a shock from the slumber of monotony. A decision breaks the magic spell of custom. A decision breaks the long row of weary thoughts. A decision pronounces its blessing upon even the weakest beginning as long as it is a real beginning (Moore 1999: 3).

Carl Schmitt secularizes Ockham's and Kierkegaard's insights and radicalizes Hegel. He is probably the most influential figure of the last century in terms of his critique of liberal ethics and legality, and he poses the main threat to liberal legality (Dyzenhaus 1998; Mouffe 1999; Holmes 1993; Scheuerman 1994). Some of his ideas make one shudder – to say nothing of his activities as a Third Reich intellectual – while others force us to rethink liberal ideals. If the strength of liberal morality is its emphasis on norms, the power of the Schmittian approach is its fascination with moments of exception, crisis and revolution, wherein lies its dangerousness, too. In these moments there is a celebration of the will, a certain vitality that is not covered by the norm, where the activity is not mere repetition.

These ideas are covered in three of Schmitt's books, *Political Theology* (1922), *The Crisis of Parliamentary Democracy* (1923) and *The Concept of the Political* (1928). The ideas in these books are complementary, though each introduces a main theme. In *The Concept of the Political*, Schmitt wonders what the 'political' is. If ethics is the distinction between the good and the bad, aesthetics is the distinction between the ugly and the beautiful, and economics is the distinction between the efficient and the non-efficient, what, then, is the main distinction that defines politics? (Schmitt 1976 [1928], 6–27). Schmitt wants politics to stand alone and not be reliant on ethics or economics, and his answer is that, 'The specific political distinction to which political actions and motives can be reduced is that between friend and enemy' (26). This distinction gains its full meaning because it refers to 'the real possibility of physical killing' (33). That is not to say that politics equals a continuous real war and actual killing; rather it means 'living in the shadow of the possibility of a radical moment of war in which one may be asked to give one's life for one's fellow citizens' (37).

Without this antithesis there can be no politics; take away the possibility of conflict between groups, and politics would come to an end (35). Thus, by foregrounding the question of friend/enemy and establishing it as the main distinction that constitutes politics, Schmitt argues that one's enemy need not be 'morally evil or aesthetically ugly' (27), which is why 'the enemy in the political sense need not be hated personally' (29).

Schmitt opens *The Concept of the Political* with the words, 'The concept of the state presupposes the concept of the political.' In Schmitt's theory, the state is born without the anguish of liberal theory over the enclosure represented by the state. The Schmittian state is born with the distinction built into its definition: friend and enemy, those who are in and those who are out. And by definition, each has different duties.

This takes us to the second important concept in Schmitt's scheme: that of homogeneity (while not connected by definition, when we study the case of Israel we see the connectedness between these two concepts). He treats this point in his book on *The Crisis of Parliamentary Democracy* (Schmitt 1985a [1923]), locating one of the basic problems in liberal legal and political theory in the question of enclosure: how are we to decide who is in the state and who is left out? Who is a citizen and who is not?

Well aware of this problem, Schmitt argues that the universal ideal of liberalism is unattainable. With such universal ideals there cannot be a moment of closure and there will be no political boundaries, which is tantamount to saying that there will be no states and thus no politics. Schmitt thus argues that internal equality between citizens is based on inequality – the exclusion of those who are not citizens from the benefits and the rights that the system grants to those included within it. He is also well aware that the ideas of universalism and citizenship are mutually exclusive, if not contradictory: 'in the domain of the political, people do not face each other as abstractions but as politically interested and politically determined persons, as citizens, governors and governed, politically allied or opponents' (Schmitt 1985a [1923]: 11).

Our abstract humanity cannot provide the basis for equality within the state itself; there must be some substantial commonality beyond the mere abstract legal persona stripped of all particularities and affiliations. This leads Schmitt to demand a certain level of homogeneity within the state, a sort of common substance. Without such homogeneity democracy is impossible: 'democracy requires, therefore, first homo-geneity and second – if the need arises – elimination or eradication of heterogeneity' (Schmitt 1985a, [1923]: 9).

Schmitt's obsession with the friend/enemy distinction and with homogeneity meets the radical decisionism he expresses in *Political Theology* (Schmitt 1985b [1922]). Here, Schmitt deals with the concept of sovereignty, which he defines in the opening sentence of the book thus: 'sovereign is he who decides on the exception' (5). This decision is existential, not governed by a norm: 'The decision on the exception is a decision in the true sense of the word. Because a general norm, as rep-resented by an ordinary legal prescription, can never encompass a total exception, the decision that a real exception exists cannot therefore be derived from the norm.' (6) This is a decision (regarding) when the norms run out and one is faced with a sheer moment of decision, an unbounded decision. It is exactly in these heated moments that the sovereign reveals his true nature: 'the exception reveals most clearly the essence of the state's authority. The decision parts here from legal norm, and authority proves that to produce law it need not be based on law' (13).

Schmitt's decisionism and the distinction between friend and enemy spares him the need to justify himself to the rest of the world. The theory itself creates the border between those who are in and those who are out. The constitution is not a contract but a decision. The creation of the state, the moment of the revolution, takes place outside the norm, and is an assertion on the part of a homogenous group, 'the nation', that wants to live within a political entity of its own – a state. All else follows – constitution, norms, legality, etc. – but first there is the ethnos. But what is unique in Schmitt's theorization is the idea that the shadow of this moment of birth never disappears; the whole legal system lives in its shadow and remains immanent within the system. There is an ongoing need for the 'exception' for both 'decision' and for the 'ethnos'.

Israel: the ideological/political story

If Zionism is a national movement, then it possesses a combination of the following characteristics of exilic/settler/ethno-primordial/religious nationalism.

One of the main themes in Zionism as an ideology is the idea of the 'negation of exile' (Raz-Krakotzkin 1993). According to this, life for the Jews in exile is unbearable, unnatural, incomplete and inferior compared to life in the Land of Israel. The only solution for the Jewish question is the creation of a state for the Jews, where they can govern and ensure a safe place for themselves (Herzl 1997 [1896]). Here, Jews can normalize their existence, bring an end to their estrangement and become a nation like all other (European) nations (Avinery 1981).

Second, Zionism was greatly influenced by eastern European national movements (Sternhell 1992), according to which the (ethnic) nation precedes the existence of the state. In western European nationalism, the existence of the state precedes the nation, the state has defined borders and institutions, and the nation is a byproduct of the state in which many different ethnic groups participate. The eastern European model of nationalism is a primordial ethnic nationalism in which the nation's existence precedes the formation of the state, and the nation is defined mainly by its primordial ethnic/linguistic/cultural origins (Brubaker 1992). In this model the nation establishes the state, which becomes an instrument in the service of the nation.

To this one must add a third element, the complex relation of Zionism to religion. While Zionism began as a revolt against Jewish orthodoxy in Europe, it constantly deployed religious language in its discourse and it has been extremely difficult to separate the national from the religious (Friedman 1989; Weissbrod 1983).

The fourth characteristic of Zionism relates to its mission as a comprehensive political, ideological and social revolution that aims to touch and completely transform almost every aspect of the life of the Jews. The Zionist revolution was to change the relation of the Jews to land and agriculture, revive their language, and create a new image of the self-reliant Israeli pioneer-settler (Ben-Gurion 1958).

The analysis should also bear in mind several material facts. The first concerns the demography of Palestine. In 1917 Jews constituted only around 11% of the total population and owned a negligible amount of land (Horowitz and Lissak 1978: 19–20). By 1947 Jews in mandatory Palestine accounted for approximately 650,000 people or 30% of the total population of 1,900,000, and owned only around 7% of the land. The area assigned to the Jewish state in the 1947 partition plan included approximately 600,000 Palestinians. Thus the existence of several hundred thousand Palestinians within the Jewish state was clearly a real problem to which a 'solution' should have been found. Similarly, as it would have been almost impossible to build a Jewish homeland while most of the land remained in Palestinian hands, Israel needed to take over this land in order to control it. Thus the negation of exile was complemented by the negation of the Palestinians.

The second material fact we need to consider is that the state was established through a war that resulted in dramatic demographic changes and produced hundreds of thousands of refugees (Morris 1987; Pappe 2006). The borders of the new state were not recognized by its neighbours and merely represented the ceasefire line, with the result that hundreds of thousands of Palestinians are still demanding to return to their homes. In these circumstances the borders of the state, which as apolitical borders are meaningless, represent only the limits of power.

Some of these beliefs/facts are manifested in the Declaration of the Establishment of the State of Israel. The bodies that declared the establishment of the state are Jewish national bodies representing not only the Jews in Palestine/Israel (the *Yishuv*), but rather Jews all over the world. Second, the Declaration itself stipulates that the state's mission is to absorb Jews from all over the world, so that the creation of the State of Israel is only one stage in a long journey. Accordingly, three years after the establishment of the state, David Ben-Gurion, Israel's first prime minister, declared (in a speech made to the American Zionist Organization/Movement) that establishing the state was less (and more) than Zionism, because:

> Zionism is a dream while the state is a fact. The state only speaks in the name of its citizens and its laws are only valid for its citizens within its

sovereign borders. However, not all Jews can take part in this sovereignty, but rather only few of them... As a citizen of Israel my relation to the people of Israel has priority over my relation to my state because the state is just a tool, and at this point in time the state has absorbed only a small part of the nation... the state is a tool and an instrument, but it is not the only tool (Ben-Gurion 1951).

The emerging picture is as follows: the borders of the state are almost meaningless in that being a Palestinian citizen *inside* Israel does not mean that you are part of the collective [national] project, while being a Jew living *outside* the state does not mean that you are *not* part of this project since, according to the ethos of the state (and the Law of Return), every Jew can become a citizen at any point in time. All of this renders the difference between the actual and the potential (Jewish) citizen marginal and blurs the concept of borders (Yiftachel 1999).

Constitutional tensions

The story I am about to recount about the birth of Israeli constitutionalism is familiar and has been told several times in different ways (Gavison 1985; Klein 1971; Rubinstein and Medina 2005).

The first point I want to stress relates to the transfer of powers from the People's Council (PC) – a purely ethnic, national Jewish body – to the Provisional State Council (PSC), putatively a state organ. The chain starts with the Declaration of Independence:

WE DECLARE that, with effect from the moment of the termination of the Mandate being tonight, the eve of Sabbath, the 6th of Iyar, 5708 (15th May, 1948), until the establishment of the elected, regular authorities of the State in accordance with the Constitution which shall be adopted by the Elected Constituent Assembly not later than the 1st of October 1948, the People's Council shall act as a Provisional Council of State, and its executive organ, the People's Administration, shall be the Provisional Government of the Jewish State, to be called 'Israel'.

This is a moment of creation, *ex nihilo*, of a new legal order. The 'we' that opens the above paragraph is the Jewish 'we', and the PC is a body that represents other Jewish bodies.

It appears from the above paragraph that the PC opted for what might be termed two levels, or two tracks, of politics: one for everyday, legislative politics, and the second for superior-historical (constitutional) matters, which would set the rules of the game for the former (Ackerman 1991). The mission assigned to the Constituent Assembly (CA) was to write a constitution, and the PSC's task was legislative.

This original plan was, however, abandoned for several reasons – among them Ben-Gurion's hostility to a written constitution – and another path was chosen that combined both powers in one body. The PSC passed the Law and Administration Ordinance, granting itself legislative (not constitutional) powers.[2] Only a few days before the elections to the CA it passed the Constituent Assembly (Transition) Ordinance (1949),[3] which stipulated that when the CA was first convened following the elections, the PSC was to be dissolved and the CA was to assume its powers. Thus the CA was accorded both legislative and constituent powers.

When the CA convened it renamed itself 'The First Knesset.' It also adopted the Second Knesset (Transition) Law (1951),[4] which stipulated that the Second Knesset was to enjoy all the powers of the First Knesset, as was, *mutatis mutandis*, every subsequent Knesset.

In the event, the First Knesset was unable to reach an agreement over the constitution. Part of the opposition came from religious groups and the difficulty of reaching a compromise in matters of state and religion, but it was in part also due to the fact that many saw the state as having been established to serve all Jews, and as only a minority of them were present at that moment, they should not restrict future generations and immigrants. The debate for and against the constitution ended in what became known as the 'Harari Resolution', in which the Knesset charged the Knesset's Constitutional and Legislative Committee with preparing a draft constitution containing different chapters, each of which would be considered a 'basic law', and these basic laws would together constitute a constitution.[5]

Ever since there has been an ongoing debate in Israel over the power of the Knesset to endorse a constitution and whether the First Knesset – as a constituent assembly – squandered the golden 'constitutional moment' to enact a constitution, or whether the Knesset still possesses all the powers held by the CA.

A decade ago this question was brought to the Supreme Court, which decided that the Knesset does have the power to create a constitution – constituent power – and the power to amend the constitution – legislative power. Thus the initial constituent power extends in time and still exists today.[6] Israel has passed several basic laws over the years, but there is lack of consistency in terms of the supremacy of these laws and their entrenchment, which create a certain confusion (which is beyond the scope of this chapter).

From revolution to statehood

The crucial moment in my analysis is the move from the People's Council to the PSC, which is a move from revolution to statehood and from national-ethnic to state-civic.

The constituent power is regarded as 'The secularized version of the divine power to create the world *ex-nihilo*' (Preuss 1994: 144). This constituent power is an 'all powerful... all embracing power'; 'It is the source of production of constitutional norms... constituent power as all-embracing power is revolution itself' (Negri 1999: 2).

There are two approaches to the relation between the constituent power and constituted powers – the constitution and other state organs. In one reading the constituent power can use its authority only once and then disappear. By using its power and creating the constitution it takes us from the lawless revolution to the institutionalized/ordered/ state. 'Making a constitution, the revolutionary forces are digging their own graves; the constitution is the final act of the revolution' (Preuss 1994: 145). After the constitution has been created we move into a new gravitational field in which the supreme arbiter is the constitution itself. In terms of the norm and the exception we have entered a new normative order, through the lenses of which every act is to be viewed. In some ways the case of the United States, where there was a clear formative constitutional moment of before and after, and where the constitution is clearly the supreme law and acquires part of its supremacy from 'the sanctity of the founding act' (Preuss 1996), is representative of this model. This might be called an 'institutional approach', because it allows the people – the revolutionaries – to revert to their daily lives and politics (Preuss 1994: 146). The revolution consummates itself and its aims are fully achieved by creating the constitution and the state's institutions.

However, another strand does not accept the total disappearance of the constituent power. Here, that power remains latent and it has an immanent nature. Advocates of the immanence thesis might be considered radical democrats in that they never relegate the people to everyday politics; rather, the power vested in the people to make a new order never completely vanishes. Constitutions are the embodiment of the will of the people and the will of the people is ultimately the final arbiter in potential future political conflicts. The revolution is never fully completed but takes on another form. However, it never relinquishes its aims. The people are the perpetual guards of the constitution. If what matters is the will of the people, then it is of no crucial importance how it expresses this will: 'the manner in which a nation exercises its will does not matter. Any procedure is adequate, and its will is always the supreme law' (Sieyès 1963: 128). France is an example of this version of radical, heightened democracy, in which the constitution does not enjoy the same supremacy as in the United States, for instance (Henkin 1989), which might explain the instability of and frequent amendments to the French constitution.

Conclusion: the case of Israel

Where, then, does Israel stand? Here are some preliminary remarks. First, Israel clearly does not follow in the footsteps of the United States. Israel has no clear 'constitutional moment' and no clearly identifiable constitutional document.[7] Legally and politically, Israel has certain affinities with the radical French pattern. Indeed, Israel appears to me as a very radical case of this model.

Second, as the aforementioned quotation from Ben-Gurion indicates, the establishment of the state is just an instrument. The main task − to gather all Jews and to take over the land − remains to be accomplished. In this respect, the case of Israel is very different from that of France by virtue of two crucial facts: while in the French case the nation is constituted as a contract bringing together people of different ethnic origins, in the case of Israel the nation is ethnic-religious-primordial. The French case represents the ongoing tension between all French citizens and the French constitution, between democracy and constitutionalism, and between the promises of the revolution (freedom, equality, fraternity) and its institutional achievements. In the Israeli case, however, the tension is between the ethnic nation and the constitution itself, representing the civic state. Thus instead of the French dichotomy of radical democracy/constitutionalism, in Israel the dichotomy is one of ethno-religiosity/constitutionalism. In Israel permanent revolution as a sort of radical democracy − which aims to preserve the constituent power − means the predominance of the ethnic over the civic, with all the implications this entails. In fact, this is one of the radicalizations that Schmitt makes by insisting on the concept of homogeneity, and thus retaining the concept of absolute power but transferring it from the demos to the ethnos.

While not the only ethno-religious country, Israel is unique due to the fact that many of the beneficiaries of the state project (all Jews) still live outside Israel, and are only potential citizens. This keeps the state 'on hold' as an unending project of absorbing immigrants and taking over Palestinian lands. Here, too, the dynamic aspect is radicalized and taken to the extreme.

The special case of Israel keeps it in a type of emergency or 'state of exception'. It encompasses the Holocaust, the war for the establishment of the state, the creation of the Palestinian refugee problem, the massive waves of immigration, and the ongoing state of war. Regardless of whether there still exists a genuine threat, emergency remains a dominant conception. In these circumstances every decision can appear to be existential; the moments of crisis are permanent, and according to many, the people (in the ethnic sense) must defend the state institutions which are the embodiment of the spirit of the people.

The tension between the definition of the state as democratic and Jewish appears as the readiness of sectors of the Jewish population to accept the institutional approach, and to declare that the revolution is over and the state is the only site for making decisions over the future of its citizens. Over the years tensions have developed between the creator – the Zionist movement/ethnos – and its creation – the State of Israel/demos. While the establishment of the state may be a major achievement, from another perspective it is a moment of crisis as it subjects the pure nationalistic-ethnic logic to the logic of the state. This tension has never been resolved. In fact, when Yigal Amir, the assassin of Prime Minister Yitzhak Rabin, was asked about the motives behind the assassination, his first response was that the Oslo Accords had been endorsed with the votes of Arab Knesset members, which for him was illegitimate (Peri 2000: 30; Grinberg 2000: 130, 154, 160).

Israel is clearly an extreme case, but one that nevertheless falls within a paradigm (of permanent revolution). Israel did not manage to push the exception to the margin, could not conceal its ethnic nature, with the result that in Israel the revolution is never completed. What surfaces in other countries only from time to time, in cases of national emergency, appears in Israel on an almost daily basis. Israel is a scandalous case of the modern paradigm of sovereignty because it reveals what lies beneath the smooth surface of other countries. The persistence of the exception in Israel, the ongoing state of emergency, the violent moment of birth, and the persistence of its ethnic nature are features that one might find in some countries at some points in time. Israel is unique in that all of these features are present most of the time.

Notes

1   For a general review of Ockham's political thought see McGrade (1974). McGrade tries to show that in spite of Ockham's voluntaristic approach, one can nevertheless find some support in his text for a theory of natural law based on reason.
2   The Law and Administration Ordinance 1 L.S.I. 7 (1948).
3   The Constituent Assembly (Transition) Ordinance 2 L.S.I. 81 (1949).
4   (1951) 5 L.S.I. 94.
5   See Knesset Protocols 1953, 1743.
6   See *Bank Mizrahi v. Migdal* P.D 49(4) 221.
7   See Justice Cheshin's decision in the *Mizrahi* case, note 6

References

Ackerman, B. (1991) 'The lost opportunity', *Tel Aviv University Studies in Law,* Vol. 10, 53–68

Agamben, G. (1998) *Homo Sacer: Sovereign Power and Bare Life*, Stanford University Press, Stanford

Agamben, G. (2005) *The State of Exception*, University of Chicago Press, Chicago

Avinery, S. (1981) *The Making of Modern Zionism: The Intellectual Origins of the Jewish State*, Basic Books, New York

Ben-Gurion, D. (1951) Speech delivered to the American Zionist Movement in May 1951 in New York, in 'Collected papers: David Ben-Gurion', *Figures and Leaders*, published by the former Israeli Ministry of Media and Propaganda (*Misrad Hahasbara*). A copy of the document is on file with the author.

Ben-Gurion, D. (1958) 'The imperatives of the Jewish revolution', in A. Hertzberg (ed.) *The Zionist Idea: A Historical Analysis and Reader*, Temple Books, New York

Brubaker, R. (1992) *Citizenship and Nationhood in France and Germany*, Harvard University Press, Cambridge, MA

'Declaration of the Establishment of the State of Israel' «http://www.knesset.gov.il/docs/eng/megilat_eng.htm»

Dyzenhaus, D. (ed.) (1998) *Law as Politics: Carl Schmitt's Critique of Liberalism*, Duke University Press, Durham, NC

Friedman, M. (1989) 'The State of Israel as a theological dilemma', in B. Kimmerling (ed.) *The Israeli State and Society: Boundaries and Frontiers*, SUNY Press, Albany, NY

Gavison, R. (1985) 'The controversy over Israel's Bill of Rights', *Israel Year Book on Human Rights,* Vol. 15, 113

Grinberg, L. (ed.) (2000) *Contested Memory: Myth, Nation and Democracy. Thoughts after Rabin's Assassination,* Humphrey Institute, Ben Gurion University, Beer Sheva

Grotius, H. (1901 [1625]) *Laws of War and Peace,* Walter Dunn Publishers, New York

Henkin, L. (1989) 'Revolutions and constitutions', *Louisiana Law Review,* Vol. 49, 1023–56

Herzl, T. (1896/1997) *The Jews' State* (trans. H. Overberg), Jason Aronson, Northvale, NJ

Holmes, S. (1993) *The Anatomy of Antiliberalism,* Harvard University Press, Cambridge, MA

Horowitz, D. and M. Lissak (1978) *Origins of the Israeli Polity: Palestine under the Mandate,* University of Chicago Press, Chicago

Klein, C. (1971) 'A new era in Israel's constitutional law', *The Israel Law Review,* Vol. 6, no. 3, 376–97

McGrade, A. S. (1974) *The Political Thought of William of Ockham,* Cambridge University Press, New York

Moore, C. (1999) *Provocations: Spiritual Writings of Kierkegaard,* Plough Publishing House, Farmington, PA

Morris, B. (1987) *The Birth of the Palestinian Refugee Problem, 1947–1949,* Cambridge University Press, Cambridge

Mouffe, C. (ed.) (1999) *The Challenge of Carl Schmitt,* Verso, London

Negri, A. (1999) *Insurgencies: Constituent Power and the Modern State,* University of Minnesota, Minneapolis

Pappe, I. (2006) *The Ethnic Cleansing of Palestine,* Oneworld Publications, Oxford

Peri, Y. (2000) 'The assassination: Causes, meanings, outcomes,' in Y. Peri (ed.) *The Assassination of Yitzhak Rabin,* Stanford University Press, Stanford

Preuss, U. (1994) 'Constitutional power making of the new polity: Some deliberations on the relations between constituent power and the constitution', in M. Rosenfeld (ed.) *Constitutionalism, Identity, Difference and Legitimacy: Theoretical Perspectives,* Duke University Press, Durham

Preuss, U. (1996) 'The political meaning of constitutionalism', in R. Bellamy (ed.) *Democracy and Sovereignty: American and European Perspectives,* Avebury Publishing, Aldershot

Raz-Krakotzkin, A. (1993) 'Exile within sovereignty: Toward a critique of negation of exile in Israeli culture', *Theory and Criticism,* no. 4, 23–56

Rubinstein, A. and B. Medina (2005) *The Constitutional Law of the State of Israel,* Schocken Publishing, Tel Aviv

Scheuerman, W. (1994) *Between the Norm and the Exception,* MIT Press, Cambridge MA

Schmitt, C. (1976 [1928]) *The Concept of the Political,* Rutgers University Press, New Brunswick, NJ

Schmitt, C. (1985a [1923]) *The Crisis of Parliamentary Democracy,* MIT Press, Cambridge, MA

Schmitt, C. (1985b [1922]) *Political Theology*, MIT Press, Cambridge, MA

Schmitt, C. (1986 [1919]) *Political Romanticism*, MIT Press, Cambridge, MA

Sieyès, E. (1963) *What is the Third Estate?* in S. E. Finer (ed.) Praeger, New York

Smooha, S. (1990) 'Minority status in an ethnic democracy: The status of the Arab minority in Israel', *Ethnic and Racial Studies*, Vol. 13, 389–413

Sternhell, Z. (1992) *The Founding Myths of Israel: Nationalism, Socialism and the Making of the Jewish State*, Princeton University Press, Princeton

Taylor, C. (1989) *Sources of the Self: The Making of the Modern Identity*, Harvard University Press, Cambridge MA

Weissbrod, L. (1983) 'Religion as national identity in secular society', *Review of Religions Research*, Vol. 24, no. 3, 188–205

Yakobson, A. and A. Rubinstein (2003) *Israel and The Family of Nations – Jewish Nation State and Human Rights*, Shocken Publishing, Tel Aviv

Yiftachel, O. (1999) '"Ethnocracy": The Politics of Judaizing Israel/Palestine', *Constellations*, Vol. 6, no. 3, 364–90

Yiftachel, O. (2006) *Ethnocracy: Land and Identity Politics in Israel/Palestine*, University of Pennsylvania Press, Philadelphia

Ilan Pappe

8 The *Mukhabarat* State of Israel:
A State of Oppression is not a State of Exception

On 29 May 2007, the Israeli Knesset revalidated, as it has done annually in recent times, the Emergency Regulations that had been imposed in Palestine by the British Mandate in 1945 and re-adopted by Israel on the day of its foundation in 1948 (*Ha'aretz*, 30 May 2007). There are almost 200 such regulations that enable the state legally to declare any part of the country a closed military area, exercise administrative arrest without trial, expel and even execute citizens. From the establishment of the state until 1996 there was no need to extend this validation annually as it was regarded as a permanent situation. In 1996, in a celebrated display of democratic histrionics, official Israel announced the annulment of the permanent status and the government decreed a need for an annual approval. The recurrent approval, needless to say, was taken for granted (partly because, even without the annual approval of the mandatory regulations, the government was still able to impose the same regime of terror and intimidation on the basis of the general State of Emergency declared in Israel on the day of its establishment, still intact in 2007). But for many observers, the 1996 annulment, or rather charade of annulment, was the last attempt to democratize the country. After that, and particularly in the wake of the second Intifada, the legislative effort in Israel focused on restricting even further the limited rights citizens had enjoyed under the State of Emergency Rule and Regulations.

It is very tempting to view these recent developments in contemporary Israel as a prime example of Giorgio Agamben's 'state of exception' (Agamben 2005). The dark side of democracy as described in this short book seems to prevail everywhere in the oppressive Jewish state. The doomsday scenarios of persons stripped of any human or civil rights, the rule of emergency regulations and the overall state of siege are familiar features of Israel as they have become also all over Europe and the United States in the wake of the 'war on terror'. Has democracy been seriously eroded in Israel as well? Is Israel also under a state of exception? My brief answer is no.

This chapter argues that the inclusion of Israel within the state of exception debate is wrong, even dangerous. I wish to challenge this inclusion and warn that, tempting as it might be, it can reinforce the global immunity Israel receives for its membership in the camp of democratic states. This immunity enables Israel to continue the dispossession of Palestine commenced in the late nineteenth century. The importance of such an inquiry – whether the democratic paradigm in general, and Agamben's in particular, is applicable to Israel and Palestine – goes far beyond the question of scholarly compatibility. The very discussion of Israel within the parameters of this debate assumes that Israel is another case of a western liberal democracy dangerously deteriorating into the abyss dreaded by Agamben. In all the cases discussed by Agamben, the state degenerates from a point to which it can return. It can slide dangerously into Nazi Germany but it can recover as a post-World War Two Germany. This debate was never and can never be applied to the Arab states and it was never applied to Apartheid South Africa, states that could not be analysed either as 'defending democracies' or suffering from a 'state of exception'. They were always examples of essentially non-democratic entities. The latter case, this chapter argues, suits Israel. Not because – as others have shown in this volume and elsewhere – the paradigm offered by Agamben does not *describe* correctly the situation in Israel vis-à-vis the Palestinian minority or the Palestinians under occupation; the descriptions befit the local situation perfectly. But they are the wrong *analysis,* reference and departure point, adding little to our understanding of how Israeli oppression actually works, while on the other hand, inadvertently contributing to that oppression.

If Israel can be judged within Agamben's terms of reference, then it must be regarded a variant of democracy – flawed or otherwise. However, Israel, I argue in this chapter, is neither in, nor a state of exception; it is rather in, and a state of oppression. Such states exist within the very region where the state's founding fathers attempted to build a European enclave: the Arab world. Of the models typifying the Arab world, one in particular applies to Israel: the Arab *mukhabarat* (secret services) state. The processes taking place in the state in Israel in recent years do not fit the twilight zone between democracy and dictatorship, which concerns Agamben. If they did, the deterioration could be halted or slowed down by reinforcing democracy. But because Israel is an oppressive state, the deterioration will surely continue unabated unless the state is de-Zionized from within or pressured from without. De-Zionization can bring about the democratization of the country as a whole, and only then will we be able to examine how far in this post-Zionist phase the state of exception has affected it.

Discussing Israel as an oppressive entity relates to its relationship with the indigenous population of Palestine, not necessarily with Jewish society. Israel controls the whole area that was formally mandatory Palestine and the examination of its oppressive nature concerns its relationship with about five million Palestinians who live in the mandatory area. In more ways than one, the oppression also affects the lives of the millions of Palestinians who live in exile or in refugee camps as a result of the ethnic cleansing Israel carried out in 1948.

My concern in showing that the Israeli case study is not applicable to the paradigm of the state of exception is not a value judgement of western democracies. Nor does it question the state's membership in the Western democratic world. This membership places Israel together with the US in Agamben's categorization of states of exception that are undergoing the worst phase in abusing democratic rights, or in a lesser category such as Agamben's own Italy, or France. In all these cases, restraining the present phase and returning to better days is within the realm of democratic activity: from writing books, as Agamben does, to demonstrating in the streets of the western capitals, and playing an active role in local politics. This was never a recipe for change in Apartheid South Africa or Pinochet's Chile. Had not a drastic action been taken both within and without, these oppressive regimes would have still been with us today. Attempting to activate the democratic formula for change in other contemporary oppressive states would be akin to throwing pebbles at a steel wall.

This chapter examines two paradigms in relation to contemporary Israel and its Palestine policies: a non-applicable one, the state of exception, and an applicable one, the state of oppression. The non-applicability is proven by the enthusiastic support for Agamben's warnings in Israel on the one hand, and the irrelevance of Agamben's concerns to the contemporary reality in Israel, on the other. The applicability is shown diachronically by following the circumstances which produced a kind of *Herrenvolk* democracy (van den Berge 1980) on the land. In reality, and in my analysis, the paradigm is applied only to part of the population in the country, while the other part of the population is aware of the oppression and fully endorses and supports it. Therefore this paradigm of the state of oppression is not an attempt to analyse Israel or Zionism in their totality as historical, cultural or political phenomena. Rather, it segregates the analysis since the reality is segregated, making the paradigm of the state of oppression more apt. The democratic paradigm, as well as that of the state of exception, on the other hand, assumes one state, one society and one territory, as the taken-for-granted subject matters of analysis and prognosis. Such an approach could never apply to Apartheid South Africa and does not apply to the reality in Israel. Synchronically, the applicability is argued through a comparison of Israel to the *mukhabarat* states in the region: the very region in which the founders of Zionism wanted to build a central European liberal democracy, but instead created a hybrid between a colonialist state and a *mukhabarat* regime imposed on its Palestinian population.

The concluding part of the chapter deals with the first decade of the twenty-first century, taking issue with those who describe this period as an indication that Israel is a democracy slipping into a state of exception. I reject the notion that the violation of human rights signifies the onset of an exceptional oppressive state in the history of the country. Instead I see the decade as a period in which the state has abandoned the charade of democracy due to what I term 'navigation fatigue' and as a result is escalating its violence against the oppressed people. This is not a new *phase*, but rather a new *cycle* of violence that occurred in the past and would recur again as long as Israel is exempt from scrutiny as an oppressive state.

Not a state of exception: an inapplicable paradigm

The inapplicability of Agamben's paradigm can be illustrated both discursively and analytically. Discursively, it is possible to show that there is nothing alarming in Agamben's concern in the eyes of Israeli Zionist scholars and jurists, both left and right. Both can use Agamben's analysis and prognosis as apt to their state, not necessarily because they have read the book but because they understand they can easily join a fashionable western self-flagellation, as long as their state is identified as a legitimate member of this community of self-suffering. As in any other *Herrenvolk* democracy, the concerns are exclusively about the rights of the whites (namely the Jewish population) and therefore Agamben's work does not constitute any challenge to the very nature of the state or the *raison d'être* that brought it into existence.

Analytically, the paradigm and the debate are not applicable because both the mechanisms that bring about a state of exception, in Agamben's paradigm, and the indicators that a given democracy is already deeply submerged in a state of exception either do not exist in present-day Israel or are very marginal elements in the overall oppression. For Agamben, the ominous indicators of the decline are in the realm of sovereignty, constitution and law. Human and civil rights are abused because something very fundamental changes in these realms of statehood. A new abusive reality unfolds, one which was not sanctioned by the idea of democratic sovereignty or by the original constitution and laws. The mechanisms that allow such an abuse are the transition of sovereignty from the legislative to the executive, the suspension of democratic laws and the legislation of oppressive ones.

Oppression in Israel has very little to do with these mechanisms, therefore there is a difference between the trajectory in Agamben's analysis and in the case of Israel. In the former, democracy fluctuates between greater or lesser democratic phases. In the latter, oppression vacillates between severe and more relaxed cycles of state violence against its oppressed citizens. Admitting such a reality is beyond the wishes and capacity of the local academic elite, which has warmly embraced the analysis of Israel as a democracy undergoing a constitutional crisis.

The righteous discourse of democracy

The discourse and debate on the state of exception assume a liberal democratic potential and a European/Western political culture. This is why Agamben's paradigm appeals to mainstream Israeli academics who wish to belong, even if the discussion is about Israel's disgrace. The analysis reinforces the Israeli media assertion that after 9/11 and in the aftermath of the London and Madrid bombs, Israel's security agenda was fully endorsed and respected by all western liberal democracies (as argued by Bhattacharyya in this volume). This has assured the inclusion of Israel in the civilized world fighting against the 'Axis of Evil'. It also protects Israel academically from any embarrassment, not to mention comparison with repulsive historical case studies such as Apartheid South Africa or Pinochet's Chile.

One of the first venues that favourably discussed Agamben's state of exception was *Tchelet*, the scholarly journal of the New Right in Israel (Sagiv 2007). It is published by an ultra neo-con Zionist think-tank, the Shalem Institute that advocates the advance of free market economy with a strong commitment to expansionist Zionist values. It emulates and is financed by similar neo-conservative think-tanks in the US. *Tchelet* welcomed Agamben's warnings, and recommended that local politicians heed these warnings and watch the pitfalls incurred by anti-democratic legislation that follows a legitimate wish of the democracy to defend itself.

The Zionist left welcomed the book and the paradigm for similar reasons. In 2007, progressive film-makers devoted a special festival to the state of exception. The lectures and accompanying texts centred on the dangerous abuses of human rights in the West, which included Israel.[1] The festival presented brave film-makers who exposed, in Israel and elsewhere in the West, the state of exception as a dangerous illusion and warned that it may be irreversible or lead to dictatorship; they also blamed the big film companies for producing this illusion in the West. Though totally disconnected from the source of the violation of basic human and civil rights in Israel, the festival offered a democratic agenda that was supposed to rectify the evils without altering the racist nature of the state or ceasing the oppression of anyone who is not Jewish.

The concrete discussion of Agamben's work is part of an older wish to stress the inclusion of Israel in the western democracy agenda, especially after 9/11. A typical example of this academic concern was a 2001 Open University conference titled 'The State of Emergency'.[2] The basic assumption of the debate was the interplay between democracy and the state of exception. Many similar interdisciplinary conferences followed. The most interesting contribution was by Claude Klein, one of Israel's leading jurists, who noted that, since the state of emergency declared in Israel on the day of its establishment was never annulled, citizens face the banalization of the state of emergency, taken for granted as a fact of life. Klein did not explain why – the obvious answer is that it applies in practice only to the five million Palestinians in the Occupied Territories and in Israel itself.

At the same conference, historian Shlomo Sand stressed the tension between liberalism and democracy, presenting a very well-argued case of how a state of exception undermines liberalism in the name of democracy, but totally irrelevant to Israel. Israel as a liberal case was favoured by Yael Tamir, the Israeli minister of education in Ehud Olmert's government, who received her D.Phil. from Oxford as Isaiah Berlin's student and was a leading light in the Peace Now movement (Tamir 1993). For her and for the liberal Zionist camp in general, the discussion of the state of exception strongly grounds the Zionist case within the liberal democratic camp. This allows Israel to continue benefiting from this membership financially, politically and more importantly, morally, despite the abuses on the ground. The inevitable result is that this privileged position empowered Israel's already very strong military power, enabling it to continue the destruction of Palestine and the Palestinians. At the end of his contribution Sand asked whether a state that is not a state of all its citizens could be a democracy, yet without re-injecting the question into a discussion which firmly placed Israel within the liberal democratic world.

In the same conference a media expert, Hilel Nossak, warned that in a state of exception the media cannot fulfil its role as democracy's watchdog. However, in Israel, he asserted, the state of exception can provide the media with a positive role in 'enhancing solidarity and social cohesion'. The paradoxical wish to present the media both as a watchdog and as the state's puppy is only one of many, characterizing an oppressive state wishing to be recognized as a democracy. This is a far cry from the way Agamben explores the dangers incurred in a state of exception, but it is very close to the popular Israeli definition of democracy as an exclusive majoritarian Jewish licence to oppress the Palestinian minority. To ensure that there will always be a Jewish majority, every means is justified, including ethnic cleansing.

This righteous discourse is not new. Already in 1993, Shimon Shitrit, professor of law and minister of justice, led a group of jurists who pontificated against the dangers of allowing an expansion of the state of emergency in Israel. He advocated adhering to 'international standards' and demanded a 'narrow and limited definition' of this state of emergency. Shitrit was minister of justice in a system that used the widest possible definition when it came to the lives of Palestinians under occupation and oppression on both sides of the Green Line. He argued against granting the authorities in cases of emergency the right to initiate anti-liberal and anti-democratic legislation; a practice which had full academic support for the policies of discrimination and oppression. Pledging loyalty to what the West cherishes as sublime human values and exercising a policy of what it abhors most seemed to be a formula for protecting the state against external rebuke (Shitrit 1993).

The issue has also won new impetus within the Israeli political and social sciences in recent years. Two schools of thought developed: a noncritical liberal Zionist school and a critical Zionist one. Both strive to present Israel as a democratic case study, the former as a paragon of the model, the latter as a more flawed specimen.

The liberal position was articulated in a book by Amnon Rubinstein and Alexander Jacobson, *Israel among the Family of Nations* (2006). Like so many who teach the history of ideas and political thought in Israeli universities,[3] they not only integrate the Israeli system into the debate on European democracy, but rather claim it is a superior case study. Several leading liberal pundits, such as Michael Walzter (2003), some of whom supervised Israeli academics in their initiation stage, provide the international umbrella for such claims. Sami Smooha represents the other point of view, seriously critiquing the flaws of Israeli democracy (Smooha 2000); however his bottom line is that Israel is an 'ethnic democracy', perhaps not the best, but still a democracy like any other Western democracy.

The analytical discrepancy

There are three major indicators that attest to the existence of a state of exception according to Agamben's analysis, all irrelevant, I argue, in the analysis of the present state of oppression in Palestine. They concern changes in sovereignty, amendments of constitutions and transformations on the ground, based on new legislation or de-legislation.

The shifting power of sovereignty is the first indicator of the transition from democracy to dictatorship. Agamben cites Carl Schmitt's argument that the power to decide on the initiation of a state of emergency in a democracy defines sovereignty itself (Agamben 2005: 1). The powers pushing this transition forward are allegedly the people themselves, but quite often it is motivated by a fanatic or greedy ruler. And yet, this transition often enjoys popular support – as Agamben's historical survey so clearly demonstrates. This did not happen only in Nazi Germany; it was also the case in the US of President Abraham

Lincoln. 'Whether strictly legal or not', as Agamben quotes Lincoln on the day he declared a state of exception, the measures Lincoln had adopted had been taken 'under what appeared to be a popular demand and a public necessity' in the certainty that Congress would ratify them. They were based on the conviction that even fundamental law could be violated if the very existence of the union and the juridical order were allegedly at stake (Agamben 2005: 20–21). Popular intoxication was also an important factor in other historical junctures, leading Agamben to argue that when the legislature delegates sovereignty to the executive, with wide popular support, democracy is slipping into a state of exception.

However, in Israel 'naked citizens' (or 'bare life', to use Agamben's term), are not oppressed because there was a shift in the source of sovereignty. Paradoxically, from the oppressed Palestinian's point of view, Jewish sovereignty is illegal and non-existent, and thus shifts in sovereignty are irrelevant. The state rests on its power to oppress – regardless of whether the power lies with the government or the parliament. As Palestinian subjects of the Jewish state, we learn very little from Agamben's learned discussion of Schmitt and Benjamin. As Jewish citizens of Israel, we are disinterested in this debate, since we accept the state's racist ideological infrastructure and trust it to disallow any legal or real parallels between 'us' and 'them', the oppressed Palestinians.

The second indicator is a transformation of the constitutional reality, especially the termination of the classical separation of powers. Agamben states very clearly that, in the state of exception, the democratic principle of the separation of powers collapses and the executive partially absorbs the legislature. Parliament loses the right to protect the citizens through constitutional checks and balances (or basic laws, as is the case in Israel). Under the state of exception the parliament's role is limited to ratifying the decrees issued by the executive. And, Agamben continues,

> it is significant that though this transformation of the constitutional order (which is today underway to varying degrees in all the Western democracies) is perfectly well known to jurists and politicians, *it has remained entirely unnoticed by the citizens*. At the very moment when it would like to give lessons in democracy to different traditions and cultures, the political culture of the West does not realize that it has entirely lost its canon (Agamben 2005: 14).

It should indeed regain its canon, but it has a canon that can be retrieved. Israel's anti-democratic canon, however, is still alive and kicking.

In other words, a total revolution of the existing order without the citizens noticing it, or noticing it too late, is the second indicator. By contrast, the Israeli state of oppression is noticed, acknowledged and welcomed by its Jewish citizens who leave it in the hands of the political elite to vacillate between *de facto* and *de jure* acknowledgement. The paradigm might be relevant if ever the abuse encompassed Jewish society. But this has not happened yet, and is not likely to happen when state ideology is that of ethnic supremacy and racist purism.

When discussing the birth of the Fascist and Nazi regimes in Italy and Germany, Agamben argues convincingly that they emerged out of the 'pressure of the paradigm of the state of exception' in which 'the entire politico-constitutional life of Western societies began gradually to assume a new form' (Agamben 2005: 13). Agamben attempts to understand how Hitler's rise to power was connected to the uses and abuses of article 48 of the Weimar Constitution, which defined national security and measures to protect it. He notes: 'the last years of the Weimar Republic passed entirely under a regime of the state of exception; it is less obvious to note that Hitler could probably not have taken power had the country not been under a regime of presidential dictatorship for nearly three years and had parliament been functioning' (Agamben 2005: 14). The reappearance of these trends, which affect all western societies as Agamben chooses to call them, has motivated his brilliant book *The State of Exception* (2005). And yet the 'assumption of new roles' which emanates from faulty constitutions, lax enough to allow the loopholes from which the state of exception emerges, are not applicable to the oppression of human and civil rights in Israel.

The source of worry in the case of Israel is the opposite: it is not the use or abuse of a certain law that is the omen of worse things to come. It is rather the legalization of current abuses in the name of national security that accentuates an already existing reality. The law does not transform the reality, it affirms it.

Indeed the wordings used by practitioners and legislators in the western state of exception and in the Israeli state of oppression are very different. The diachronic span that Agamben so skilfully draws for us comes back to the state of exception as 'defending democracy'. Israel uses oppression to defend it *against* democracy, not only in practice but also in the discourse used, leading to the maintenance of the state of oppression. The Weimar coalition wanted to defend the constitution with the state of exception; Israel wants to defend a permanent state of oppression with its constitutional law. This is why genuine supporters of democracy, as I point out later, are branded as the arch-enemies of the state.

Agamben draws our attention to the importance of the very act of legislation for declaring a state of exception. For the State of Israel the least important condition for producing oppression is declaration by law. The law can only be used to de-declare the state of oppression, not initiate it. However, in the Israeli state of oppression, the very act of legislation comes when 'navigation fatigue' sets in. The law is needed to reflect reality without any need to present it, mainly for external consumption, as something else. In other words, unlike the state of exception, in the state of oppression the very act is to institutionalize, rather than legalize, oppression.

A state of exception needs legislation and de-legislation (passing emergency laws, suspending constitutions or even abolishing them). Whereas 'navigation fatigue' in Israel prepares the ground for legislation of the *de facto* reality of apartheid, ethnic cleansing and occupation, such legislation does not change the constitutional or legal nature of the State of Israel. It rather reaffirms it, and, when this happens, it cannot be understood through the paradigm of the state of exception.

The third indicator is the relation between law and reality. According to Agamben, abnormal and exceptional state behaviour becomes norm in the state of exception, as in rites of sublimation such as carnivals that allow citizens to play with forbidden taboos becoming reality (you no longer play an imagined executor, you become one for real). Another way of tracing the state of exception, before it is too late, is through instances where the legal system is heavily politicized. But all these very dangerous indicators that democracy is falling into the abyss of dictatorship are within the realm of legality. The Israeli charade of democracy is not played on this field at all, but rather in the realm of self-conviction, indoctrination and external presentation.

In the historical and contemporary examples he surveys, Agamben asks why vague democratic articulations enabled clearcut dictatorial situations. When the citizen engages in such a search he discovers, often too late, that a state of exception was imposed in the name of an unclear law. However, this debate is of no great significance for Israel, where there is no need for an elaborate and twisted search for the tension between vague legislation and clearly oppressive political realities. One of Agamben's favourite examples is Article 14 of the French *Charte* of 1814 that granted the sovereign the power to 'make the regulations and ordinances necessary for the execution of the laws and the security of the state' (Agamben 2005: 11). Israel does not have a constitution, but the infrastructure of its emergency regulations is neither vague nor hidden in obscure articles of basic law; unlike in France, it is integrated into something more substantial and formative than the constitution of any republic.

The integration of these abuses of power, law and sovereignty into the ideology of a colonizing regime is beyond Agamben's discursive and analytical framework. And these elements that are basically racist and colonialist and not the outcome of a collapsing republic or democracy are far more sustainable as facts of life. They remain so pervasive in the lives of citizens not because of laws, their interpretation or even their abuse, but because of the way the State of Israel came into being, and due to an element that is totally absent from the paradigm of the state of exception: the hegemony of the security apparatuses. Let us now examine these two elements: the history of oppression and the security apparatus, as the two components of my alternative paradigm.

The historical context of the state of oppression

Zionism was born out of two impulses. The first was a wish to find a safe haven for Jews after centuries of persecution and perhaps an insight that worse was to come. The second was the desire to reinvent Judaism as a national movement, a drive inspired by the Spring of Nations and similar developments in Europe. However, as soon as these two impulses were territorially realized in Palestine, the national and humanist project became a colonialist one. Inside Palestine a third impulse was added, the wish to create a pure Jewish space in whatever part of Palestine was coveted as the future Jewish State. And when that part was finally delineated in 1947/1948 as consisting of 80% of historical and mandatory Palestine, it was clear that the only way of achieving it was by ethnically cleansing the one million Palestinians who lived there (see Pappe 2006).

The ethnic cleansing of Palestine that depopulated half the country's people as it destroyed half the country's villages and towns was never acknowledged or condemned worldwide. The Jews became a decisive majority in the land and claimed their state was a democracy, whose leaders were committed to ensuring that 'the democracy' meant the permanent dispossession of the indigenous population of Palestine.

The global message for the State of Israel was that it could be included in the democratic world despite this crime against humanity. The result was that ethnic supremacy was cast as superior to any other values. Most importantly, it was maintained despite Israel's wish to be recognized as 'the only democracy in the Middle East'. Indeed it was the only democracy in the world where the inhabitants' ethnicity and religion defined their citizenship, and where a racist state posed as a democracy. Moreover, the ethnic cleansing left 160,000 Palestinians inside the Jewish state whose territorial expansionist appetite led to the incorporation of another 2.5 million Palestinians in 1967 (now numbering almost four million). Indirectly, the state also controlled the lives of the 5.5 million refugee community emerging out of the 1948 ethnic cleansing and of subsequent waves of expulsion. While after 1967 Israel chose not to use the same drastic means for ensuring its ethnic supremacy, it substituted them with the creation of an oppressive state.

The presence of Palestinians in what was supposed to be exclusive Jewish space determined the nature of the state dictated by a set of assumptions manifested in daily reality rather than law. However, a certain foundational legislation was deemed necessary, and was useful, as it attracted very little external attention, despite scholarly Palestinian attempts to show that only minimal legislation was sufficient to brand Israel as an apartheid state. The end result of minimal legislation and extensive practices was the total violation of the right to own property, land, identity or culture, or to receive full state benefits and rights. This was sometimes achieved through military rule, sometimes by direct or indirect occupation, and sometimes through semi-apartheid policies. However, the wish to be recognized as a democracy demanded impressive navigational skills by the political class in order to steer the state between apartheid, oppression and occupation on the one hand, and the pretence that these did not exist on the other. With American backing and European support this pretence became strategy, enabled by the quality of the leaders and by a certain regional and global constellation, as Israel was accepted globally as a member in the club of western democracies. This could not have been achieved without the assistance of the Israeli academia, Supreme Court and media, which re-cast the oppressive reality as democratic.

It is from this perspective that one understands why Agamben's work was discussed in Hebrew very early on as a guide that warns against the perils of emergency rules and civil rights abuses in genuine democracies. Despite the popularity of the state of exception paradigm in Israeli academic discourse, Israeli intellectuals felt nervous at attempts to apply Agamben's *homo sacer* definition to the Palestinians (but see Ghanim in this volume).

However, it must be emphasized that Israeli navigators embrace the state of exception paradigm because it is a Eurocentric perspective that assumes that any oppression such as the one existing in Israel is always a dangerous, albeit temporary, condition that stems from flaws in the constitutional situation of democracy, not from the ideological infrastructure of the Jewish state.

While Agamben was adopted as part of the navigation effort, the best navigators in the land – the liberal (or 'diet') Zionists – know how difficult it was to navigate between the belief in the necessity of oppression and the wish to appear to oppose it. You end up lying to yourself. A new language had to be invented and things that are said in close quarters cannot be repeated in public.

While liberal Zionists were at the centre of power in Israel, the navigation produced two golden rules about the Palestinians governed by Israel. One was that there are two kinds of Palestinians, the 'occupied' with no rights whatsoever, and 'our Palestinians', the citizens of the state, who have no collective rights apart from formal democratic rights such as voting. Unlike the Jewish majority, they have no right of land ownership, they cannot publicly identify with their national movement, or build autonomous educational or cultural systems. For most of the time this was sufficient for presenting Israel as the 'only democracy in the Middle East'. But the apparition disappeared when, after 1975, the Palestinians in Israel increasingly demanded collective rights. Then, in October 2000, the state reacted brutally and violently in driving its message home.

The navigation fatigue of the oppressive state

The navigation fatigue was fully exposed when the Palestinians citizens of Israel fundamentally challenged the definition of the state as a democracy. The serious challenge commenced in 1976, with the campaign against the vast land expropriation in the north, and culminated in the widespread show of solidarity with the second Intifada, resulting in 6 deaths in the first instance and 13 in the second, not to mention hundreds of wounded and thousands of arrests, marking the beginning of the end of the navigation efforts.

But these two challenges, in 1976 and 2000, were low intensity actions compared with the deeper process of change that was affecting the Palestinian minority in Israel, producing unprecedented challenges to the state in the first seven years of the twenty-first century. The most active and self-assertive sections of the Palestinian minority made clear and unequivocal demands for the construction of a genuine democracy in a state which they branded a racist ethnocracy (Yiftachel 2006). This was a new chapter in the life of a community used to responding to governmental initiatives rather than initiate action. Whereas in the past the state responded with violence, it now responded through its security apparatuses by dispensing with the charade of democracy, among other things thorough legislation, leading to the illusion that this was democracy deteriorating into a state of exception.

The latest challenge revolves around one party – the National Democratic Assembly (NDA) – and four documents of self-identity produced by Palestinian civil society in 2007. The NDA was founded in 1995 as a direct response to the Oslo process. It centred on the Palestinian intellectual Azmi Bishara, by all accounts one of the most important political figures in the Palestinian community in Israel in recent years. After receiving a Ph.D. from Humboldt University in Berlin, Bishara returned to Israel where he injected new life into the local political discourse, first as an academic and later as the founder of the NDA. He unnerved the certainties of the Israeli political system, leading a group of activists, mostly originally from the Communist Party, dissatisfied with the Oslo process and its implications. His declared aim was to reassert the collective identity of the Palestinian citizens of Israel by directly connecting them not only to other Palestinian groups but also to the Arab world at large. With the platform that called for making Israel a state of all its citizens, the NDA, headed by Bishara, competed in the 1996 elections.

Ever since 1999, Bishara was running an individual campaign inspired by these ideas and which the state found difficult to tolerate and accept. His eloquent television appearances defeated both many of Zionism's best spokespersons and Palestinians who collaborated with the state. In 1999, he nearly ran as a candidate for the prime minister's post, stretching the pretence almost to breaking point (Barzilai 2002).

The state's response came in 2007 as Bishara was expelled from political life through allegations that he spied for Hizbullah in the second Lebanon war. Bishara has been roaming the Arab world ever since he founded the NDA: kings, prime ministers, leaders of revolutionary organizations, such as Hassan Nasrallah, were among the many he embraced and with whom he discussed the future of the area in general and Palestine in particular. Some of the leaders he met – such as Syria's Bashar Assad, who still holds political prisoners without trial – did not add to his popularity among his voters. But during his decade of activity, no other Palestinian intellectual or politician has achieved what he did in terms of self-assertion and dignity. His last series of visits before and during the second Lebanon war, according to the allegations, were used to pass secret information and even money to the 'enemy'. This is a ridiculous charge as Bishara could not have been of any help to those on the ground in southern Lebanon, who studied every possible piece of intelligence that helped them to defeat the IDF. Nor was Bishara likely to be engaged in such activity – he enjoyed provocative and open gestures, such as sitting in public next to Nasrallah – rather than meetings in Beirut's back alleys.[4]

We have been there before. In 1999, Sheikh Raed Salah, the leader of the Islamic Movement in Israel, was charged with similar crimes. He was imprisoned for more than a year without trial and, when finally brought to court, it transpired that none of the charges could be validated. But the secret service was content: it punished another charismatic Palestinian leader so as to deter others from taking a firm position against Israel's right to exist as an exclusive and supremacist Jewish state. Bishara, who has lost a kidney, felt he could not survive under Israeli jail conditions for such a long period. This is why his supporters see the whole affair as an attempted politicide, or worse.

The second challenge was a set of documents published by Palestinian organizations in Israel in 2007, delineating the collective identity of the Palestinians in Israel and their future vision. On 13 March 2007, the daily *Maariv* reported a closed meeting of the Shabak (the Israeli secret service) in which the head of the organization described these documents as indicating a 'dangerous radicalization of Israeli Arabs; they tend not to identify with the state and this is caused by the rise of subversive elements among them'. This remark related to four documents published by Adalah (the Legal Centre for Arab Minority Rights in Israel whose members still desperately believe Israeli law has enough loopholes to improve the lot of Palestinians in Israel), the Follow-Up Committee for Arab Citizens in Israel (consisting of most of the heads of local councils and municipalities together with Arab Knesset members), MADA al-Carmel (the Arab Centre for Applied Social Research) and Mussawa (an NGO monitoring occupational and educational discrimination). The four documents called for the creation, within the 5 June 1967 borders, of a state for all its citizens that would respect Jewish and Palestinian sensibilities and strive to a fair solution of the Palestinian refugee problem and the end of the 1967 occupation. When asked to respond to the piece in *Maariv*, Yuval Diskin, the head of the Shabak, reiterated his view that the documents were subversive, endangered state security and could lead to the closure of these NGOs.

These remarks were accompanied by legislative efforts to curb this 'subversive' trend, by amending the laws so as to de-legitimize and strip the citizenship from anyone who did not declare his or her faith in the Jewishness of the state, or supported Palestinian organizations such as Hamas.

The new discourse signalled a violent response to any attempt to express a collective Palestinian identity or challenge the ethnic state, denoting clear signs of the descending fatigue. At the beginning of the twenty-first century official Israel was tired of navigating between an actual policy of ethnic discrimination and the formality of a democratic state. The regional and global balance of power – as understood in Israel – made such navigation skills redundant. No one in the US or the Arab world seemed to expect Israel to be a democracy.

The fatigue was also the inevitable result of the mediocrity of the political leadership, whose corruption and narrow-mindedness meant that any serious acts of navigation – or indeed any decisions about the future – were beyond its capacity. This came to light in the summer of 2006, when the prime minister and several other ministers were busy fighting legal battles against charges of corruption. They showed very little skill and dragged Israel into the second Lebanon war, universally regarded as the first ever Israeli military defeat. The vacuum of ruling was filled by two outfits that never had much faith in the need to appear 'democratic' for domestic or foreign consumption: the army and the secret services. These two organizations were above the law anyway, and their position testified that Israel was not a democracy transgressing into a state of exception, but rather a *mukhabarat* state, a local Arab and Middle Eastern variant of the oppressive state.

The applicable model: the *mukhabarat* state of Israel

Politically, the *mukhabarat* state exists mostly within the Arab world (although there are similar states elsewhere). Such a state is characterized as a mass mobilizing state, run by an all-pervasive bureaucracy and ruled by military and security apparatuses (Entelis 2005). The variants of this model range from robust to liberal autocracies, and the span is wide enough to include Israel.

What characterizes such states is the sustainability of their security establishment (the *mukhabarat*) in the face of internal challenges and external pressures. This sustainability is ensured by a strong connection to an outside power: 'the *mukhabarat* state cannot long endure, if it lacks the financial resources to pay its soldiers, purchase arms, upgrade equipment, maintain supplies, and acquire externally-gathered intelligence data' (Entelis 2005: 1). These are apt descriptions of the State of Israel, not found in the literature about the state of exception.

One of the experts on the subject, Nazih Ayubi, described such states as 'fierce', as distinguished from a 'strong' (democratic) state (Ayubi 1996). The relationship between the state and its citizens is not legal, but purely a function of fierce power relations (remember this is a typology of Israel's relations with the Palestinians, not with Jewish society). A fierce state resorts to the use of raw power as its default function – whereas in the state of exception the use of such power is a deviation from a set of non-violent default mechanisms of maintaining the state.

Readers versed in the critique of Israel are familiar with its depiction as 'an army with a state'. This is actually a common reference to the *mukhabarat* state of Algeria, about which it was written that 'every state has an army but in Algeria the army has a state', describing the deeply enmeshed linkage between the state and the security apparatuses (Bellin 2004: 144).

This is not dissimilar to the bold attempt by several critical Israeli sociologists to define Israel as a militarist society (Ben-Eliezer 1995; Erlich 1987; Karmi and Rosenfeld 1989). The role of the army or the security apparatuses in these studies appears not to be the outcome of anomie, as it would be in the state of exception, but part of the state's foundation and *raison d'état*. Critical sociology points to the oppression as stemming from a non-democratic founding ideology and a colonialist reality, not from any internal contradictions in the democratic system that can produce states of exception. The ideology and colonialist reality produced a state in which the army and the security services reign not in exceptional situations, but as a rule. While the militaristic model mobilizes Jewish society, as a typical *mukhabarat* state it oppresses the Palestinian population.

The role of the army and security service is not central to Agamben's analysis; he refers to it only marginally when he discusses martial law. When the military assumes power during times of war, it is a governmental policy rather than a drastic change in the constitution or sovereignty – which for Agamben are the main indicators of a state of exception. This is why he disagrees with Carl Schmitt when the latter referred to martial law as a constitutional issue. In Israel, martial law is the legal and political reality for almost all its Palestinians citizens at any given time, directly or indirectly.

The authoritarian, rentier militaristic state of the Arab world is a model that better corresponds, historically and theoretically, with the state within the State of Israel: the state of the Palestinians within the Jewish state. However, as argued by others before me (see, e.g., Ram 1993), it is a hybrid with another model, the settler-colonial state, which can be presented as a mixture of an Arab post-colonial model and a colonialist model such as Apartheid South Africa.

Conclusion and future trends

Agamben's paradigm of the state of exception does not directly include an intrinsic hegemonic role for the secret services or the army, one which is enshrined not by law but by historical circumstances and practice. And yet, I can fully understand why recent policies and discourses adopted in Israel, especially towards its Palestinian citizens, seem as though they come directly from Schmitt and Agamben. Indeed, one Palestinian scholar in Israel, Issam Abu Raya, wrote in response to Diskin's remarks: 'Diskin's statement fits beautifully with [Carl] Schmitt's arguments' about the sovereign having the final say under the law of a defending democracy (Abu Raya 2007). This was a line of reasoning that pushed Schmitt into the Nazi embrace. However, although – if one follows Diskin's words on several other occasions – one can see the similarities with Schmitt, Schmitt's analysis of Germany is of a deteriorating democracy that became a dictatorship and was then salvaged. This trajectory is inapplicable in Israel unless one accepts the liberal

Zionist claim that pre-1967 Israel was different. My argument is that the Israeli paradigm is a colonialist and post-colonialist mixture, a political outfit of a settler state ruling through a *mukhabarat* state.

Israel is neither in, nor a state of exception. Rather it is in, *and* a state of oppression, the kind that typifies both settler states and *mukhabarat* states. Therefore the navigation fatigue, the harsh response to new challenges and the overall political situation at the beginning of the twenty-first century are not indicators of an Agamben nightmare come true in the holy land. They rather indicate an escalating cycle which carries the potential to end the pretence and the false inclusion of Israel in the western democracy frame of analysis. This escalating cycle is made up of a series of legislative waves, all intended to continue the oppression of the Palestinian population under Israeli state rule.

The first wave was in 1948, leading to the rights to own land and water and to buy and sell land being denied to the Palestinians by law, as was the right for full citizenship. This was followed by discrimination in every aspect of life, while welfare, education and protection from abuse of the law were all practised systematically and efficiently but not legalized.

The second wave was legislation through the imposition of the Emergency Regulations on the occupied West Bank and Gaza Strip in 1967 that denied basic human and civil rights to the millions who lived there. It began with ethnically cleansing 300,000 Palestinians and then constructing the oppressive regime we are familiar with today. All this was achieved without undermining Israel's membership in the exclusive democratic club.

The third wave is the one that points to navigation fatigue. It concerns greater Jerusalem, defined as one-third of the West Bank, where potential Palestinian citizens of Israel have lived since it was officially annexed to Israel in 1967. A set of municipal regulations, town planning ordinances and other municipal legislation enabled the ethnic cleansing of the 200,000 Palestinians who live there – an operation that needed time and has not yet been completed at the time of writing (40% have already been transferred; see report on East Jerusalem at btselem.org).

And there is a fourth wave of legislation that began in 2001. A series of parliamentary initiatives led to new discriminatory laws, among them 'The Nation and Admittance to the Country Law' which disables any reunion of Palestinian couples living on either side of the Green Line and of families separated for whatever other reason. In practice it is a means of preventing the return to the homeland of any Palestinian who 'overstayed' abroad. Other laws institutionalized discrimination in the realms of welfare and education (including the secret service's right to determine the employment of school principals and teachers). And finally, there are the laws, already mentioned, equating opposition to the Jewishness of the state with treason.

According to the scenario described and analysed in this chapter, the short-term repercussions are catastrophic, as we can expect either escalating state violence against the Palestinians, wherever they are, or further oppressive legislation. However, in the long run, this may rob Israel of the moral and political shield with which the West has provided it. If Israel continues its oppressive regime, it may be South Africanized or Arabized and thus be judged by harsher criteria, much harsher than the current soft rebukes Israel receives as a democracy. This would be taken more seriously by the Israeli elite, both culturally and economically, as it may mean that Israel would be regarded as a pariah state, and it would bring an end to the dispossession and occupation. Moreover, de-democratizing Israel could give Palestinian resistance hope for change and lead it to abandon tactics rooted in despair and anger, born not just of a response to the actual oppression, but also of a reaction to the hypocritical dishonest brokery of the West in the conflict. If Israel is seen as a permanent state of oppression, the Palestinians may glimpse a light at the end of their tunnel of suffering and abuse.

Notes

1　Festival Cinema South, 2–7 June 2007, under the auspices of Sapir College.
2　The lectures are in «http://www.maager.openu.ac.il/opus»
3　A fine example is Fania Oz-Salzberger (2001).
4　See interview with *al-Jazeera,* 25 April 2007.

References

Abu Raya, I. (2007) 'The Shabak is the sovereign', *Machsom website* «http://www.machsom.com»

Agamben, G. (2005) *State of Exception,* Chicago University Press, Chicago

Ayubi, N. (1996) *Over-Stating the Arab State: Politics and Society in the Middle East,* IB Tauris, London and New York

Barzilai, G. (2002) 'The case of Azmi Bishara: Political immunity and freedom in Israel', *MERIP online*, January

Bellin, E. (2004) 'The robustness of authoritarianism in the Middle East: Exceptionalism in comparative perspective', *Comparative Politics*, Vol. 36, no. 2, 144–9

Ben-Eliezer, U. (1995) *The Emergence of Israeli Militarism; 1936–1956*, Dvir, Tel-Aviv

Entelis, J. P. (2005) 'The democratic imperative vs. authoritarian impulse: the Maghreb state between transition and terrorism', *Strategic Insights*, Vol. 4, no. 6, 1–15

Erlich, A. (1987) 'Israel, conflict, war and social change', in C. Creighton and M. Shaw (eds), *The Sociology of War and Peace*, Routledge, London

Karmi, S. and H. Rosenfeld (1989) 'The emergence of national militarism in Israel', *International Journal of Politics, Culture and Society*, no. 31, 5–49

Oz-Salzberger, F. (2001) *Israelis, Berlin*, Keter, Jerusalem

Pappe, I. (2006) *The Ethnic Cleansing of Palestine*, Oneworld Publications, London and New York

Ram, U. (1993) 'The colonization perspective in Israeli sociology: Internal and external comparisons', *Journal of Historical Sociology*, Vol. 6, no. 3

Rubinstein, A. and A. Yakobson (2006) *Israel et les Nations: L'état-nation juif et les droits de l'homme*, Presses universitaires de France, Paris

Sagiv, A. (2007) 'The state of exception and the state of freedom', *Techelet*, no. 27, 3–27

Shirtit, S. (1993) 'Emergency legislation in Israel in view of the foundational law', in Y. Zamir (ed.), *Law and Government*, Vol. 1, no. 2, 433–37

Smooha, S. (2000) 'The regime of the State of Israel: Civic democracy, non-democracy or ethnic democracy', *Sociologia Yisraelit*, Vol. 2, no. 2, 565–630

Tamir, Y. (1993) *Liberal Nationalism*, Princeton University Press, Princeton

Van den Berge, P. (1980) *South Africa: A Study in Conflict*, Greenwood Press, Westport, CT

Waltzer, M. (2003) 'History and national liberation', in A. Shapira and D. J. Pensler (eds) *Israeli Historical Revisionism: From Left to Right*, Frank Cass, London and Portland

Yiftachel, O. (2006) *Ethnocracy: Land and Identity Politics in Israel/Palestine*, University of Pennsylvania Press, Philadelphia

PART III
Palestine: Contested Representations

Nahla Abdo

9 Palestinian *Munadelat*: Between Western Representation and Lived Reality

Introduction

In the current context of globalization (read, uni-polar US imperialism) the 'Palestine issue' continues to receive the lion's share of debates. Whether the context of debate is related to 'democracy', 'Islam', 'terrorism', or even 'fundamentalism', Palestinians continue to be cast outside international legitimacy. Yet, as Edward Said has often reminded us, Palestine (and Palestinians) is a state of 'consciousness', a representation of 'a vast collective feeling of injustice [which] continues to hang over our lives with undiminished weight' (in Turner 2003: 139). It is this state of feeling and being which has been and continues to be the driving force behind Palestinian women's (and men's) struggle for life and survival.

Western discourses on Palestinians have gone beyond mainstream official discourses of demonizing and inferiorizing Arabs (and Palestinians), and cross over into the wider academic and feminist community. Of particular concern in this chapter are western feminist discourses on Palestinian women freedom fighters or *munadelat* – women who participate in the armed struggle against Israeli colonialism and military occupation. Western discourses, this chapter argues, continue to orientalize and racialize Palestinians by de-contextualizing and de-historicizing them, while simultaneously upholding their colonizers/occupiers as superior beings who maintain liberationist and democratizing values. This chapter explores and counters cultural imperialism as expressed in western feminist discourse on Palestinian women freedom fighters, using a feminist approach based on historicizing Palestinian women's activism in the anti-colonial resistance movement.

During the hype of 11 September 2001, which coincided with the Palestinian second Intifada, a plethora of writings about Palestinian women involved in armed struggle emerged, albeit with a convoluted bent. Stripped of any contextual or historical background, Palestinian women were depicted as inhuman 'suicide bombers' who resort to acts of violence for 'personal/cultural' reasons. These women were described by the late feminist author Andrea Dworkin as 'idealists who crave committing a pure act [which] will wipe away the stigma of being female... After all those women were sexually abused by their men and threatened to be killed by them.' Palestinian women's 'terrorism', Dworkin asserts, is 'a life-saving procedure used by women as a trade off between the lowly status of the raped woman for the higher status of a martyr' (Dworkin 2002: 21). Like Dworkin, Barbara Victor (2003), while praising Israel for its 'democracy', treatment of women, and superior values, vilifies Palestinian mothers and families for sending their children to death. 'Suicide bombing', 'Islamism' and 'Palestinians' have in fact become the western media's sexiest and hottest items in recent years. In this vein, Palestinian women have been cast as 'uneducated', 'powerless' 'controlled by their men' and 'willing to die and be rewarded in the after-life in Paradise'.[1] Nowhere in this feminist literature is there an attempt to understand the context of women's military resistance, let alone appreciate Palestinian women's long history of struggle, including military struggle.

Against this background, the main argument underpinning this chapter is that, short of a comprehensive understanding of Palestinian women's history and daily experiences, any discourse on women which focuses on 'cultural' attributes, such as Islam, the family, personal attributes or social norms is little more than an imperialist/colonialist tool reaffirming white western hegemony and moral grounds over Arab, Middle Eastern and Palestinian women (and men). This chapter, based on extensive interviews conducted with *munadelat* in 2006/2007 and other research conducted during 2004, addresses two major questions. Firstly, why do Palestinian women partake in the military struggle? And, secondly, what role does the colonial state (Israel) play in promoting Palestinian women's racialization? Finally, using Palestinian women's own voices, experiences and narratives, this chapter aims to contribute to de-orientalizing and de-racializing Palestinian *munadelat*.

Colonialism, occupation and resistance

The global context within which the Palestinian polity was formed is contextualized by Israel's unrelenting brutal policies of economic strangulation, political suffocation and the social destruction it has and continues to wreak on the Palestinians in the Occupied Palestinian Territories (OPT). Thus in addition to the Apartheid Wall and the hundreds of military checkpoints erected throughout the West Bank and the Gaza Strip, Israel has intensified its policies of closures, land confiscation, house demolitions and assassinations since the second Intifada, leading to widespread poverty, especially in the Gaza Strip.

A response to white western sexist and racist depictions of Palestinian women (and men) fighters takes many forms. One such form would be following authors such as Bryan Turner (2003) who contextualized Palestinian resistance by acknowledging the historical and contemporary injustices afflicting the Palestinian people, primarily as a result of the global neo-liberal capitalist economy and the consequences of a long process of injustice that befell the Palestinians, alongside the 'the failures of authoritarian nationalist governments, and the socio-economic divisions that have been exacerbated by neo-liberal globalization' (Turner 2003: 140).

Other scholars, such as Edward Said (2001), Mahmoud Mamdani (2002) and Eqbal Ahmad (2000), have situated the issue of military resistance and suicide bombing in a historical comparative context, pointing to other historical experiences of anti-colonial resistance. This includes the very history of the Zionist movement which used Jewish terrorist groups to kill innocent Palestinian women and men in the prelude to the establishment of the State of Israel. This chapter locates women's military involvement in the context of Arab resistance to western colonialism.

In 'Why We Have Become Suicide Bombers', Eyad Sarraj (2005) recounts the devastating effects of the Nakba, documenting the countless 'peaceful' 'negotiations', 'agreements', 'dialogues', 'treaties' and 'deals' the Palestinians have entered into and accepted, albeit, as he argues, 'to no avail':

> We simply became the slaves of our enemy. We are building their homes on our villages, and we clean their streets. Do you know what does this do to you when you have to be the slave of your enemy in order to survive? No, you will never understand how painful it is unless your country is occupied by another force. Only then will you learn

how to watch in silence pretending not to see the torture of your friends and the humiliation of your father [mother, brother and sister].

Do you know what it means for a child to see his father spat at and beaten before his eyes by an Israeli soldier? Nobody knows what happened to our children. We don't know ourselves except we observe that they lose respect for their fathers. So they, our children, the children of the stone as they became known, tried the Intifada, the Uprising. Seven long years our children were throwing stones and being killed daily. Nearly all our young men [and many of our young women] were arrested and the majority [were] tortured. All had to confess. The result was every one suspected that all people were spies. So, we were exhausted, tormented and brutalized. What else could we do to return to our home? We had almost forgotten that and all what we wanted was to be left alone (Sarraj 2005).

Sarraj's response echoes that of Frantz Fanon who almost half a century earlier described the Algerian anti-colonial resistance as follows:

The native's violence was not life denying, but life affirming... for he knows that he is not an animal; and it is precisely when he realizes his humanity that he begins to sharpen the weapons with which he will secure its victory... What distinguished native violence from the violence of the settler, its saving grace, was that it was the violence of yesterday's victims who have turned around and decided to cast aside their victimhood and become masters of their own lives... He, of whom they have never stopped saying that the only language he understands is that of force, decides to give utterance by force. Indeed, the argument the native chooses has been furnished by the settler, and by an ironic turning of the tables it is the native who now affirms that the colonialist understands nothing but force... (Fanon 1970: 15–16).

Distinguishing between 'terrorist' and freedom fighter, 'fidai', a concept also used by Palestinian women and men martyrs, Fanon added:

The 'terrorist', from the moment he undertakes an assignment, allows death to enter into his soul. He has a rendezvous with death. The 'fidai', on the other hand, has a rendezvous with the life of the Revolution, and with his own life. The 'fidai' is not one of the sacrificed. To be sure, he does not shrink before the possibility of losing his life or the independence of his country, but at no moment does he choose death (Fanon 1970: 43).

Fanon has gone one step beyond Sarraj, acknowledging the role of

Algerian women fighters in the anti-colonial struggle, and suggesting that the colonial battle in Algiers was primarily fought on the bodies of Algerian women. The case of Palestine is not much different. All women interviewed for this project, as we see below, exhibit characteristics that are totally alien to how the West imagines them, explaining their involvement in the military struggle against Israel in ways that western white feminists cannot begin to fathom.

To begin to unpack western images of Palestinian *munadelat*, I begin with a question.

Why do Palestinian women partake in the military struggle?

The one single event mentioned by all the women as a primary reason for their political and military activism was the Nakba (catastrophe), the first Palestinian ethnic cleansing of 1948-9 and its consequences of forced exile and trauma. Of course each woman had a personal/ intimate experience of loss, torture and humiliation, and experienced forced exile and refugeehood differently. For example, Aida was forced in 1948 to leave the Jaffa area and became a refugee in Gaza, and also witnessed the killing of both her sisters by Israeli shelling during the 1956 Suez War. Itaf, from Lidd (1948 Palestine), who also became a refugee, witnessed, in her own words: 'the cruelty of the Israeli enemy in 1956 and 1967. I heard about the massacres in Deir Yassin and the one in a mosque in Lidd. This mosque served as a refuge to many Palestinians who hid in it, thinking they would be safe in this holy place, but to no avail. All the people who were in it were massacred...' Still, a common experience to all the women interviewed was the one which was eloquently articulated by Aisha:

> To wake up one day and find out you are under military occupation; robbed of your land, home and identity; your basic human rights have been taken away from you; you were turned into a refugee; suddenly living under occupation, while at the same time the whole world, including the Arab world, is watching with a deafening silence, unable to do anything about it....

Or in the words of Aida: '... deprived of your land, home and identity, turned into a refugee in your own country, forced to survive on rations, under the mercy and charities of UNRWA.'

In addition to the experiences of the Nakba, 'exile and refugee-ism' both inside and outside your own country in the twenty-first century, especially since the second Intifada, a number of other forms of colonial humiliation and torture have been added to the women's lexicon of military subjugation. These include women's experiences of the Apartheid Wall and the Israeli military checkpoints designed to further isolate Palestinians and restrict their basic rights of movement even further, as the following two examples illustrate.

Nesreen from Abu Dis relayed the following about her sister's experience at one military checkpoint:

> You know, the worst... is during labour as the woman cannot climb hills or jump over fences. The other day when my sister felt she was due to give birth and began to experience labour pain, my mother and I took her to the hospital. As the line up was huge and we were not allowed to cross [the military checkpoint], my sister who was in a lot of pain decided to climb a brick wall which was very narrow... only 15 centimetres wide – you could hardly put one foot on it. Her labour pain was intensified while walking on the fence [wall], neither she nor we could hold ourselves... we were almost sure she was going to lose her balance, fall down and die along with her unborn baby.

Samia from al-Azariyyah explained the humiliation women go through while crossing the checkpoints:

> Once I got very sick with a terrible headache and unable to walk... On my way to al-Maqased hospital I was stopped at the checkpoint and the soldier started shouting at me using coarse language and laughing at me. When I told him I was too sick, he responded 'come, I will check you', and added, 'all of you say you are sick and need to go to the doctor![2]

While my own experience at the Qalandya checkpoint pales by comparison with that of most other women, it undoubtedly confirmed, at least to me, how Palestinian women feel under such circumstances.

Unlike the western image of the Palestinian *munadelat*, except for Aida who was financially unable to complete high school, all the women interviewed completed post-secondary education and had left their villages and lived on their own, whether in Beirut attending university or in Ramallah which hosted the only Women's Teachers College in the OPT. Without exception, all the women interviewed were secular and defined their political affiliation as left. None was religious and most belonged to Marxist Leninist wings of the PLO. Equally important, all the women interviewed described their relationship with their families as very good, and some went to great lengths to describe the mutual respect between them and male members of their families and communities.

While the role played by sex, sexuality, 'family' and the perceived 'traditional culture' in the discussion of Palestinian *munadelat* is important, it does not equate with western perceptions of the role of culture, religion, family, male oppression and women 'dishonouring their families' in the lives of Palestinian women.[3] Discourses about women's bodies, sexuality, family, honour, or virginity during this period of the struggle must be located in Israel's colonial policies, especially as expressed in its prison policies, as I demonstrate below.

In the context of the colonial state, sexual abuse, harassment and torture are often used as direct tools for enforcing women's submission, compliance and obedience. These means are enforced in order to quell women's participation in the resistance movement. It is no surprise, therefore, that indecent language, which often makes reference to women's sexual organs, is heavily used in the encounters between colonial/state agents (soldiers, police or prison guards) and Palestinian women. Under military occupation where the occupying state and its institutions are heavily militarized, violence against the subject/occupied female sexuality becomes a major tool for releasing the military's hatred and contempt for the colonized.

This direct relationship between the subject woman and the occupying state is best exemplified in prison, during the detention of political prisoners. Prisons and detention camps represent a primary site for state control. The rest of this chapter deals with encounters between Palestinian female prisoners and the Israeli state. More specifically I argue that, in addition to the physical, psychological and sexual abuse and torture Palestinian female (and male) prisoners endure, the focus on the body and sexuality is more prominent in the case of female political prisoners.

Sex and family as colonial tools of control

The targeting of the Palestinian home, house and family has been and continues to be used as Israel's systematic policy for controlling the Palestinians. House demolitions are only one example of this policy. Founded on its perception of the importance (read, demographic danger) of the Palestinian family and home and the special value it places on the 'purity' (read, virginity) of its female members, Israel has always tried to meddle with this institution. Depending on the historical moment and the political gains the state seeks to achieve, it either targets female members to threaten the family, or, in what seems contradictory, it cements 'family unity' by controlling the 'head of the family'. The first instance became clear through the publication of works by Israeli revisionist historians, most notably Ilan Pappe (2006). These studies have confirmed Israel's belief that it was able to expel the majority of the Palestinians by sheer force, including killing and raping women or threatening to do so. Similar methods have been and continue to be used by Israel against female political prisoners. On the other hand, and in an attempt to solidify its control over the remaining Palestinian population, the state has created the position of the *mukhtar* (head of *hamula* or *ashira*) in a move to generate alliances and mediators between the state and ordinary Palestinians (Nakhleh 1977; Zeidani 1995). Of particular concern here is the first policy, namely the colonial state's targeting of women's bodies and sexuality as a mode of political control over the Palestinian family and society.

The complex relationship between Palestinian social values, family unity, women's image and position on the one hand, and Israeli state policies on the other is best highlighted through the narratives of Palestinian women political prisoners. It is worth noting that in almost all the interviews conducted, the state has tried to present the female subject in discord with her family, using various methods of torture, fear and threat in an attempt to force the women to submit. To illustrate, the stories of two Palestinian women ex-political prisoners, Aisha and Halima, will be presented.

Our first *munadelat* (freedom fighter) is Aisha, who received multiple life sentences but was released after about ten years of prison through an exchange deal between Israel and the PLO. Aisha is a highly educated and intelligent woman who came from a loving family. She was a maths and science teacher when she decided to become a *munadelat* and take up arms against the Israeli occupation in 1969. From a young age she learnt the rules of society vis-à-vis its female members. She had a strong personality and was able to convince her mother to allow her to leave the village and go to Ramallah for her secondary education. This happened despite the fact that her mother, as she stated, 'was under a lot of pressure from our neighbours and other women from the village, who used to tell her: "Ya Khaibah, you failed to raise your daughter...

your daughter lives alone without any man looking after her" '.
Reflecting further on this issue, Aisha added, 'my mother used to tell
herself "why should I, the widow, send my daughter to school while
the village mukhtar who was much richer and more powerful did not
do this to his daughter".'

Aisha's appreciation of social values allowed her to pursue further
education and gave her more space for social mobilization. This is how
Aisha put it:

> At an early age I understood the traditional deal for the women in my
> society: do very well at school and avoid relationships with men. I also
> learnt that people respect those involved in the national struggle and that
> served me well... my high grades and national political activities enabled
> me to gain a lot of respect and I became the village example to emulate.

This is the personality with which Aisha confronted her Israeli prison
interrogators every single day for forty-five days until she was sentenced
to multiple life imprisonment.[4] This was the personality Israeli prison
guards sought to destroy in order to control her, as with any other
woman, to reach the wider political resistance movement. A couple of
weeks after her detention, the Israeli authorities demolished Aisha's
family home – collective punishment has been extensively used by
Israel against all Palestinian political prisoners – and used all forms of
physical and psychological torture on her including *'shabeh',* which is
often used on males.[5] Sexual harassment and torture appear to have
been more pronounced for Aisha, who was called *'sharmouta'* and
'qahbah' (whore) dozens of times. In one interrogation session, to which
she refers as *'jura'at ta'adhib'* (a taste of torture), she recounts:

> He slapped me on the face. I screamed and asked: why are you doing
> this? He said 'because you are *sharmouta.*' 'I am not,' I replied. 'What are
> you then? Tell us how many men did you fuck?' Unable to use the same
> language, I responded, 'I did not sleep with any man and this is none of
> your business.'

She narrates that, during another interrogation session,

> He grabbed his whip and whipped me on the legs, then on my shoulders
> and back and said: 'You *sharmouta* want to be stronger than men... we
> shall see if you can take this.' He continued to whip me all over my
> body while uttering every dirty word in and out of the language dictio-
> nary: 'How many men did you sleep with, *sharmouta*?' 'None', I
> answered. 'Do you want to tell me you have not been fucked at all?' He

then handed me to another one saying: 'This *qahba* does not want to talk.'

Again:

> They dragged me to a room where there was one man pacing the room. He leaned on the table, put one hand there and the other on his waist and started to check me out from head to toe, he then ordered me to sit down. He came closer to me and leaned his back on the table and said: 'You are *sharmouta* and you know it.' I answered 'I am not *sharmouta*'. He said back: 'The difference between the ordinary *sharmouta* and yourself is that you are *sharmouta* with brain, but the other who sells her body has more honour than you. I want you to say: "I am *sharmouta*" ten times.' 'I will not say,' I said. 'I order you and you have to obey.' 'You cannot force me'. 'I will show you how you have the brain of *sharmouta*!' He sat on the table, surrounded me with both of his legs, pulled my hair back and started slapping me on the face… He would only stop to remind me of what he wants me to say. After a while he stepped down, approached me and repeated: 'How many men did you sleep with?' I answered 'None!' He said: 'You want to convince me you are still a virgin?' His eyes became red and the fire which appeared in his eyes scared the hell out of me… I was sure he was going to rape me…
>
> I was then dragged to a room where in the middle of it there stood a short man with thick black moustache and a big belly. Moments later a tall blond female guard with army uniform joined in. The man whom I called '*Uzraeel*' (Satan, because he killed comrade Ya'aqoub and is here to kill me) looked at me and said: 'Take off your clothes!'
>
> I shrank, crossed my arms and put them on my chest to protect my body, the same moment he ordered other men who came to the room to undress me. I resisted with all my force but was unable to prevent them. He pulled my arms behind my back and cuffed them with a sharp chain and pushed me on the floor naked…. Then '*Uzraeel*' came closer to me, pushed his two knees against my belly. Then, using a stick, he pushed my legs apart and put them under his knees. The woman put her foot on my head so I wouldn't move… he started pressing on my chest with his huge disgusting hands, then he began to push the stick into my vagina. I resisted so hard as never ever before… that moment I felt stronger than ever before… Minutes later and after pouring a lot of cold water on my body, one held me from one arm and the other from one leg and started to wipe the floor with my body… then they dragged my body outside the room, parading me in front of a row of young men who were lined up against the wall. After a couple of rounds in the corridor, they brought me back to the room, threw me on the floor and left.

Aisha, who understood 'the deal' of her traditional society, was not only aware of the social pressure placed on a woman who loses her virginity outside of marriage, but also recognized how Israel uses sexuality to quell women's participation in national resistance. After one episode of interrogation/torture she recounted the following:

> Back in my cell I started thinking: was it worth the torture of last night? So what if I said what he ordered me to say? Saying 'I am *sharmouta*' does not turn me into one! I think I was unable to think straight, after all, sex issues are not treated as individual matters in my society, especially the issue of virginity… the latter is society's concern… the woman must be virgin until married…. This is the shame which is washable only with her blood – by killing her – and this is a major constraint placed on women's movement and development in my society. I learned my lesson at a very young age and realized that to gain my social and political freedom I have to sacrifice my individual freedom…. Being a virgin is a major factor when you confront the Israeli enemy in prison, for they always play on this issue… spreading rumours about non-married *munadelat* surrounding their sexuality (e.g., she has a boyfriend or was sexually involved) is a major method used by prison authorities to quell women's participation in national resistance.

When social, psychological, physical and even sexual torture fail to satisfy the prison establishment, it resorts to using family members to bring more pressure on the detainees. To Aisha, this was very painful:

> One very painful moment during my interrogation was when one came with a whip and said: 'You do love your mother and sister-in-law, don't you?' Suddenly he raised his voice very high and asked men from the next room to come and said: 'Go bring her mother and sister-in-law and hang them from their breasts so she could hear their screams!' He spoke and left the room and I felt a thunder gripping me, thinking what if this does happen!

Bringing family members into prison and using them as a threat to force confessions out of female prisoners is a well-known practice in Israeli prisons. In fact, Aisha's cousin was picked up on his arrival from Beirut, where he was a student, and brought to prison and tortured in front of her. It is important to understand that almost all *munadelat* who become political prisoners were/are well aware of the possibility of sexual abuse and family pressure by the Israeli prison authorities. The work of Israeli and Palestinian lawyers, like Felicia Langer and Walid Fahoum (1980), is replete with such incidents.

Israel's racist/orientalist nature is evident in the prison establishment through the 'nice cop'/'bad cop' routine performed by Israeli interrogators. Almost all *munadelat* interviewed raised this issue. The 'nice cop/interrogator' is often a soft-spoken blond Ashkenazi (European) Jew who presents himself as someone who is there to 'help' you, while the 'bad cop/interrogator' is depicted as a short, fat, ugly and scary-faced Mizrahi or Arab Jew, who speaks Arabic and has an Arab name. Like Aisha, Halima was also raised in a loving home:

I was the youngest, I was very spoiled... people used to tell my father to marry another woman for boys but he refused saying: 'for me the girl is worth a million boys'. I had a very special relationship with my father who was uneducated but on the left. My father was imprisoned under the British and his cousins were killed in 1948... Although my father was not an activist, he had an activist and revolutionary spirit...

Halima was highly educated, practising law at the time of her arrest. Similar to Aisha, Halima was also respected by her family and society and would not hide her activism – albeit not that relating to the organization – from her mother: 'What my mother knew well is that I was a great admirer of Laila Khaled and [PFLP Leader] George Habash and always welcomed male and female comrades to our house... We used my room as the space for discussion and organizational matters.'

The strong character and personality of most of the *munadelat* were targeted by the prison guards and interrogators. Describing one episode of interrogation, Halima recounted: 'He started his first question with a well-known Arab idiom: "One thousand eyes can cry but not my mother's... you have gone out with [dated] all of these men who have wives, yet none of them married you!" I answered: "What does this or that have to do with me..."' Halima understood what her interrogator meant without his being explicit; she knew he was threatening to tell her mother about what he alleged were her illicit sexual relations with different men in the organization she worked with. On the very first day of her arrest Halima experienced her first taste of sexual and physical humiliation:

At my arrival to al-Mascoubiyyah prison, a female soldier ordered me to take off all my clothes including my underwear and bra. She kept me naked for a whole hour, then ordered me to put on my clothes and took me to the interrogation room... Then along with a male interrogator, they ordered me to carry a chair and go with them. I refused to carry the chair, he carried it by himself and I followed them… we walked through a deep path which seemed to me like a death road… on our way I saw '*Mashbooheen* on the chair' [men with hands and feet tied to the back of a chair] and heads covered with long sacks… then a prison guard took me to a small corner surrounded with prison cells, tied both feet with hooks placed on the wall and raised my hand 'like this' (imitating the act)…[at this point Halima was very emotional], then they covered my head with a very long khaki sack full with the stench of urine and defecation.

In addition to personal humiliation, a common form of sexual torture experienced by most of the women involved forcing them to witness or listen to Israeli Jewish female prisoners performing sexual acts:

During my interrogation in al-Mascoubiyyah prison, I wished many times to face all the deprivation of being in isolated cells with no air, light or sun, than to be in the rooms reserved for us under interrogation. To these rooms they would bring us female drug addicts, others performing same-sex porno… all naked, and they would perform sexual intercourse in front of us… these women would also tell us that our turn will come. We were very scared… the five of us would hold each other and climb to the bunk bed for protection. One of them [the Jewish prisoners] would spend most of the night screaming at an imaginary prison police urging him to come and fuck her, using dirty swear words. Both Itaf and I were terrified of these women.

Like Aisha, Halima was also tortured by a Mizrahi/Arab Jew, named Shawqi. She described the man as 'terrifying', commenting, 'I would call him Farid Shawqi because he was huge,' adding:

Once they brought me to the interrogation room and left me alone with a tall and wide interrogator named Shawqi … At that time I had my period for the second time, I was never able to find sanitary pads or change my underwear. I smelled awful and my clothes were full of blood… whenever I asked for sanitary pads or undergarment change they would respond: 'If you talk we give you.' Shawqi came close to the chair I was sitting on, placed one of his feet between my legs and the second around my leg and told me: 'So Halima, is it only George Habash who is allowed to fuck you… I also want to fuck you now!' I was wearing pants and a shirt … I opened the two upper buttons of my shirt and told him … 'Here do whatever you wish…'

Halima explained that she was fully confident that she would deter him by showing him that she understood his intentions: 'I knew they exploit Palestinian traditional social values and especially the issue of sex... I felt like telling him that this kind of cheap pressure does not scare me... I know your aims – but I did not. Then he told me, "go fuck off, you smell terrible"; he pushed me with his foot and repeated: "you stink and you guys disgust me... you are used to move from one man to the next in the PFLP [Popular Front for the Liberation of Palestine]".'

Detailing the above experiences of Palestinian women *munadelat* serves to highlight the reality that, while under occupation women share with their male counterparts the daily endurance of poverty, harassment and humiliation, their gender and sexuality make their experiences quite different. However, I also want to emphasize that Palestinian women are not just victims and silent recipients of their subjugation, but rather have agency, acting and reacting against their oppression.

Conclusion

This chapter has argued that a proper understanding of Palestinian women's involvement in the anti-colonial armed struggle requires an adequate appreciation of their history and lived experiences. Without presenting examples of women's actual lived experiences, the western orientalist 'feminist' representation of Palestinian women fighters is an imaginary construction, ideologically and politically oriented in the service of the US and Israeli imperial colonial hegemonic projects.

The history of Palestinian women's participation in the armed struggle against Israeli colonialism and military occupation is replete with examples of strong, opinionated and committed women who, through understanding their/our own society and its traditional/patri-archal limits, are nonetheless able to challenge these through their political involvement.

The western emphasis on reactionary Palestinian social norms, par-ticularly around women's bodies and sexuality, which in abstract terms might have been raised as a legitimate issue, in the particular context of Palestinian anti-colonial resistance is misplaced. Palestinian women's bodies and sexuality, not unlike other cases such as in Algeria during the anti-colonial struggle, are best understood as tools used by the colonizer/occupier to quell the occupied/colonized resistance.

Notes

1 For more on the western discourse, see Reuter 2006. See interview with Pierre Rehov, a French documentary film-maker, on 'the psychology behind suicide bombings' in «http://counterterror.typepad.com/the_counterterrorism_blog/2005/07/interview_with_.html».

2 For more on this, see Shalhoub-Kevorkian and Abdo (2006).

3 One day in May 2004, Salwa (deputy minister for women's affairs) and I decided to join a large peaceful demonstration against the Wall and the military checkpoints. After crossing Qalandyia checkpoint, we suddenly found ourselves in what seemed to be a war zone with gun-fire, sound bombs and gas bombs filling the air. Instantly, women, young and old, along with men and children, started running in every direction. As we were unable go back to Ramallah, Salwa and I decided to go to Jerusalem. As we turned back to go to Jerusalem a 'flying' checkpoint was immediately erected in front of our eyes. Using my foreign passport as a shield, I started arguing with the soldiers, demanding they allow us to pass.

In the meantime, a young pregnant woman with her husband showed up and started to ask, then beg, the soldier to let them cross to the hospital. The encounter between the young man (husband) and the soldier was quite surreal: 'She is pregnant and in her ninth month,' the husband said in Hebrew. 'Do you have a proof that she is pregnant? What if she is carrying something else in her body?' answered the soldier. Humiliated and helpless, the husband responded: 'You can check her and find out for yourself.' 'This is not my job... I need the proof', the soldier retorted. Apparently the husband was prepared for such an event. He immediately pulled out a medical document from a plastic bag he was carrying, showing what was believed to be the expected due date for his wife's delivery. By the time the soldier finished his questioning and decided to let them pass, the woman had almost collapsed with tears all over her face and in incredible labour pain. Partly stunned and partly humiliated, I decided to leave the soldiers and look for Salwa. It was equally painful, if not surreal to find Salwa, who otherwise commands strength and control, standing far away from the soldiers, helpless, silent and even fearful... humiliation beyond imagination!

4 I would like to note that my assertion here is true for the overwhelming majority of Palestinian fighters who joined the struggle with high political commitment and a sense of national responsibility.

5 *Shabeh* is an infamous mode of physical and mental torture where the political prisoner is often forced to stand facing a wall with tied feet and hands held up against the wall. The ordeal can last for many hours and even overnight. There are other forms of *shabeh* with hands behind the back and feet tied to the chair.

References

Ahmad, E. (2000) *Confronting Empire: Interviews with David Barsamian*, South End Press, Cambridge, MA.

Dworkin, A. (2002) 'The women suicide bombers', *Feminista* Vol. 5, no. 1, 19–28

Fahoum, W. (1980) *Toyour Nve-Tertza (The Birds of Nve-Tertza Prison)*, Al-Hakim, Nazareth

Fanon, F. (1970) *A Dying Colonialism*, Penguin Books, Harmondsworth

Langer, F. (1975) *With My Own Eyes: Israel and the Occupied Territories, 1967–1973*, Ithaca Press, London

Mamdani, M. (2002) 'Good Muslim, bad Muslim: A political perspective on culture and terrorism', *American Anthropologist*, Vol. 104, no. 3, 766–75

Nakhleh, K. (1977) 'Anthropological and sociological studies of the Arabs in Israel: A critique', *Journal of Palestine Studies*, Vol. 6, no. 4, 38–53

Pappe, I. (2006) *The Ethnic Cleansing of Palestine*, One World Publishing, Oxford

Reuter, C. (2006) *My Life is a Weapon: A Modern History of Suicide Bombing*, Princeton University Press, Princeton

Said, E. (2001) 'Afterwords', in E. L. Rogan and A. Shlaim (eds) *The War for Palestine: Re-Writing the History of 1948*, Cambridge University Press, Cambridge, MA

Sarraj, E. (2005) 'Why we have become suicide bombers', «http://www.mission islam.com/conissues/palestine.html»

Shalhoub-Kevorkian, N. and N. Abdo (2006) *Palestinian Women's Ordeals in East Jerusalem*, Women's Studies Centre, Ramallah

Turner, B. S. (2003) 'Review article: Class, generation and Islamism – towards a global sociology of political Islam', *British Journal of Sociology*, Vol. 54, no. 1, 139–47

Victor, B. (2003) *Army of Roses: Inside the World of Palestinian Women Suicide Bombers*, Barnes and Noble, New York

Zeidani, S. (1995) 'Al-hizbel siyasi, wal-mujtama's al-madani, wal-nizam al-dimocrati' ('The political party, civil society and democracy'), in *Azmat al-Hizb al-Siyasi (The Crisis of the Palestinian Political Party)*, Muwatin, Ramallah

David Landy

10 Authenticity and Political Agency on Study Trips to Palestine[1]

'Our presence there will bring hope to those who feel so forgotten and misunderstood by the outside world, and we will return enlightened and inspired' (Israeli Committee against House Demolitions brochure, 2006).

Israeli Ministry of Tourism sign at the Separation Wall, Bethlehem

Political tourism to Palestine – of which study trips are an important part – are key in shaping western solidarity activists' understanding of Palestine and Israel, constructing their identity and informing their activism. The significance of these trips lies in their promise to offer relatively unmediated and experiential knowledge to participants so they can fulfil the role of political activists upon returning home. The customary representation by participants is of having been vaguely interested in 'the situation' beforehand and committed to 'the cause' after the trip.[2]

This chapter examines the representations made by study tours and what effect these may have on the participants' understanding and future activism. Though these tours may be a useful way of creating activists in the Palestinian solidarity movements of Europe and America, I explore the possibility that in creating out of the self a subject fit for activism, and out of Palestine an object worthy of this activism, these tours position western activists as dialectically superior partners in this activism, thereby silencing Palestinian subjectivity.

After describing these study trips, I examine how both tourist and activist discourses veil Palestine with an authenticity that constricts the manner in which it is represented. Nevertheless these tours are an effective way to forward a Palestinian point of view. I examine how this occurs and look further into the political construction of Palestine made by these tours, focusing on how the discourse of developmentalism invests tourists, and often well-meaning Israelis rather than Palestinians, with political agency.

As an academic studying the Palestinian solidarity movement and an activist centrally involved in the practices of this movement in Ireland, I situate this work in the field of critical activism research, believing that a theory/practice dialogue between academics and activists enables reflection by participants.[3] This critique should not be seen as aloof academic criticism of the shortcomings of a movement, but hopefully as a site for productive tension and discussion – research which is detached, yet involved (Elias 1987).

Veiling Palestine with authenticity

Political tourism and other forms of volunteer tourism can be classed as forming a continuum with more conventional alternative tourism such as cultural and education tourism in that the object-related authenticity of this experience is crucial to its success (Wearing 2001). In this, it can be contrasted with mass tourism where the bodily experience of the tourist is foregrounded (Wang 1999).

Political tourism to Palestine can be further divided into activist tourism and study tourism, though there is considerable overlap. Both are organized by Palestinian solidarity or Israel-critical groups in western countries in association with Palestinian alternative tourism operators and/or Israeli peace groups. The average duration of study tours is between a week and two weeks, that of activist tours – where practical activism such as picking olives or monitoring checkpoints is the main purpose of the trip – is three weeks (Dudouet 2006). Both are intense experiences combining an exhausting schedule of meeting Palestinian and left-wing Israeli groups with tours of specific sites. These sites are seen as a means of framing and explaining the conflict from a pro-Palestinian, if not Palestinian point of view.

The ten-day study tour I participated in provides a good example of these tours. It was organized by an Israeli peace group – the Israeli Committee Against House Demolitions (ICAHD) and based in Bethlehem and East Jerusalem. From there our sixteen-strong group from Britain and North America toured Israel/Palestine, our itinerary including walking tours of Jerusalem, Bethlehem and Hebron, trips to Palestinian Bedouin groups in the Negev, to Palestinian representatives in Ramallah, and to Israeli peace groups in Tel Aviv and Jerusalem. In addition there was one day off in the middle of the trip. Of the twenty groups we visited, about half were Israeli peace groups and half were Palestinian institutions, charities and civil society organizations. While this itinerary is representative of Israeli-organized tours, those organized by Palestinian groups focus less on these tiny Israeli groups and are almost exclusively based in the West Bank.

While demanding and occasionally harrowing, the trip was also very fulfilling for participants. During the trip a strong sense of group solidarity developed, with group members taking their role as conveyors of information extremely seriously; there were no attempts to skive off meetings, on the contrary much of the group's free time was devoted to discussing the issues raised and there have been serious efforts to convey this information on returning home.

The experience received on these tours – especially its visceral emotional impact – goes beyond merely providing a back-up story to one's pre-existing perception of the situation. These trips can be viewed as a means of establishing participants as actors who receive the ability to interpret what Israel/Palestine means for them and their social network and the authority to act on this information. Such authority is based on the perceived genuineness of what is experienced and so the prism of authenticity through which Israel/Palestine is seen – which one might expect from the tourist discourses of the trip – is reinforced by its activist dynamic.

Authenticity can be seen first as a means of drawing a boundary between tourists and locals. From its inception as a means which Rousseau used to describe the human condition, authenticity has been held to be a feature of primitive society, a mirror with which to critique modern inauthentic society. Especially in tourism, a temporal watershed is established and the authentic is assigned to one side of the divide – where the present and the tourist are seen as representing the inauthentic, or at least fleeing from it (Taylor 2001).

This has led tourists to classify the authenticity of destination cultures in terms of the degree to which they have not been 'spoilt' by contact with tourists. For instance, on our trip to the Negev some participants expressed horror about how the presence of a McDonalds was spoiling the desert, as well as more conventional disapproval of Israeli destruction of Bedouin life. This was part of a general counterpoising of the Bedouin way of life with our inauthentic modern 'civilization'.

At its extreme, the discourse of making natives repositories of authenticity may strip them of the rights of citizenship. For instance, in New Zealand tourist brochures, Maori are portrayed as part of the magical natural world laid out for discovery by tourists (Taylor 2001: 11). This portrays certain racialized locals as 'bare life', opposed to the sphere of modernity, somehow outside human laws and the rights of citizenship (Agamben 1998). Tourism theory has long suggested that the tourist experience militates against it being a site for solidarity, as what is seen, especially in alternative tourism, is mediated by 'the romantic tourist gaze' (Urry 1991) – an anthropological endeavour seeking to establish discursive mastery over the destination country.

The other problem with the patina of authenticity is that what is sought in Palestine is, to a large extent, what one already knows. The invocation of authenticity-in-others requires a denial of that complexity which may confuse the extent to which they are not actually the perfect others of modernity. This leads to a process of stereotyping which, in Palestine, appears to draw upon pre-existent orientalist framing.

Orientalist discourses of remaking and interpreting the East were evident on my trip, especially the use of women's rights dialectically to construct a picture of Palestinian society as 'primitive', and the tendency to present Palestinians as 'native informants' rather than experts. Such tendencies draw upon western feminism's 'discursive colonization' of Third World women whereby, 'universal sisterhood, defined as the transcendence of the male world... ends up being a middle-class, psychologized notion which effectively erases material and ideological power differences within and among groups of women, especially between First and Third World' (Mohanty 1992: 83–4). Feminism, thus articulated, allows western visitors to legitimize their otherwise troubling positionality and constitute themselves as dialectically superior actors vis-à-vis the Palestinians.

An illustration of this is the treatment our tour accorded a Palestinian director of a women's centre. In her talk, she drew on her personal experiences to present the difficulties that women face owing to the occupation, which she expanded into a more general political critique. However, in the question-and-answer session that followed, these political issues were mostly ignored in favour of asking her for more personal stories. While some of these questions, which the speaker invited, were justified, the almost exclusive concentration on her private life and suffering was noteworthy. This recalls bell hooks's criticism of how the experiences of blacks are mined and their suffering highlighted in order to provide middle-class whites with the raw material for their theoretical constructions (hooks 1989).

Politics intervened only when the director was asked several times about the dangers of Shari'a law. Some participants disagreed with her reply that this really wasn't an issue in Palestine. Their instancing of having seen women being oppressed in other (Muslim) countries was both a way of claiming for themselves expertise she did not possess and a disturbing flattening of a homogenous Islamic world. It is ironic that in representing themselves as defenders of women, tour participants appeared to silence Palestinian women, both by demanding that these women subscribe to specific strands of western feminism and by the fact that the speaker was chiefly given authority to talk about women's problems rather than wider political affairs.

This stark declaration needs to be qualified: Palestinians aren't simply accorded native informant status by these tours. It is more that they were asked about specific political issues such as the Wall or the Occupation, while participants were not interested in hearing Palestinians present any overarching political narrative (see also Davie 2004). Furthermore, the process whereby Palestinians were accorded local interpretative control while tour participants retained general control is perhaps stronger in Israeli-run tours than in Palestinian ones, since the heavy concentration on Israeli organizations encouraged the tendency to think of Palestinians as storytellers and Israelis as those to whom the stories needed to be directed.

That said, why are these tours, despite their caveats, still used by Palestinian groups as a means of forwarding their points of view?

Tourism as a site of resistance

> I would allow a Palestinian to fly a fighter plane before I would license a Palestinian tour guide (Moshe Dayan, attributed)

> Only by living what Palestinians experience all the time can a visitor come to recognize the injustices that are their daily bread. With this understanding comes a desire to try to help end the accumulated injustices in Palestine (Kassis 2004).

Any examination of the role of Israel-critical study tourism must recognize its counter-hegemonic nature. The Israeli tourist industry has long been treated as an arm of Zionism (Cohen-Hattab 2004) and contributes to Israel's attempts to efface the existence of the Palestinians. Conventional tours visit the West Bank merely to see Christian or Jewish holy sites and then get out, or increasingly ignore it entirely (Trainor 2006). Palestinians are often referred to on these standard tours as well as on explicitly Zionist pilgrimages in a derogatory fashion (Bowman 1992; Shabi 2006).

In the fight against such dominant narratives that render Palestinians invisible or represent them as terrorists, the concept of tourism as solidarity becomes legitimate. The attack on all aspects of Palestinian life by Israel makes this representation believable, as does the interweaving of political and tourist symbols in Palestinians sites. Tourism in the West Bank may reify Palestinian culture, but at least it accords it value and acknowledges Palestinian existence. In addition, tourism is seen as a means of resisting the Israeli onslaught on the Palestinian economy (Trainor 2006).

Nevertheless, Palestinian groups are not content with simply encouraging traditional pilgrimage tours, dismissed by one interviewee from the Alternative Tourism Group (ATG), as 'visiting stones and ignoring Palestinians'. In seeking to undermine such classic tourism essentializations and encourage solidarity activism, Palestinian groups promote personal contacts with Palestinians. ATG tours, sold to tourists as a means of experiencing authenticity, involve participants living and eating with Palestinians. Such staged back areas provide an income for Palestinians and present visitors and Palestinians with an important opportunity for one-to-one contact which may transcend any pre-arranged discursive structures.

Likewise, Christians are invited to pray with the local community in an effort to create a common link (Bernath 1999). This may be done to counteract the sense of identification which it is feared many western visitors have with Israeli society. One Palestinian interviewee contrasted images of Israelis in nightclubs with Palestinians in markets, with sheep and goats around them, remarking ruefully, 'Whether we like it or not, in your head you associate differently with Israelis than you do with Palestinians.'

Such an easy association with Israelis compared to Palestinians was a feature of the trip I was on. While encounters with Israeli organizations were characterized by informality, back-channel communication and individual contacts, meetings with Palestinian organizations were largely formal and polite. Interestingly, participants sought to challenge this lack of personal contacts. On the 'free day' on the trip almost all went to Palestinian areas, articulating their motivation as a desire to establish personal contacts or maintain previous contacts with Palestinians, a feature they felt was lacking on the trip.

Despite such efforts, study tours chiefly operate within the restricted parameters of the group tourist experience, providing Palestinians with an effective means to establish a measure of interpretative control over their land.

This is achieved primarily through the establishment of new Palestinian tourist/pilgrimage sites. Such sacralization (McCannell 1976) is conducted through both tourist and political discourses – thus people were interested in seeing a Palestinian village as representative of authentic traditional Palestine, *and* as an example of the encroachment of Israeli settlers on Palestine. Other sights which formed the tourist economy on our trip included the dispossessed Bedouin in the middle of the desert, the nets in Hebron that Palestinians put up to protect themselves from missiles thrown by Jewish settlers above them, the half-demolished village reached through the affluent and illegal Jewish settlement, and above all else – the image that serves as the new emblem of Palestine – the Separation Wall. On first encountering this, our group was horror-struck and dumbfounded; it is precisely the emotional intensity of this experience that engenders the need to convey it.

There were also positive sights such as Beit Arabiya, the rebuilt house which serves as a marker of non-violent (foreign-backed) resistance and as demonstration of Palestinian attachment to the land. But such sites are outnumbered by sites of tourist pilgrimage which portray Palestinians as victims, and which implicitly urge tourists to help these victims. The political meetings and the reading material participants are provided with should be seen, among other things, as ensuring they appreciate the meaning of these sites and can convey their message.

The attempt by Palestinian tour operators to control certain discourses was highly successful. Nobody we met advocated or defended armed struggle, despite its centrality in Palestinian political life. Without exception, all Palestinian groups that we met were eager to portray themselves and their society as 'reasonable', advocating peaceful change and putting forward moderate demands. In this, as my interviews indicate, our trip was not unique (see also Carroll 2004; Fox 2005).

Furthermore, the presence of Palestinian Christians is promoted by Palestinian tour guides and organizations, not simply because many guides are Christian, but also because foregrounding Christians whose presence has been effaced by Israeli narratives is a way of presenting Palestinian society as multicultural and complex. Participants on the ICAHD tour increasingly internalized the ideas presented by the people they visited. This was evidenced in the adoption of key phrases – at the beginning, the tour was repeatedly enjoined by Palestinian groups not to forget Palestine, as the tour went on, participants were discussing what they could do *so as* not to forget Palestine.

Beyond tourism?

> On several occasions in group meetings the topic of our privilege as Westerners arose and was duly acknowledged, but there can have been no greater privilege than that of being admitted into the lives of our extraordinary Palestinian friends (Ward 2004).

The last point indicates that political tourism is not fully contained within the logic of tourism. Participants' self-definition is less that of tourists than of students and potential activists; the alternative master frame of political activism challenges tourist discourses and enables the othering gaze of the tourist to be ruptured.

This can be seen in the way study tourists are constantly presented with a frustrating counter-hegemonic narrative of the landscape. Through having the landscape continually re-presented from the vantage point of those not in control and who are suffering from the changes in it, study tourists are continually asked to question what they see. This disconcerting contestation of an unsettled landscape affords them an insight into their own limited understanding and helps prevent the overlordship of the tourist gaze from coming into effect.

Another criticism of tourism is the absence of the principle of exchange between tourist and destination culture. It can be argued that this principle has been maintained by political tours in Palestine as the demand of the destination country is precisely to be represented – not to be forgotten – and the tourists, should they become active at home, are fulfilling their part of the bargain.

The last key distinction refers to how the tourist gaze is directed at the exotic and unusual. It could be argued that by attempting to incorporate the everyday experience of oppression into one's activities back home, these tours are antithetical to other forms of tourism. Our group's experience at Bethlehem University illustrates this point. Here, our mainly middle-class group encountered Palestinians as equals, with the political impact of the stories of occupation heightened precisely because we were made aware that this was being experienced by 'people like us', rather than objects of the classical tourist gaze.

However, it may not only be distance from Palestinians that militates against understanding, but also a false sense of closeness. By valorizing the depths of this awareness, tourists run the risk of effacing unpleasant complexities about their positionality and about Palestine.

As in gap-year tourism (Simpson 2004) these tours have been sold for their life-changing effects. The idea that tourist-activists are engaged in a transcendental experience that brings them closer to Palestinians was often referred to in my tour and others. It is not difficult to see why study tourists need to convey this trip as successful and spiritually fulfill-ing; in the spirit of pilgrimage with which tourists approach these trips, it is their very centrality to identity production which makes it difficult to acknowledge failure. Most accounts, including newspaper reports (Tickle 2005), speak of participants receiving an intense and occasionally life-changing experience, and achieving depths of understanding that can be used to re-place the self within the tourists' society, often at a higher level within localized hierarchies.

But does this contradict my earlier comments about participants accepting the limitations of what they see? The valorization of being uncomfortable and unknowing, which occurs on these trips,[4] seems to be an acceptance that political tourists need to recognize the 'cognitive limits of the anthropological endeavor' (Stein 1996). Ward's excerpt above illustrates how discomfort can be raised and disposed of in the same sentence. Though the two parts of the sentence are not logically connected, it appears that in the mind of the writer any awkwardness in his positionality is effaced both by 'duly acknowledging' it and by being accepted by Palestinians.

Of course Palestinians have other priorities than providing meaningful experiences to westerners, and – partly owing to the increased difficulties of solidarity activism in Palestine – the emphasis appears to have turned from activism in Palestine to advocacy back home. One interviewee working in Palestinian tourism was sharply critical of activist tourism. While recognizing the good intentions behind it, she characterized it as a disempowering activity – a means for the activists to portray themselves as heroes and then walk away from the situation, leaving locals to feel that political action is a seasonal foreign-orientated activity.

She contrasted this process explicitly – though perhaps unfairly (Dudouet 2006) – with study tourism, seen as a means of obtaining the tools by which foreigners can carry out activism in their own country. However, the goal of ensuring that participants engage in home-country activism does not necessarily lead to deeper understanding. It is precisely because the role of political tourists is to convey advocacy information that uncomfortable complexities and failures are hidden and forgotten. Even if it were possible to acknowledge failures as a tourist, it is less easy to do so when one is called upon to convey a political message which boosts Palestine.

Returning to the principle of exchange, the argument that it exists sidesteps the one-sided relationships formed between Palestinians and study tourists. It fails to question whether the former's vulnerability legitimizes the latter's one-sided intrusion into their lives, or whether this imposition, on the contrary, contributes to Palestinian powerlessness. This intrusion is not reciprocated; Palestinians are urged to share their stories, to open their workplaces and homes to well-meaning foreigners, yet in common with developmentalist practices elsewhere, there is rarely reciprocal openness or opening of borders by these foreigners (Goudge 2003).

Developmentalism and political agency

While political discourses may help rescue study tourists from the pitfalls inherent in tourism, the politics of study trips are strongly informed by the developmentalist idea, replete with traps of its own. I now examine the process whereby both Israeli peace groups and local Palestinian charities assist in the construction of Palestine as a place of despair which 'good Israelis' and foreigners are granted agency to change.

Criticism of the effects of development on the recipient country has been so extensive (Crush 1995; Escobar 1995; Rahnema and Bawtree 1997) that one expert in the field was moved to pose the significant question: 'What do aid programmes do besides fail to help poor people?' (Ferguson 1997: 231). In part answer, critics of development focus on the motives of volunteers and argue that the only development promoted is the volunteer's self-development; the destination country being reduced to a means by which volunteers can become enlightened. Criticism has been levelled at both gap-year tourists (Simpson 2004) and longer-term development workers – that in order to do one's work, as well as to account for failure, it is necessary to construct an image of the self as active, rational and progressive in contradistinction, necessarily, to the passive, irrational and backward society where one works (Baaz 2005).

Happily, the most rampantly imperialist (Escobar 1995) elements of developmentalism are largely absent from study trips. This may be because participants are not cast as activists able to indulge latent fantasies of heroism against a backdrop of passivity, but as students trying to learn from those more knowledgeable.

However, classic imperialist tropes weren't totally absent from the trip I participated in. Palestinians were continually portrayed as being grateful for our presence, and the structure of our trip ensured that we were represented as important. The high level of access to Palestinian groups, the rushing around from significant meeting to significant meeting, our special status at the hotels – all this made us feel we were part of a special elite, and gave us a status we do not have in our home society.

More significant was the prevalence of charity practices. Before the trip we were asked by the organizers to fundraise at least £100 each and to bring second-hand clothes for a village we visited. During each presentation an envelope was passed around into which participants put money; this was then handed to the speaker(s) with a little thank-you speech, a practice which reinforced the construction of these groups as charity cases rather than autonomous political actors. While such an elaborate organization of charity practices may have been particular to our trip, the wider charity discourse is more general. This allows Palestinians to be seen as victims of 'the situation', a construction that accords them a status of dependency and passivity.

This despair was not simply a construct of the tour participants – several Palestinian organizations we visited were complicit in presenting Palestine as prostrate and needing our charity. Again this fits into common practices of developmentalism whereby the Third World is represented as primitive and chaotic by local development agencies, for purposes of fundraising and of enhancing their own role (Griesshaber 1997). One must also recognize the very genuine and realistic feelings of despair among Palestinians in the face of global complicity with successful Israeli practices of occupation, mass imprisonment and disempowerment.

Nevertheless, pitying Palestine as a victim locates the focus of activism among outsiders – both Israelis and international visitors. It is hardly surprising, then, that the Israeli peace groups we encountered were complicit in this construction, and that one of the messages of the tour was that hope was located in Israel and specifically in those Israeli groups working to challenge the Israeli consensus.

Cynically, one could say that it was important for participants to declare belief in the possibility of 'good Israelis' to avoid being labelled anti-Israeli, seen as a variety of antisemitism. However this does not account for the fervour, throughout the trip, with which all evidence possible was mobilized to prove the existence of 'good Israelis', nor the enthusiasm with which these miniscule organizations on the fringes of Israeli society were treated. The search for 'good Israelis' may lie in the success of the 'Jewish story' in the west, seen as a story of an oppressed people with whom one feels sympathy.[5] While not all study tours had such a close connection with left-wing Israeli organizations as ours did, many do, and many study trippers – not just Jewish ones – appear impelled to confirm the existence of noble Israeli groups.

The consequent status accorded to Israeli peace groups allows them to maintain their position – for which they have been severely criticized – as gatekeepers of what action or political frame is acceptable to western liberals (Laor 2001). One Palestinian activist referred to an effective Israeli peace group vetting that Palestinian groups need to pass in order to access the western world (personal communication). This locks Palestinians into a frustrating and often immobilizing relationship of dependency with these tiny Israeli groups who – partly because there is no structural reason for doing so – do not see themselves as answerable to Palestinian leadership (Bronstein 2005).

Conclusion: the mystery of the missing right of return

The contradictory effects of these political tours should hardly come as a surprise: all political action comes equipped with opportunity costs and negative effects. While it is legitimate to ask whether study trips are successful, we must bear in mind that the alternative to 'going there' is often 'doing nothing', rather than 'doing something better'. While one can question whether study tours grant discursive dominance to western tourists over their Palestinian hosts, nevertheless this feeling of discursive control seems to afford them political agency as advocates for the Palestinian cause upon returning home.

Yet such discursive dominance can militate against study tourists being able to conduct the political work they are expected to undertake. Highlighting the tourists' own subjectivities and (occasionally) those of Israeli peace groups, rather than Palestinians', may silence the diverse voices from Palestine, prevent communication and promote a politics which may enhance the participants' self-image and identity, but not necessarily allow for Palestinian subjectivity.

This can be illustrated with reference to the right of return for Palestinian refugees, central in Palestinian political discourse and yet almost completely absent on study trips. At best it is supported with the addendum that very few people would actually come back – in other words, people should be allowed to return, because after all they won't return (see also Lentin this volume).

As one Palestinian speaker pointed out, the right of return is an issue which Israeli organizations need to promote more than Palestinian ones. Yet since Israeli peace groups rarely consider themselves answerable to Palestinians, and because they have constructed their field of activities to focus on the occupation, they have chosen not to address this issue.

One reason for Palestinian groups not mentioning it may be the irrelevance of the demand for their immediate work. They may feel that tourists have full opportunity to listen to Palestinian exiles, and that their job is to present the situation in the Occupied Palestinian Territories. However such explanations do not explain why, for instance, we could visit a refugee camp in the West Bank without raising the obvious right of return that this entails. There are three possible explanations for this.

Firstly, the tour I was on was regulated by ICAHD's political vision, which sees the occupation as the main focus for action. Furthermore, given the primacy these tours afford to 'seeing' the political situation, there is an unconscious framing of the situation which excludes that which isn't seen – Palestinian refugees outside Israel/Palestine – from a political solution.

Second is the issue of interpretative control. If, as I argue, Palestinians encountered on study trips (especially trips organized by Israeli peace groups) are urged to be experts on issues within their immediate knowledge, then this excludes them from speaking of wider political-legal issues, such as the right of return. Thus, Palestinians were not allowed the discursive space within which to articulate a political analysis which would have included advocating the right of return.

Third, in their self-presentation, Palestinians were keen to present themselves as reasonable in contradistinction to the unreasonable, unfathomable behaviour of the Israelis. Their demands were presented as modest and achievable without causing major political upheaval. Emphasising immediate goals such as the lifting of sanctions on Palestine was based on a perception of what the tourists could achieve and what would appeal to them. This strategy of dealing with the noose that's nearest one's neck is sensible, and Palestinian groups seemed well aware of what could and could not be achieved by western activists. The right of return does not fit into such a framework and thus was not forwarded by Palestinian groups.

Nevertheless the effacement of this central demand of Palestinian people and their leadership during the trip is cause for concern. It illustrates the wider issue that while this tour and others like it are effective in their very necessary central aim of rendering participants fit for advocacy work in Europe and America, such an aim may be achieved at the expense of the subjectivity and political aspirations of Palestinians themselves.

One may see the various discourses of these trips – the tourist gaze, imperialist feminism, developmentalism and associated charity practices – as being aspects of the same thing, a discursive colonization of Palestine by well-meaning Western activists. This is not to assert there is no discursive space within the trips to undermine the aura of authenticity, to create relations of mutual understanding, and to promote Palestinian political objectives – there clearly is, which is why Palestinian organizations increasingly promote study tourism.

However, while each separate discourse contains the possibility of contesting and undercutting the imperialist tendencies in others, it appears that by being used by the activist tourists to form their own coherent identity, these practices serve mainly to reinforce each other. It would be a cruel irony if, through producing the identities of Palestinian solidarity activists, there is complicity with a discursive colonization of Palestine which silences Palestinians themselves by allocating them a subordinate place in the conduct of these activities.

Notes

1   I wish to thank Ronit Lentin for her invaluable support and helpful comments throughout this research. I would also like to acknowledge the support of the Irish Research Council for the Humanities and Social Sciences for funding my research

2   This chapter is based on participant observation of one of these study trips, on analysis of other accounts of trips, and on interviews with their participants and with people involved in the tourist industry in Palestine.

3   A comparison can be made with critical research on fair trade initiatives – another 'partial, imperfect, yet significant praxis' (Johnston and Goodman 2006: 17).

4   The experience the group had of being crammed into a house in a refugee camp was praised for that very reason, and one participant persuasively argued that the stress and overwhelmed feeling many experienced was preferable to the distancing vantage point of comfort.

5   On the first day of the trip many of the participants indicated it was an interest in Israel and the Jewish story, not Palestine, which had sparked their interest in going on this study trip.

References

Agamben, G. (1998) *Homo Sacer: Sovereign Power and Bare Life,* Stanford University Press, Stanford, CA

Baaz, M. (2005) *The Paternalism of Partnership: A Postcolonial Reading of Identity in Aid and Development,* Zed Books, London

Bernath, K. (1999) 'Ghassan Andoni offers alternative tourism to Palestine', *Washington Report on Middle East Affairs,* Jan/Feb 1999

Bowman, G. (1992) 'The politics of tour guiding: Israeli and Palestinian guides in Israel and the Occupied Territories', in D. Harrison (ed.) *Tourism and the Less Developed Countries,* Belhaven, London

Bronstein, E. (2005) 'The *Nakba* in Hebrew: Israeli-Jewish awareness of the Palestinian catastrophe and internal refugees', in N. Masalha (ed.) *Catastrophe Remembered: Palestine, Israel and the Internal Refugees: Essays in Memory of Edward W. Said,* Zed Books, London

Carroll, D. (2004) *Zaytoun Tour,* November 2004 «http://www.olivecoop.com/reviews.html#donal»

Cohen-Hattab, K. (2004) 'Zionism, tourism, and the battle for Palestine: Tourism as a political-propaganda tool', *Israel Studies,* Vol. 9, no. 1

Davie, M. (2004) *Palestine Trip* ‹‹http://www.apocalypse.gen.nz/palestine/›

Desforges, L. (2000) 'Travelling the world: Identity and travel biography', *Annals of Tourism Research,* Vol. 27, no. 4

Dudouet, V. (2006) 'Cross-border non-violent advocacy during the second Palestinian *Intifada*: The case of the international solidarity movement', paper presented at Coventry International Seminar: Unarmed Resistance – The Transnational Factor, 13–17 July

Elias, N. (1987) *Involvement and Detachment,* Basil Blackwell, Oxford

Escobar, A. (1995) *Encountering Development: The Making and Unmaking of the Third World,* Princeton University Press, Princeton

Ferguson, J. (1997) 'Development and bureaucratic power in Lesotho', in M. Rahnema and V. Bawtree, *The Post-Development Reader,* Zed Books, London

Fox, D. (2005) *Dennis Fox's Weblog* «http://blog.dennisfox.net/ »

Goudge, P. (2003) *The Power of Whiteness: Racism in Third World Development and Aid,* Lawrence & Wishart, London

Griesshaber, D. (1997) *Challenging Perspectives: The Majority World on Irish Television,* Comhlámh Action Network, Dublin

hooks, b. (1989) *talking back: thinking feminist, thinking black,* Sheba, London

Johnston, J. and J. Goodman (2006) 'Hope and activism in the ivory tower: Freirean lessons for critical globalization research', *Globalizations,* Vol. 3, no. 1

Kassis, R. (2004) *The Palestinians and Justice Tourism,* Alternative Tourism Group, Beit Sahour, Palestine

Laor, Y. (2001) 'The tears of Zion', *New Left Review,* Vol. 10

McCannell, D. (1976) *The Tourist: A New Theory of the Leisure Class,* Macmillan, London

Mohanty, C. (1992) 'Feminist encounters: Locating the politics of experience', in

M. Barrett and A. Phillips (eds) *Destabilizing Theory: Contemporary Feminist Debates*, Polity, Cambridge

Rahnema, M. and V. Bawtree (1997) *The Post-Development Reader*, Zed Books, London

Shabi, R. (2006) 'Come, see Palestine!' *Spiegel Online International*, 5 June 2006 «http://service.spiegel.de/cache/international/0,1518,419696,00.html»

Simpson, K. (2004) '"Doing Development": The gap year, volunteer-tourists and a popular practice of development', *Journal of International Development*, Vol. 16, no. 5

Stein, R. (1996) 'Political tourism in Palestine. Review of Sherna Berger Gluck, An American Feminist in Palestine: The *Intifada* Years (Philadelphia: Temple University Press, 1994).' *Stanford Humanities Review*, Vol. 5, no. 1

Taylor, J. (2001) 'Authenticity and sincerity in tourism', *Annals of Tourism Research*, Vol. 28, no. 1

Tickle, L. (2005) 'Education in olive branches', *Guardian*, 12 December

Trainor, P. (2006) *Hiding their Crimes, Destroying Livelihoods: The Effect of the Israeli Occupation on Tourism in Bethlehem*, Alternative Tourism Group, Beit Sahour, Palestine

Urry, J. (1991) *The Tourist Gaze*, Sage, London

Wang, N. (1999) 'Rethinking authenticity in tourism experience', *Annals of Tourism Research*, Vol. 26, no. 2

Ward, R. (2004) 'Putting Palestinian homes back together: Two weeks in Beit Arabiya', *CounterPunch*, September, no. 18/19 «http://www.counterpunch.org/ward09182004.html»

Waterman, P. (1998) *Globalization, Social Movements and the New Internationalisms*, Mansell, London

Wearing, S. (2001) *Volunteer Tourism: Experiences that Make a Difference*, CABI Publishing, Oxford

Ronit Lentin

11 The Contested Memory of Dispossession: Commemorizing the Palestinian Nakba in Israel

Introduction[1]

> Do you think we can create our homeland on the basis of this vague story? And why do we need to create it at all? A person inherits his homeland just as he inherits his language – why should we, of all the peoples of the world, have to invent our homeland anew every day? (Khouri 2005: 384)

> According to Gush Emunim's ideology, the land signified deep, ancient Jewish memory... The prohibition on Jewish presence on the land... was seen as a continuation of the persecutions, dispossessions and expulsions, and also of the Holocaust, which the Jews were victims to throughout history... In the settlers' discourse, death was seen as life-enhancing and territory-creating (Eldar and Zertal 2004: 279, 324)

> It's dehumanizing: to protect your victimhood, you have to ignore others' pain (Etgar Keret, in Jaggi 2007).

In September 1967, as a group of Israeli Jews who had been expelled from Kfar Etzion during the 1948 war was preparing to settle Gush Etzion, the first West Bank Jewish settlement, settler leader Hanan Porat recalled the Palestinian poet Mahmoud Darwish describing the return to his western Galilee village. Startled by the association, Porat rejected any similarities: 'An Arab returning to his village', he would later write, 'is human and moving. But a Jew returning to his village is beyond nostalgia. It is history. It is meta-history' (cited in Eldar and Zertal 2004: 14). This juxtaposition illustrates what Edward Said (1980) saw as the encounter between Palestinian and Zionist histories, a dialectic contestation of the right to what both Jews and Palestinians call 'the land', though even when they are aware of Palestinian claims, Zionists put their own claim on a higher level. Following Said, this dialectic encounter means that it is fruitful to theorize Palestine in tandem with theorizing Zionism and the State of Israel.

At the centre of the contested rights stands the struggle regarding the memory of the 1948 war, which the Israelis call their War of Independence and the Palestinians their Nakba, the 1948 catastrophe when 800,000 Palestinians were expelled or escaped from their homes. Uniquely, the inclusion of the second and third generation brings the number of Palestinian refugees, according to the UNHCR, to four million people (Kuperman 2005).[2]

In this chapter I locate the Nakba as a specific site of contested commemoration. I do not theorize memory in relation to judicial accountability, truth and reconciliation committees, human rights, healing and social justice (see, e.g., Amadiume and An-Na'im 2000). Rather, my intention is to interrogate the complex issues surrounding the specific commemorization of the Nakba in the self-narration of its Israeli Jewish rememberers. While the entitlement of Palestinian refugees has been globally accepted as central to 'Palestinian society of today and Palestinian history, memory and collective identity... [and] to the future of Palestine and Israel' (Masalha 2005a: 3-4), many questions remain open, including the issue of the internally displaced (Kanaaneh 2007; Masalha 2005b). Another contestation is between the Palestinian claim of refugee status for the second and third generation, and the Israeli threefold claim, first, that internal refugees are an 'internal Israeli problem', second, as Israeli historian Hillel Cohen argues, that 'Israel is the only state to have solved the problem of Palestinian refugees' (personal communication, November 2005), and third, that the 'definition of refugee status that allows it to be passed on from generation to generation' is unacceptable (Alpher 2002).

Some Palestinians (see, e.g., Khouri 2005) argue that the past and its narration are a burden which does not allow them to live in the present. I want to argue that the debates on the place of the memory of the Nakba past stand at the heart of the 'memory boom' in relation to the Palestinian question regarding homeland, rights, entitlements, refugeehood, against which Israelis position Israeli Jewish victimhood (and at times also the divine Jewish right to the land) as an opposing narrative.

The Nakba is increasingly commemorized, discussed, contested, by Palestinian and international scholars, and Palestinians are increasingly taking charge of commemorating their Nakba, in Palestine as elsewhere (see e.g., Sa'di and Abu-Lughod 2007). However, as I am interested here in questions of representation and appropriation, this chapter focuses on the contested commemoration of the Nakba by Israeli Jews. I begin by outlining Pierre Nora's concept of *lieux de mémoire*. I then briefly survey work by Israeli 'new historians' whose excavations of official Israeli archives since the 1980s have been shattering the Zionist consensus by introducing the Israeli public to the events of the Nakba. To explore what I see as the colonization of Palestinian memory, this chapter critically examines *Zochrot*, an Israeli group dedicated since 2002 to commemorating the Nakba in Hebrew, arguing that its commemorative work, while welcome, is a deeply problematic *lieu de mémoire*.

As an émigré Israeli, opposed to Israeli state policies since 1967 (Lentin 1980, 2002, 2004), aware of the problems of writing as an Israeli about the meanings of the Nakba, I acknowledge that awareness of othering in social research is never 'directly soluble by methodological rules' (Ramazanoğlu 2002: 120). I am guided by what the Palestinian-Israeli activist Ghared Nabulsi said to me in an interview in May 2006: 'You can use the term Nakba but you cannot talk about the real experience of those who lived it'. Elsewhere (Lentin 2007a) I discuss my own responsibility – through being the daughter of one of the pre-state Israeli soldiers who conquered the mixed city of Haifa. Set against the backdrop of the daily practices of the Israeli racial state (Goldberg this volume; Lentin 2004), this chapter explores the contested relationship between commemoration and appropriation from the standpoint of a member of the perpetrators' collectivity, whose politics align her with the colonized.

Lieux de mémoire: memory or memoricide?

> Is memory but a disease? A strange disease afflicting a whole nation, a disease for which you imagine the past building your lives on an imagined memory… (Khouri 2005: 339–40)

Pierre Nora's seminal 1989 article can be read as an elegy for the decline of 'authentic' memories. Nora argues that we continue to speak of memory because there is so little of it, and contrasts 'real memory – social and unviolated' (Nora 1989: 8) – in primitive societies and among peasants, with contemporary memory. Claiming that we can retain sites of memory because this is the best we can do now there is no spontaneous memory, Nora writes that *'lieux de mémoire* are fundamentally remains, the ultimate embodiments of a memorial consciousness that has barely survived in a historical age that calls out for memory because it has abandoned it' (Nora 1989: 12). According to Nora, people are increasingly attempting to research their individual memories, with archives being kept not only by states and large institutions, but by everyone. Memory thus becomes an individual duty, and *lieux de mémoire* come in various shapes as 'memory attaches itself to sites, whereas history attaches itself to events' (Nora 1989: 22).

In Israel, the valorization of certain sites of memory over others is an ongoing process – see for instance the juxtaposition of *Yad Vashem*, The Holocaust Martyrs' and Heroes' Remembrance Memorial, a site of Israeli collective memory – with Deir Yassin – the neglected and deliberately forgotten site of the 1948 massacre – only 1400 metres away. The State of Israel has engaged in an active memoricide of both the Nakba and the ethnically cleansed Palestinians through establishing new Jewish settlements on the lands of destroyed Palestinian villages, renaming the places seized, and, with the help of archaeologists and biblical experts, 'hebraicizing' Palestine's geography (Pappe 2006: 225–6). The link between remembering and forgetting in constructing collective memories (Forty and Küchler 1999; Zertal 2000) entails a memory boom, as each generation invests *lieux de mémoire* with different interpretations so they become their own referent.

Debates on the centrality of memory in theorizing catastrophe have proliferated in relation to the Nazi Holocaust. Marianne Hirsch (1997) posits 'postmemory', mediated through photographs, films, books, testimonies, and distinguished from memory by generational distance and from history by deep personal connection. Young calls this 'the afterlife of memory represented in history's after-images: the impressions retained in the mind's eye of a vivid sensation long after the original, external cause has been removed' (Young 2000: 3–4). Postmemory is one facet of 'collective memory', theorized as different from 'history' in being shaped by society's changing needs, or, conversely, as shaping both political life and history itself. The politics of remembrance in the current 'era of testimonies' includes the trauma experienced by contemporary bystanders – often reluctantly forced to listen to the voices of victims and survivors.

This also entails collective forgetting, which 'we', who survived after the catastrophe, have to struggle with in the face of our shame (Agamben 1999). Notions such as 'postmemory', or 'received history' (Young 2000) put memory – via, among other things, victims' and perpetrators' testimonies accessed through oral history, and told and retold from generation to generation – on a plateau with history. Sites of memory, including archived survivors' testimonies, museums, monuments, public exhibitions, and artistic representations, vie with written history in keeping traumatic events alive, often serving the political purpose of the collective (documented in the case of Israel, by e.g., Lentin 2000; Segev 1991; Zertal 2005). Israeli novelist Etgar Keret – speaking about the legacy of the Holocaust, employed to perpetuate Israeli victimhood, but also to justify the ongoing dispossession of the Palestinians – reminds us that protecting Israeli victimhood means having to ignore Palestinian pain (Jaggi 2007).

Writing about the inability to proceed from Holocaust past to post-Holocaust present, Laurence Langer distinguishes between 'common memory' which 'urges us to regard the Auschwitz ordeal as part of a chronology, (freeing) us from the pain of remembering the unthinkable', and 'deep memory' that 'reminds us that the Auschwitz past is not really past and never will be' (Langer 1991: xi). This distinction, while helpful in understanding Shoah survivors' difficulties in living in the present, is not helpful in the situation of the Palestinians internally dispossessed, who live side by side with those who re-possessed their lands, continue to confiscate their lands, deprive them of their refugee identity, triumph at their expense, and erase the memory of their catastrophe through legal and governmental technologies which cast them as second-class citizens (Kannaneh 2007). While the experiences of Palestinian refugees vary greatly, depending on their gender, class and diasporic location, and, above all, on whether or not they are refugee camp dwellers, it is useful to theorize the memory of their catastrophe in terms of Langer's 'deep memory', in that their dispossession is 'not really past and never will be'.

Of course there are differences between the Holocaust and the Nakba and between Holocaust and Nakba commemoration. According to Hanafi, 'the Israeli colonial project is not genocidal but "spacio-cidal" ' with land being the main target (Hanafi 2005: 159). Signposting locations of deportations and Jewish dwellings in contemporary Germany monumentalizes and counter-monumentalizes genocide

(Young 2000), but financial retribution was usually not contested; nor were there questions of 'return' or of territorial claims, central in the case of Palestinian refugees, where, despite widespread massacres and dispossession, the term genocide does not apply. However, on the testimonial level some similarities do exist, particularly in relation to self-silencing.[3]

Although Palestinians began telling the Nakba immediately after the 1948 war (Masalha 2005a), the story is still full of silences regarding the experiences of different Palestinian communities, some living in the western diaspora, others living in refugee camps; it is also marked by the erasure of the struggle of internal refugees who remained in Israel after 1948. The latter struggle was not helped, according to Waqim Waqim, chairperson of the Association for the Defence of the Rights of the Displaced Person in Israel, by the refusal of the PLO – under pressure from Israel – to include the issue of the internally displaced in any negotiations (interview May 2006). There was also a degree of self-silencing of Nakba memories, due, some argue, to *shame* at not having fought (Khouri 1998; Tamari 2002), but also to *fear*, particularly during the military government which ended only in 1966.[4] However, according to Waqim, the fear is beginning to be assuaged due to the Association's annual march of return to the destroyed villages:

> Until a few years ago, the memory of the *Nakba* was private, not collective...they were afraid... remember people lived under military government until 1966... My father for instance... When father is asked where he is from – and he is from el Bassa – he would say I am *not* from here, I am not from Me'ilia... this is negative identity... But today if you ask him, he would say 'I am from el Bassa'... I think that the new discourse of the Committee of the Internally Displaced has contributed to people's new identity, allowing them to identify positively with their original villages (interview May 2006).

Evading the continuous past: the treatment of the Nakba and its aftermath by Israeli academics

According to Benny Morris, one of the Israeli pioneer revisionist historians of the Nakba, the turning point in relation to re-telling the Nakba was his 1988 article, in which he contrasted the phrase 'new historians' with 'old historians', many of whom wrote the history they had participated in making as officers in the pre-state and state armies (e.g., Lorech 1958).

At the same time works by several other Israeli revisionist historians began shattering the Zionist consensus that the majority of Palestinians either left their homes because they were instructed to do so by the invading Arab states, fled in ill-informed fear, or departed along with the defeated Arab armies. The accepted Israeli narrative was that the plight of the Palestinian refugees was neither the fault nor the responsibility of the Zionist leaders. The work of 'new historians' Benny Morris (1987, 1994, 2004), Simha Flappan (1987), Ilan Pappe (1988) and Avi Shlaim (1988) made it clear to many Israelis that 'the maps of meaning provided by Zionism are simply no longer adequate' (Silberstein 2002).[5] However, with the exception of Pappe and Shlaim, Israeli Nakba historiographies, following Morris, believe that '*war and not design* (Jewish or Arab) gave birth to the Palestinian refugee problem' (Morris 2004: 588, emphasis added). While Morris was the first Israeli historian to publicly uncover material delineating individual cases of expulsions and massacres as well as plans – notably Plan *Dalet* (D) – for the removal of Palestinians, he was unwilling to accept the Palestinian contention that Plan *Dalet* was a Zionist masterplan for ethnic cleansing, as has been argued by Pappe (2006) and others. In 2000 Morris did acknowledge that 'the leadership entered the war with the belief that transfer was desirable and even necessary for the establishment and preservation of a Jewish state... this mindset enabled the limited ethnic cleansing... [about which] there was wall to wall consensus in the Zionist leadership' (Morris 2000:15). However, in a 2004 interview in *Ha'aretz*, Morris declared his disappointment that the Nakba was not more thorough (Shavit 2004). Israeli 1948 historiography, again with the exception of Pappe, placed the Palestinian refugee problem within the timeframe of the war, closing the problem off from the present. It can thus be presented as an episode of history which is now over, a position which accords with Israeli policies that seek to dissolve the political dimension of the refugees' dispossession (Masalha 2003; Piterberg 2001).

Furthermore, and central to questions of representation and appropriation discussed in this chapter, for most 'new historians' 'Jews are the subjects of history. Arabs are objects of Jewish action' (Beinin 2004).[6] Even when the suffering of the Palestinians is acknowledged and highlighted, they are rarely allowed interpretive possession of their history, as my discussion of *Zochrot* demonstrates.[7]

Zochrot: remembering, commemorating, appropriating

> No need to hear your voice when I can talk about you better than you
> can speak about yourself… Only tell me about your pain. I want to
> know your story. And then I will tell it back to you in a new way. Tell it
> back to you in such a way that it has become mine… Re-writing you, I
> write myself anew. I am still author, authority. I am still the colonizer,
> the speaking subject, and you are now at the centre of my talk (hooks
> 1991: 151–2, cited in Goldstone 2000: 313–14).

Zochrot was founded in 2002 when members joined the annual march of
return, initiated by the Association for the Defence of the Rights of the
Displaced Persons in Israel on Israel's Independence Day. From that first
march, *Zochrot,* a group of Israeli Jewish intellectuals, set about *performing*
the memory of the Nakba, through giving a 'sermon' on the Nakba in
Hebrew (Bronstein 2005: 217; Lentin 2007b). *Zochrot* organizes tours to
Palestinian villages and towns destroyed during and after the 1948 war,
during which members post clearly visible signs to commemorate the
sites and provide the Israeli public with information about the Nakba.
The tours include the distribution of printed material written by former
Palestinian inhabitants and the unveiling of often-masked remnants of
destroyed villages and urban quarters. *Zochrot*'s practices aim to uncover
'a kind of memory that was deliberately and systematically hidden' from
Israeli Jews, and, crucially, 'Hebraicize' the Nakba by creating a space for
it in the 'written, spoken and public discourse of Hebrew Israel', and
promoting an 'alternative discourse on memory'.

According to Said (Said and Mohr 1986), the dominance of the
Israeli historical narrative and the present geographical fragmentation of
Palestinian society block attempts to present historical accounts of the
lived experiences of Palestinians. While oral history projects documenting the stories of Nakba survivors ('Issa 2005; Masalha 2005a) target
Palestinian and global consumption, *Zochrot*'s activities explicitly target
a Jewish Israeli public.

However, *Zochrot*'s ambitions go beyond commemorating or
'Hebraicizing' Nakba memory. In the spirit of global paradigms of truth
and reconciliation, according to *Zochrot*'s chair, Eitan Bronstein,
acknowledging Israeli Jewish responsibility for Zionist ethnic cleansing,
massacres and property confiscations aims to 'bring about an end to the
conflict and promote true *reconciliation* between the two peoples'
(Bronstein 2005: 217).

One illustration of this ambitious aim is *Zochrot*'s proposal in relation to Kufr Hittin, a sacred Druze site destroyed in 1948. Following the appeal by the Druze in Israel to the Regional Committee for Planning and Construction in Northern Israel against the re-designation of the ruins, *Zochrot* proposed turning the Palestinian remains into a site of reconciliation between Palestinians and Jews, by conserving them and emphasizing their Arab history. Emphasizing parallelism and the importance of memorizing the Nakba for Israeli Jewish identity, Bronstein argues that re-designating the ruins of Hittin

> should also worry Jewish Israelis interested in understanding the country's history since 1948 and the prevention of the return of most of its Palestinian inhabitants. The Hittin remains are testimony to this past and represent the violent origin of our conflict. We can now choose between continuing destruction and respect for this past, respect for the vanquished and expropriated Palestinian nation; this can be the beginning of a process of reconciliation (Ali 2007).

My argument is that *Zochrot*'s commemorative acts, though a welcome negation of the ongoing Israeli erasure of the Nakba, constitute a problematic, very Israeli, *lieu de mémoire,* in two main senses, the first relating to subsuming the Palestinian voice by *Zochrot*'s Israeli Jewish narrative of the Nakba, the second concerning the contested issue of the right of return.

Discussing Primo Levi's proposal that the witness whose testimony we most need to hear, the only 'complete witness', is she who had reached bottom and who therefore cannot testify (in Levi's terms, the *Musulman*), Giorgio Agamben argues that this makes the true testimony of catastrophe unspeakable: 'the relation… between language and the archive demands subjectivity as that which in its very possibility of speech, bears witness to an impossibility of speech' (Agamben 1999: 146).

Bronstein acknowledges that *Zochrot*'s activities not only do not 'depend upon the consent or approval of the Arabs in Israel, even those internally displaced', they 'might even *exclude* Palestinian groups in Israel because the main target is to change fundamentally the discourse in the "national Jewish camp" ' (Bronstein 2005: 233, emphasis added). Merely representing Palestinian refugees as victims and stressing their ongoing dispossession compounds the trauma, while at the same time depriving them of voice. The question as to who is the Nakba's 'complete witness', whose 'unspeakable' testimony we need to hear, is neither addressed nor resolved by *Zochrot*. The material distributed by *Zochrot,* while written by Palestinian witnesses-informants, is translated, edited and produced by *Zochrot*. This emphasis on the Hebraicization of Nakba memory, despite the good intentions, is too reminiscent of the Hebraicization of the Palestinian geography that Pappe documents (see page 208).

The Druze writer and activist Salman Natur, while agreeing that 'it's possible to work with the Jewish side, through people who can break into the Israeli Jewish consciousness', cautions against 'a situation, that because of their better resources, the anti-Zionist Palestinian narrative will be written by Israeli Jews. It's not right' (interview May 2006). Ghared Nabulsi, who resigned her membership of *Zochrot* when executive members would not refuse to serve as IDF reservists, agrees: 'Why do I need *Zochrot* to write the history of a given Arab village for me? ... This is not new for the Palestinians. What is new is that this is a group of Jews doing it with groups of Jews. This is *Zochrot*'s *raison d'être*... but if they want to talk about the Nakba in general, beyond just to Jews... this is nothing new' (interview May 2006).

Another aspect of this appropriation is conquest through knowledge, as illustrated by Jewish *Zochrot* member Tamar Abraham:

> Members of *Zochrot* see the tours to the villages as a way of making them part of their own history.... As Bronstein put it... the most important thing for him personally is that these places, after he has learnt about them and made a tour to them, are no longer unknown to him, they... become part of his map of the country, belong to him, he has 'conquered' them... literally. I was quite shocked, thinking that this way the villages will be conquered for a second time (interview March 2007).

I want to suggest that by collecting testimonies of Palestinians who survived the Nakba and commemorizing the Nakba in Hebrew, *Zochrot* appropriates Palestinian memory and perpetuates Palestinian victim-hood, a position most Palestinians reject. The question must be asked whether Israeli Jews should be collecting testimonies of Palestinian victims, or rather using existing archived testimonies, and document instead testimonies of Jewish perpetrators of the Nakba, a much more difficult task.

Conclusion

An exploration of *Zochrot's* performative commemoration of the Nakba (Lentin 2007b) raises questions regarding the crisis in the Israeli resistance movement, particularly since the onset of the al-Aqsa Intifada, the erection of the Separation Wall and the deepening checkpoint regime. To maintain their funding, groups are often forced to resort to public relations strategies (Barda 2006), and *Zochrot* is particularly creative in the use of performative devices, including re-signposting ruined Palestinian villages and urban neighbourhoods with their original names. A particularly clever event used posting cartoon-style bubble signs 'I almost forgot... that the Day of Independence is the Day of the *Nakba*... that Israel had destroyed 530 Palestinian villages...' in Tel Aviv's fashionable neighbourhoods (www. nakbainhebrew.org).

However, one must question what is the ultimate aim of *Zochrot's* work 'to change Jewish public consciousness', if all its creativity does not lead to explicit support for the right of return for Palestinian refugees. Although formally in favour of the right of return through participating in marches of return and in the annual conference on the right of return, without an explicit critique of the Israeli racial state *Zochrot's* actions remain symbolic. Such critique would mean the demise of Israel as a Jewish state, a stance supported by very few Jewish Israelis, even though many more have by now moved closer to a two-state solution, which retains the recognition of 'Israel's right to exist', and a mere handful support the one-state solution (see, e.g., *Race Traitor* 2005).

An internal *Zochrot* document raises the issue of parallelism when it suggests that the right of return aims 'not merely (to) correct the historic injustice to the Palestinians, but also perhaps afford a *true return of Jews* to the land in the sense of really meeting it through the return of the Palestinians. To truly meet it and become part of it.' The document further insists that the right of return is not about nostalgia but about a 'possible future of peace and reconciliation', while also questioning 'until when can we count the refugees' offspring as candidates for return?' In the same token, Bronstein speaks tentatively about 'the return of the *sign*' and 'the possibility that Palestinians *might* return to Palestine' and suggests that the memory of Palestinian life in the Israeli Jewish space through the action of *Zochrot* 'holds the *potential* of acknowledging the "right of return" (even if not necessarily the *actual* act of returning' (Bronstein 2005, 231).[8] In contrast, the explicit aim of the Association for the Defence of the Displaced Persons in Israel in commemorating the Nakba, is to work for the right of return, according to UN Resolution 194 (Va'ad Ha'hakurim 2005) – leaving the symbolic to the privileged occupiers of the land.

Within the global commemoration discourse, Palestinian memory is not only paradigmatic of dispossession but is also a discursive shortcut to denote ethnic and political conflict – regardless of which side you are on. The 2006 war in Gaza and Lebanon made it clear that Palestine remains central to any 'new Middle East' and this must include a resolution of the refugee issue.

Zochrot engages with the Israeli landscape and the Hebrew-speaking public without critiquing the state, while retaining interpretative control over the meaning of the Nakba, implying it can do this in ways which tacitly enter the consensus and ratify the status quo. Recognizing the right of return must be a logical conclusion of any commemorizing work, but giving voice to the dispossessed does not mean that Israeli Jews – well-intentioned as they might be – can make decisions in this respect. Ghared Nabulsi, herself member of the third generation of the Nakba, insists that it is up to the refugees themselves, not those who have not lived the Nakba, to determine their future:

> We must begin by recognizing the right of return... But I do not want to speak for the refugees and the dispossessed, we need to listen to their own wishes... I do not want to perpetuate power relations, I do not want to speak for them... there are people who still keep their keys and wish to return to their houses, and there are others who say they are happy to return to another place. I don't want to decide for them without asking them (interview May 2006).

Ultimately, *Zochrot*'s actions – eye-catching and effective as they are – still remain at the level of the symbolic. It is hard to escape the feeling that, in regarding its commemorative acts as 'conquest', and in aiming at reconciliation rather than at a political solution, *Zochrot* perpetuates rather than contests the ongoing colonization of Palestine.

Notes

1 This chapter is part of an ongoing study of the Israeli politics of the memory of the Palestinian Nakba, supported by the Institute of International Integration Studies (IIIS), Trinity College, Dublin. I am indebted to my research assistant

David Landy, who, among other things, has conducted several interviews and ethnographies for this study. And thanks, yet again, to Nitza Aminov.
2   According to Palestinian sources the number is closer to six million («http://palestineremembered.com»).
3   Katalin Katz, who chairs 'Collective and individual memory and interpretation' seminars in the Hebrew University, compares the self-silencing in the families of children of Holocaust survivors and children of Palestinian refugees (Katz 2000; see also Lentin 2000).
4   In 1950 the Israeli government issued the Absentee Property Law, according to which the state confiscated the property of all Palestinians who were not present in their homes between 29 November 1947 and 19 May 1948, even if they stayed in the country and did not go farther than the few kilometres to the next village. As a result, the internally displaced Palestinians were declared 'present absentees' and deprived of the right to carry the citizenship of the new state (Kannaneh 2007).
5   Other Israeli scholars active in exploding the Nakba myth include sociologist Baruch Kimmerling (Kimmerling and Migdal 1994) and geographer Meron Benvenisti (2000).
6   Hence Morris's total reliance on Israeli sources and his refusal to deal with Palestinian sources, stemming not merely from his inability to speak Arabic, but also from contempt for their point of view (Beinin 2004).
7   Morris's view that 'There are no good Palestinian historians' (cited in Pappe 2004) appears commonplace in Israeli academia. Likewise, Benvenisti (2000) appears to believe that there are no good Palestinian geographers, ridiculing their painstaking efforts to map the land as being 'Palestinian sacred geography' comparable to pornography in its obsession with an unreal image rather than the authentic landscape, which only those living in Israel can possess.
8   Or, as Hillel Cohen puts it, for 'pragmatic reasons','the right, not the return' (personal communication, November 2005).

References

Agamben, G. (1999) *Remnants of Auschwitz: The Witness and the Archive,* Zone Books, New York
Ali, S. (2007) 'The remains of Kufr Hittin in danger of erasure', *Machsom*, 5 March 2007 «http://www.machsom.com»
Alpher, Y. (2002) 'Refugees forever?' (Originally posted on *Ramallah Online*) «http://www.artsmcgill.ca/MEPP/PRPN/papers/alpher»
Amadiume, I. and A. An-Na'im (eds) (2000) *The Politics of Memory: Truth, Healing and Social Justice,* Zed Books, London
Barda, Y. (2006) 'Peace-peace to the professional left', *Mitsad Sheni*, no. 14-5, 14-9
Beinin, J. (2004) 'No more tears: Benny Morris and the road back from liberal Zionism', *Middle East Report* 230
Benvenisti, M. (2000) *Sacred Landscape: The Buried History of the Holy Land since 1948,* University of California Press, Berkeley
Bronstein, E. (2005) 'The *Nakba* in Hebrew: Israeli-Jewish awareness of the Palestinian Catastrophe and internal refugees', in N. Masalha (ed.) *Catastrophe*

Remembered: Palestine, Israel and the Internal Refugees – Essays in Memory of Edward W. Said, Zed Books, London

Cohen, H. (2005) 'The State of Israel versus the Palestinian internal refugees', in N. Masalha (ed.) *Catastrophe Remembered: Palestine, Israel and the Internal Refugees. Essays in Memory of Edward W. Said*, Zed Books, London

Eldar, A. and I. Zertal (2004) *Lords of the Land: The Settlers and the State of Israel 1967–2004*, Kinneret, Zmora-Bitan, Dvir, Or Yehuda

Flapan, S. (1987) *The Birth of Israel: Myths and Reality*, Croom Helm, London

Forty, A. and S. Küchler (eds) (1999) *The Art of Forgetting*, Berg, Oxford

Goldberg, D. T. (2002) *The Racial State*, Blackwell, Oxford

Goldstone, K. (2000) '"Rewriting you": Researching and writing about ethnic minorities', in M. MacLachlan and M. O'Connell (eds), *Cultivating Pluralism: Psychological, Social and Cultural Perspectives on a Changing Ireland*, Oaktree Press, Dublin

Hanafi, S. (2005) 'Spacio-cide and biopolitics: The Israeli colonial conflict from 1947 to the Wall', in Michael Sorkin (ed.), *Against the Wall: Israel's Barrier to Peace*, The New Press, New York

Hirsch, M. (1997) *Family Frames: Photography, Narrative and Postmemory*, Harvard University Press, Cambridge, Mass.

hooks, b. (1991) *Yearning: Race, Gender and Cultural Politics*, Turnaround, London

'Issa, M. (2005) 'The *Nakba*, oral history and the Palestinian peasantry: The case of Lubya', in N. Masalha (ed.) *Catastrophe Remembered: Palestine, Israel and the Internal Refugees – Essays in Memory of Edward W. Said*, Zed Books, London

Jaggi, M. (2007) 'Life at a louder volume', *The Guardian*, 17 March 2007

Kannaneh, M. (2007) '"The agony of living so close to your home village": Internally displaced Palestinians in the Galilee', paper presented at the Institute of International Integration Studies, Trinity College Dublin, 13 April 2007

Katz, K. (2000) *Memory Encounters*, Alternative Information Centre, Jerusalem

Khouri, E. (1998 [2002]) *Bab El Shams*, Andalus Publishing House, Tel Aviv

Kimmerling, B. and J. Migdal (1994) *Palestinians: The Making of a People*, Harvard University Press, Cambridge, Mass.

Kuperman, Y. (2005) The *Nakba*, «www.machsom.com/article.php?id=2660»

Langer, L. (1991) *Holocaust Testimonies: The Ruins of Memory*, Yale University Press, New Haven

Lentin, R. (1980) *Sichot im Nashim Palestiniot* ('Conversations with Palestinian Women'), Mifras, Jerusalem

Lentin, R. (2002). 'If I forget thee… terms of diasporicity', in N. Abdo and R. Lentin (eds) *Women and the Politics of Military Confrontation: Palestinian and Israeli Gendered Narratives of Dislocation*, Berghahn Books, Oxford and New York

Lentin, R. (2004) '"No woman's law will rot this state": The Israeli racial state and feminist resistance', *Sociological Research Online*, Vol. 9, no. 3, «http://www.socresonline.org.uk/9/3/lentin.html»

Lentin, R. (2007a) 'The slopes of Mount Carmel: My (Israeli) Nakba story of the 1948 fall of Haifa', Phil Salmon Memorial Lecture, XVIth Auto/biography Summer Conference 2007, Trinity College, Dublin

Lentin, R. (2007b) 'The memory of dispossession, dispossessing memory: Israeli networks commemorating the *Nakba*', in K. Fricker and R. Lentin (eds) *Performing Global Networks*, Cambridge Scholars Publishing, Newcastle

Lorech, N. (1958) *The History of the War of Independence*, Massada, Tel-Aviv

Masalha, N. (2003) *The Politics of Denial: Israel and the Palestinian Refugee Problem*, Pluto, London

Masalha, N. (2005a) 'Introduction', in N. Masalha (ed.) *Catastrophe Remembered: Palestine, Israel and the Internal Refugees: Essays in Memory of Edward W. Said*, Zed Books, London

Masalha, N. (ed.) (2005b) *Catastrophe Remembered: Palestine, Israel and the Internal Refugees – Essays in Memory of Edward W. Said*, Zed Books, London

Morris, B. (1987) *The Birth of the Palestinian Refugee Problem, 1947–1949*, Cambridge University Press, Cambridge

Morris, B. (1994) *1948 and After: Israel and the Palestinians*, Clarendon Press, Oxford

Morris, B. (2000) *Jews and Arabs in Palestine / Israel 1936–1956*, Am Oved, Tel Aviv

Morris, B. (2002) 'A new exodus for the Middle East?' *Guardian*, 3 October

Morris, B. (2004) *The Birth of the Palestinian Refugee Problem Revisited*, Cambridge University Press, Cambridge

Nora, P. (1989) 'Between memory and history: *Les Lieux de Mémoire'*, *Representations*, no. 26, 7–24.

Pappe, I. (1988) *Britain and the Arab-Israeli conflict, 1948–51*, Macmillan in association with St Antony's College, Oxford, Basingstoke

Pappe, I. (2004) 'Response to Benny Morris, "Politics by other means" in the New Republic', *The Electronic Intifada*, 30 March 2004

Pappe, I. (2006) *The Ethnic Cleansing of Palestine*, Oneworld Publications, Oxford

Piterberg, G. (2001) 'Erasures', *New Left Review*, no. 10

Race Traitor (2005) Special Palestine issue (guest editor R. Lentin) «http://www.race traitor.org»

Ramazanoğlu, C. (2002) *Feminist Methodology: Challenges and Choices*, Sage, London

Sa'di, A. and L. Abu-Lughod (eds) (2007) *Nakba: Palestine, 1948 and the Claims of Memory*, Columbia University Press, New York

Said, E. and J. Mohr (1986) *After the Last Sky: Palestinian Lives*, Faber and Faber, London

Segev, T. (1991) *Hamillion Hashevi'i: HaIsraelim vehaShoah* (The Seventh Million: The Israelis and the Holocaust), Keter, Jerusalem

Shavit, A. (2004) 'Survival of the fittest: An interview with Benny Morris', *Ha'aretz*, 9 January 2004

Shlaim, A. (1988) *Collusion across the Jordan: King Abdullah, the Zionist movement and the Partition of Palestine*, Clarendon, Oxford

Silberstein, L. J. (2002) 'Problematising power: Israel's postzionist critics', *Palestine-Israel Journal*, Vol. 9, no. 3, 97–107

Tamari, S. (2002) 'Narratives of exile', *Palestine–Israel Journal* Vol. 9, no. 4

Va'ad Ha'akurim (2005) 'The internally displaced and the right of return' position paper, Committee for the Internally Displaced, Nazareth

Young, J. E. (2000) *At Memory's Edge: After-Images of the Holocaust in Contemporary Art and Architecture*, Yale University Press, New Haven

Zertal, I. (2000) 'From the people's hall to the wailing wall: A study in memory, fear and war', *Representations* no. 69, 96–126

Zertal, I. (2005) *Israel's Holocaust and the Politics of Nationhood*, Cambridge University Press, Cambridge, MA.

Conor McCarthy

12 The State, the Text and the Critic in a Globalized World: The Case of Edward Said

This chapter discusses the place and figuration of the state in the work of Edward Said. Said was best known as a literary critic, and as an advocate of the cause of the Palestinian people. Accordingly, I investigate Said's attitudes to the state, both in his literary-cultural work, and in his more directly political work on Palestine. However, as Said's work and ideas are easily separated and compartmentalized, these easy boundaries will be found to blur in significant ways.

Late in his career, Said published a massive retrospective collection of essays, *Reflections on Exile and Other Essays* (2000). For the first time in his career, Said brought together literary and theoretical essays, and essays touching directly on Palestine and the Middle East. He also wrote a lengthy introduction to the volume, entitled 'Criticism and Exile'. What we can take from this, and Said states it explicitly in that introduction, is that he sees criticism as intimately and constitutively related to exile (Said 2000, xiv–xv, xxx–iii–xxxiv). This also means that Said saw his conception of criticism as intimately related to his status as an exiled Palestinian.

One vector into this line of thinking is the relationship that Said figured between criticism and space. Exile is principally a matter of expulsion from and denial of a loved natal place. Said was interested in exiled writers such as Ovid, Dante and Joyce, but he also had critical exemplars who were exiles, most obviously and famously Erich Auerbach and Theodor Adorno (Said 1983: 1–30; 1994a: 47–64). How does this relate to the state?

The state is an important element in Said's work and yet its presence
is not theoretically uncomplicated. Said's interest in Antonio Gramsci
provides him with a model of the state, while it also offers him the
texture and density of Gramsci's thought on civil society. Gramsci also,
of course, gives Said a theory of the intellectual, a social category of
immense importance to him (Gramsci 1971: 3–23, 206–76). The com-
plication arises in his relationship to Michel Foucault, who offers Said
the idea of discourse, and of the disciplinary apparatus. So Said is interested in Foucault's ideas of the regularity, internal variation, and persistence of discourse, and in the power of discourse to produce its objects.
But Said was disturbed from early on by what he called the Borgesian
circularity of Foucault's thought (Said 1983: 246). Foucault did not
have a fully worked-out theory of the state, though he later wrote about
what he called 'governmentality' (Foucault 2002: 201–21). This is a
reference to a series of technologies or techniques of governance, but it
does not allow for a central dominating agency or source of power in
society. Foucault's theory of power, as Said was one of the first to point
out, does not seem to allow for emergent groups, or historical change.
It does not offer an explanation of why changes of power or discursive
regime occur. It is uninterested in why social groups or nations seek
power (Said 1983: 244–7). For Said, Foucault's thought risks becoming
a kind of quiescent functionalism. This is the reason for Said's interest in
Gramsci, and also, though it is hardly ever referred to, Nicos Poulantzas
(who was heavily influenced by Gramsci). Said often pointed out the
geographical or spatial vocabulary used by Gramsci in his theorization
of political struggle – his terminology of 'terrain', 'territory', 'blocs',
'region', the 'war of position' and the 'war of manoeuvre' (Said 2000:
453–73). Though he never showed much interest in the structuralist
Marxism of Louis Althusser and his circle, of which Poulantzas was a
prominent member, Said was clearly drawn to the Marxist critique of
Foucault in *State, Power, Socialism*. This book, Poulantzas's last, was
published just as Foucault was, in Said's eyes, abandoning his commitment to a radical politics, and was beginning to be lionized by conservative or technocratic intellectual currents on both sides of the Atlantic
(Poulantzas 1978). Poulantzas stresses the geographical aspect of the
state, and gives stress to intellectuals in ways that will have drawn Said's
interest (Poulantzas 1978: 54–62, 99–107). Equally, Said's essays on the
Occupied Territories are predicated on the capacity of the state to
enclose, regulate, divide, and dispose of space – described much in the

manner of Poulantzas. Both in his work on Palestine and in his criticism (and there is a very strong case to be made that his greatest work of 'postcolonial', or more accurately anti-colonial, criticism was precisely his work on Palestine, though most of his literary-critical admirers tend not to allude to that), Said is very keen to demonstrate that cultural artifacts take part in a contest waged in civil society for control of space and territory.

Said represented criticism and culture in spatial terms and in terms explicitly related to the state. In the opening essay of *The World, the Text, and the Critic,* Said explicitly suggests that there is a relationship between culture, especially a majority culture or 'high' culture, and the state (Said 1983: 9–12). Said notably understands culture as a hegemonic system, and as being, in a strong sense, *spatial.* He notes 'the power of culture by virtue of its elevated or superior position to authorize, to dominate, to legitimate, demote, interdict, and validate: in short, the power of culture to be an agent of, and perhaps the main agency for, powerful differentiation within its domain and beyond it too'. Further, culture is for Said 'a system of values *saturating* downward almost everything within its purview' (Said 1983: 9). Via Matthew Arnold, he identifies dominant culture with the state, 'insofar as culture is man's best self, and the State its realization in material reality' (Said 1983: 10). Thus the power of culture is effectively the power of the state. This interdependence of culture and the state means that 'to be for and in culture is to be in and for a State in a compellingly loyal way' (Said 1983: 11). Said offers a formulation that links culture, the state, and geography in significant ways:

> With this assimilation of culture to the authority and exterior framework of the State go as well such things as assurance, confidence, the majority sense, the entire matrix of meanings we associate with 'home', belonging and community. Outside this range of meanings – for it is the outside that partially defines the inside in this case – stand anarchy, the culturally disenfranchised, those elements opposed to culture and State: the homeless, in short (Said 1983: 11).

Said describes culture as a spatialized system, which defines itself partly by means of that which it rejects and extrudes, and suggests that the borders of culture are related to the borders of the state.

He is also suggesting that culture is a system of *authority.* Said was very interested in the idea of authority, which appears across the range of his work. For him, authority was a more analytically useful term than power. In his first major theoretical work, *Beginnings* (1975), Said discusses authority in terms that move between the idealist and the Nietzschean (Said 1985a: 83). But in *Orientalism*, he is more historical and materialist:

> There is nothing mysterious or natural about authority. It is formed, irradiated, disseminated; it is instrumental, it is persuasive; it has status, it establishes canons of taste and value; it is virtually indistinguishable from certain ideas it dignifies as true, and from traditions, perceptions and judgements it forms, transmits, reproduces. Above all, authority can, indeed must, be analyzed (Said 1978: 19–20).

Said is suggesting here that authority is something that is *made*, that it is not merely a matter of charisma, or a gift from God, or an emanation of Nature. Rather it is, to use a vocabulary favoured by Said, worldly or secular. It is related to human beings and to their institutions, such as the family, the professional organization or guild, the state, or the international political system.

Said deployed a pair of terms – *filiation* and *affiliation* – in his discussions of authority. For him, a filiative relation was one where authority or legitimacy derived from an inherited, natal, dynastic or hierarchical structure, tradition or idea. An affiliative relation was one that was forged by the subject for herself, by way of work or deliberate solidarity (Said 1983: 16–24). Seamus Deane, in discussing Said's thought on intellectuals, notes how these relationships can be figured as ones of distance or proximity (Deane 1997). In other words, Deane helps us to see that filiation and affiliation can be understood in spatial or geographical terms.

Tom Nairn, suggesting that Said was 'an intellectual earmarked for escape and successful metropolitan assimilation', noted that he instead 'has turned back, and tried to assume the burden of those left behind' (Nairn 1997: 168). Yet Said, though he was a member of the Palestine National Council for fourteen years, was never, in his own terms, a party-joiner or a true believer. He always maintained a scrupulous distance from the major Palestinian factions. Yet no one could doubt his intense commitment to the struggle. That the struggle was conducted in New York or London or Paris did not diminish the involvement or its seriousness. The theoretical point here is that Said's work moved in a kind of cycle between closeness and distance: to and from authority

(American, Israeli, Palestinian), to and from Palestinian nationalism, to and from Palestine itself. Deane argues, from Said's work and example, that this pattern is constitutive of the work of all real intellectuals. For Said, this metaphorical geography of intellectual performance has political and even epistemological implications. He sees mainstream intellectual work and culture as a spatialized system of filiative authority whose boundaries are coterminous with those of the state. But the relationship of knowledge to the state can be made yet more direct. In *Orientalism*, Said sets up a distinction between political and pure knowledge. He wishes to get beyond the general liberal consensus that putatively 'non-political' knowledge is objective and truthful. He points out that this idea clouds 'the highly if obscurely organized political circumstances obtaining when knowledge is produced' (Said 1978: 10). Arguing in a Gramscian vocabulary, Said suggests that civil society recognizes a gradation of political importance in the various fields of knowledge. He argues that this importance is related to the possible economic value of knowledge, but more to its closeness to sources of political power. Accordingly,

... because Britain, France, and more recently the United States are imperial powers, their political societies impart to their civil societies a sense of urgency, a direct political infusion as it were, where and whenever matters pertaining to their imperial interests abroad are concerned (Said 1978: 11).

So, rather than orientalism being a 'mere political subject matter or field that is reflected passively by culture', or a simple conspiracy to hold down the East, it is rather

a *distribution* of geopolitical awareness into aesthetic, scholarly, economic, sociological, historical, and philological texts; it is an *elaboration* not only of a basic geographical distinction (the world is made up of two unequal halves, Orient and Occident) but also of a whole series of interests which, by such means as scholarly discovery, philological reconstruction, psychological analysis, landscape and sociological description, it not only creates but also maintains; it *is*, rather than expresses, a certain *will* or *intention* to understand, in some case to control, manipulate, even to incorporate, what is a manifestly different ... world (Said 1978: 12).

In this passage, the terms *distribution*, *elaboration*, *will* and *intention* are all italicized for stress. Between them they display some of Said's most important influences – Foucault, Gramsci, Nietzsche, and the phenomenological tradition; however, the primary influence is Gramsci. What Said is trying to describe here is how a text of the most arcane aesthetic or formal qualities can function as part of a much broader ensemble headed up and deployed by explicitly political power.

In an essay written at the time of the publication of *Orientalism*, 'Reflections on American "Left" Literary Criticism', Said sets out what he considers to be the relationship between criticism and the primary source of authority in modernity: the state (Said 1983: 158–177). This essay is Said's most direct examination of the state anywhere in his work, but it also serves to delineate even more clearly the theoretical underpinnings of his writing about orientalism.

Drawing on Gramsci, he proceeds to suggest that the fundamental fact that most radical contemporary criticism ignores is that of the state – 'To a great extent, culture, cultural formations, and intellectuals exist by virtue of a very interesting network of relationships with the State's almost absolute power.' Yet ,

> nearly everyone producing literary or cultural studies makes no allowance for the truth that all intellectual or cultural work occurs somewhere, at some time, on some very precisely mapped-out and permissible terrain, which is ultimately contained by the State (Said 1983: 169).

Writing in 1978 or 1979, Said suggests that only a handful of people have approached this matter – he refers glancingly to Foucault, Nicos Poulantzas, and unnamed 'feminist critics'. He goes on to suggest that, if literature and art are to be understood in aestheticist or formalist terms as autonomous of the material world and of human institutions, then that autonomy of such pervasive forces as the state needs to be argued for and not simply assumed.

Said wishes to avoid the charge of reductionism, or of saying that 'it is all political'. But he does wish to argue, with Gramsci, that culture can be said to be connected to large intellectual endeavours, 'systems and currents of thought – connected in complex ways to doing things, to accomplishing certain things, to force, to social class and economic production, to diffusing ideas, values and world pictures' (Said 1983: 170). Said takes from Gramsci a number of elements. First, he is taken with Gramsci's point that no idea is produced merely for itself – rather thought is produced so that actions can be effective; it is 'diffused in order to be effective, persuasive, forceful' and 'a great deal of thought elaborates on what is a relatively small number of principal, directive ideas' (Said 1983: 170). The term 'elaborate' is specifically Gramscian, and Said notes two aspects to it. First, it means to *refine* or, literally, *to work out* a prior more powerful idea. Second, it means that culture is a quasi-autonomous extension of political society and, such is its density and complexity, it actually makes politics possible. This elaboration is what creates the strength and depth of civil society. For Said, culture or elaboration is what gives the State something to govern; it is the detail on which power depends for its focus. Said stresses that power flows through a whole array of social agencies, and that it is effective because it obtains consent – what Gramsci called *hegemony*. According to Said,

> Well before Foucault, Gramsci had grasped the idea that culture serves authority, and ultimately the national State, not because it represses and coerces, but because it is affirmative, positive, and persuasive. Culture is productive, Gramsci says, and this – much more than the monopoly of coercion held by the State – is what makes a national Western society strong, difficult for the revolutionary to conquer (Said 1983: 171).

What should the critic do in these circumstances? Said had a number of suggestions for critical action, but what I want to concentrate on here is what he referred to as *affiliation*. Here he is using the term somewhat differently from when he is talking about intellectuals and proximity and distance. Here Said is referring to 'that implicit network of peculiarly cultural associations between forms, statements, and other aesthetic elaborations on the one hand and, on the other, institutions, agencies, classes and amorphous social forces'. Affiliation, Said tells us, is what enables a text to maintain itself as a text: 'the author's status, the historical moment, conditions of publication, diffusion and reception, values drawn upon, values and ideas assumed, a framework of consensually held tacit assumptions, presumed background and so on' (Said 1983: 174). To study this is to recreate the bonds that tie texts to the world, bonds that Said says institutionalization and specialization have hidden (Said 1985b: 144).

At the same time that he was writing about criticism and the state as I have described, Said was writing *The Question of Palestine*. In this book, and in the crucial second chapter, 'Zionism from the Standpoint of its Victims', Said deploys his thinking about criticism, authority and the state to the clearest political ends. He argues that Zionism has been a highly successful project of state-construction for Jews, and, at one and the same time, a series of disasters for Palestinians. His point is that these are different aspects of the same process. Said counters the notion that Zionism is the expression of the timeless yearning of the Jewish people for self-determination in their homeland, with the historical results of the project of Zionism, on the ground, for the non-Jews of Palestine.

When Said begins *The Question of Palestine* by arguing that '[E]very idea or system of ideas exists *somewhere*', he is actually articulating in very direct terms his idea of the 'worldliness' of texts and discourse (Said 1992: 56). In an essay originally published in 1975, Said had argued powerfully for the *situatedness* or *circumstantiality* of texts. By this we can understand Said to be saying that texts are to be understood not only in historical terms, but also in a strong sense as events taking place in determinable locations. This is another instance of Said's geographical sense coming into play. This is linked to a powerful sense of texts as elements in a perpetual *agon*:

> ... all texts essentially dislodge other texts or, more frequently, take the place of something else. As Nietzsche had the perspicacity to see, texts are fundamentally facts of power, not of democratic exchange. They compel attention away from the world even as their beginning intention as texts, coupled with the inherent authoritarianism of the authorial authority (the repetition in this phrase is a deliberate emphasis on the tautology within all texts, since all texts are in some way self-confirmatory), makes for sustained power (Said 1983: 45–6).

In this light, it is not surprising that he then suggests that political ideas such as Zionism need to be examined historically in two ways:

> (1) *genealogically* in order that their provenance, their kinship and descent, their affiliation both with other ideas and with political institutions may be demonstrated; (2) as practical systems for *accumulation* (of power, land, ideological legitimacy) and *displacement* (of people, other ideas, prior legitimacy) (Said 1992: 57).

We need to note the spatial or geographical sense of the locatedness of ideas and discourse Said is putting forward here. Ideas must be investigated in terms of their historical emergence, persistence and effect, but they are also figured as occurring at points in a landscape that is at once discursive-idealist, material, and instrumental. The stress on 'accumulation' and 'displacement' suggests the Gramscian notion of ideas being produced to be 'effective, persuasive, forceful', while also tying ideas directly to struggles in the material world. What has been crucially important in the case of Zionism is that its legitimacy, as vested in the State of Israel, has mostly succeeded in erasing the political dispensation out of which it arose. When the state was founded in 1948, the combination of Israeli conquest, and the annexation of the West Bank and Gaza by Jordan and Egypt, left no location from which the idea of Palestinian community or nationhood might successfully be articulated. But Zionism's legitimacy dates back to the moment of its inception. We have to remember that Zionism took shape towards the end of the nineteenth century, at a time when the great European powers were engaged in the height of the imperial enterprise. Zionism emerged out of a context of virulent European antisemitism, but also out of a European intellectual milieu where the classification of overseas races and territories in hierarchical terms was considered canonical and natural. Accordingly, Zionism never spoke of itself unambiguously as a Jewish liberation movement, but rather as a Jewish project for colonial settlement in the Orient. For Said,

> To those Palestinian victims that Zionism displaced, it *cannot have meant anything by way of sufficient cause* that Jews were victims of European anti-Semitism and, given Israel's continued oppression of Palestinians, few Palestinians are able to see beyond their reality, namely, that once victims themselves, Occidental Jews in Israel have become oppressors (of Palestinian Arabs and Oriental Jews) (Said 1992: 69).

For Said, the fact that Palestinians have not been able to reconcile themselves to Zionism is testament to the degree to which Zionism appears to Palestinians only as a powerful colonial exclusionary practice.

Said is very clear in his sense that the power and effectiveness of the ideas of Zionism are related to the affiliation of that movement and ideology to Great Power politics, to the greatest imperial powers of the day. But he is also clear about the material base for the effectiveness of these ideas. Zionism, we can say, attached itself, or affiliated itself, to a great state, and this gave it legitimacy, force, legality, authority: it gave it values one associates with a state. When Said says that an idea or set of ideas must be analysed as a system of accumulation of power, land, legitimacy, and of displacement of other ideas, peoples, prior legitimacies, he is clear that this can take place because of the relation of that ideological system to authority and the state.

Said then examines the writings of Chaim Weizmann, the chief architect of the relationship between Britain and the Zionist movement and the first president of Israel. He detects in this writing a will to visualize and then implement a scheme for creating a network of realities – a language, a grid of colonies, a set of institutions – which would convert Palestine from its supposed state of 'neglect' into a Jewish state. This network would not so much attack the existing realities as ignore them, grow up beside them, overshadow them, eventually choke them like ivy. Weizmann, in his own text, modified the wording of the Balfour Declaration, which had promised to 'establish' a Jewish homeland in Palestine, by arguing for the 're-establishment' of a Jewish state there. Thus, the construction of the state would not be a supplanting or a breaking up of an existing society, but a reclamation, a redemption, a repetition, a realization of the Jewish hegemony over Palestine. The ancient state is repeated and realized by the new one, and so the Zionist narrative construes Israel as a return to an earlier state of affairs, and, thereby, as legitimate (Said 1992: 85–7).

Said argues therefore that the respective denials of each other by the Jewish and Palestinian communities are not comparable. The Zionist denial, he says, is strikingly paradoxical:

> Zionism aimed to create a society that could never be anything but 'native' (with minimal ties to a metropolitan centre) at the same time that it determined not to come to terms with the very natives it was replacing with new (but essentially European) 'natives' (Said 1992: 88).

The Palestinian denial, by contrast, is a much simpler thing, and this accounts to a degree for the weakness of the Palestinian position vis-à-vis Israel. According to Said, the Palestinians have failed to appreciate that Zionism is 'a policy of detail, not simply a general colonial vision' (Said 1992: 95). Palestine, to Zionism, was not simply the Promised Land, which is a highly abstract concept; it was also a territory that was to be known, surveyed, studied, planned for and worked on down to the last square metre. 'Another acre, another goat', Weizmann once wrote. Palestinians opposed Jewish settlement in general; they described it as foreign colonization (which the early Zionists admitted it to be); they said it was unfair to the natives, but they had no detailed counter-proposals or actions of their own, of a proximate or comparable kind.

The Palestinians have failed to understand the extraordinary Zionist drive not merely to take over land, but, in a real sense, to *produce* it. In his autobiography, Weizmann quotes from a 1917 document, an 'Outline of Program for the Jewish Resettlement of Palestine in Accordance with the Aspirations of the Zionist Movement'. Said finds the extraordinary language of this document a 'vision of a matrix of organizations whose functioning duplicates that of an army' (Said 1992: 96). The document speaks of 'opening' the country to 'suitable' Jews. For Said, this recalls a Foucauldian disciplinary apparatus. It is an army, after all, that 'opens' territory and prepares it for settlement, that supports immigration, shipping and supply, and, most important, that converts mere citizens to 'suitable' disciplined agents whose job it is to establish a presence on the land and to invest it with their structures, organizations and institutions. For Said,

> Just as an army assimilates ordinary citizens to its purposes by dressing them in uniforms, by exercising them in tactics and maneuvers, by disciplining everyone to its purposes – so too did Zionism dress the Jewish colonists in the system of Jewish labour and Jewish land, whose uniform required that only Jews were acceptable. The power of the Zionist army did not reside in its leader, nor in the arms it collected for its conquests and defence, but rather in the functioning of a whole system, a series of positions taken and held, as Weizmann says, in agriculture, culture, commerce, and industry (Said 1992: 96–7).[1]

But we need to note also the abstract implications of Said's analysis here, for this leads us back to his other writings on criticism, worldliness, and the state. First, he is offering us a powerful example of Zionism's ability to effect what he called in *Orientalism* 'a *distribution* of geopolitical awareness into aesthetic, scholarly, economic, sociological, historical, and philological texts'. We can now understand Zionism in the way we understand the discourse of orientalism: '[I]t *is*, rather than expresses, a certain *will* or *intention* to understand, in some cases to control, manipulate, even to incorporate, what is a manifestly different ... world' (Said 1978: 12). Further, we can go on to say, with Said and Gramsci, that what this amounts to is the marshalling of the *Yishuv* civil society into the elaboration of essentially military directive ideas. If Weizmann uses military metaphors to describe the colonial programme of Zionism, then it is worth remembering that an army is part of the repressive apparatus of a state, and also the ultimate defender of state sovereignty. Furthermore, its primary role is to control space – its task is the spatial projection of state power. But an army also functions, in Althusser's famous terms, as an 'ideological state apparatus': it turns citizens into citizen-soldiers; it inculcates in citizens values such as the paramount status of the state, its sovereignty, its territorial integrity, the legitimacy of its violence, the necessity of subsuming individuality in the corporate body that is the state (Althusser 1971: 125–86). Zionism, in this analysis, with its extraordinary powers of 'accumulation' and 'displacement', is only a particularly dramatic illustration of Said's radical reading of Arnoldian culture as a spatialized system of authority coterminous with the boundaries of the state.

In 1984, Said published a long review essay in the *London Review of Books*, under the title 'Permission to Narrate' (Said 1994b: 247–68). This was a lengthy consideration of a number of books arising out of the Lebanon war and the camp massacres, most notably of Noam Chomsky's *The Fateful Triangle* (1983). Underpinning Said's reading and analysis, however, was a linkage of *narrative* and *authority*. Hayden White, Said points out, argues that 'narrative in general, from the folk tale to the novel, from annals to the fully realized "history", has to do with the topics of law, legality, legitimacy, or, more generally, authority'. White also notes that, conventionally, the proper subject of historical narrative has been, following Hegel, the state (White 1987: 11–2). In this light, Said observes the competition and intertwining of the Israeli and Palestinian narratives, and, broadly speaking, his point is that the Israeli narrative had successfully interdicted the Palestinian one because the Israeli narrative was underpinned by the authority conferred by the possession of a state. Said argues that the target of 'Operation Peace for Galilee' was the 'coherent narrative direction towards self-determination' of the Palestinian people with their history, actuality and aspirations (Said 1994b: 249). Competing against the Zionist narrative of Jewish in-gathering, return and redemption, there has been the Palestinian narrative of dispersion, fragmentation, alienation, struggle, and hoped-for return. The Palestinian narrative, Said says, 'has never been officially admitted to Israeli history, except as that of "non-Jews", whose inert presence in Palestine was a nuisance to be ignored or expelled' (Said 1994b: 254). With the military destruction of the Palestine Liberation Organization in 1982, the narrative of the transformation of Palestinians from peasants to refugees to revolutionaries 'has... come to an abrupt stop, curling about itself violently' (Said 1994b: 252).

A crucial issue here for Said is the discourse of 'terrorism', put so firmly on the international agenda by the Reagan Administration, and now back in a new even more powerful inflection since the attacks on New York and Washington in 2001, and which is capable of both absorbing and de-legitimating a narrative such as that of the Palestinians:

> ... terrorism is the biggest and yet for that reason the most precise of concepts. This is not at all to say that terrorism does not exist, but rather to suggest that its existence has occasioned a whole new signifying system as well. Terrorism signifies... in relation to 'us', the alien and gratuitously hostile force. It is destructive, systematic, and controlled. It is a web, a network, a conspiracy run from Moscow... As such it can be used retrospectively... or prospectively... to justify everything 'we' do, and to de-legitimize as well as dehumanize everything 'they' do. The very indiscriminateness of terrorism, actual and described, its tautological and circular character, is anti-narrative. Sequence, the logic of cause and effect as between oppressors and victims, opposing pressures – all these vanish inside an enveloping cloud called 'terrorism' (Said 1994b: 257).

The point here is that societies, nations, and oppressed groups need to achieve a kind of narrative coherence in order to obtain socio-political prominence and legitimacy. The most powerful mechanism yet devised for instituting or institutionalizing this narrative is the state. Thus Zionism struggled to create a state in Palestine, and the Palestinians struggled to create a rival state-in-exile, or state-in-waiting, or, under the severely compromised Oslo process, a 'state-in-Jericho-first'. Further, the power to regulate narratives possessed by established states is, at its most extreme, that of designating groups or ideas that fall outside of the coercive or representational capacity of the state as 'terrorist' in the manner Said describes. If there is a linkage between states and narrative, then an important weapon in the arsenal of a state is the capacity to block rival narratives. It was not for nothing that the Israeli Defence Forces confiscated the Palestinian archives in Beirut in 1984. But in discourse, the blockage comes in the form of the appellation of 'terrorism'. 'Terrorism' is that which has ceased to be rational, logical, sequential, historical, causal, linear. Terrorism, one might say to turn full circle, is that which is outside culture and the state, 'the homeless, in short' (Said 1983: 11).

To conclude, the state is important to Said in a number of ways. First, he was, of course, at different times an advocate of both the two-state solution to the Israel–Palestine conflict, and of the bi-national state solution. Said famously said that he wished to argue for the setting up of a Palestinian state, and that he would be its first critic. Allowing for the greatly reduced and non-sovereign character of the Palestinian Authority, Said was one of its very first, and most potent, critics. Second, Said also tried to theorize, in ways from which we can still learn, the relationship between cultural production, intellectual activity, and the state.

This chapter has sought to trace the continuities and interrelations between Said's powerfully spatialized ideas of culture, authority and the state, and to show how he worked out, in cultural criticism and theory, ideas that would underpin his political writing and give it much of its strength and originality. In ethico-political terms, Said was never less than certain that the position of the intellectual was to be on or attendant to the margins of the state, to all that falls outside of it or that is delegitimated by it. Said can be accused of having romanticized his own exile or that of some of his intellectual heroes. But he was also clear about the capacity of states to produce that exile. His position was one of constant tension with the state, of distance and closeness, of the need to know its workings and to feel its texture, but also of the ethical requirement to examine the fragments left behind by the historical evolution and the geographical spread of the state. Said greatly admired Theodor Adorno's performance of exilic intellectualism, and Adorno aphoristically sums up Said's position with regard to both criticism and the state in the *Minima Moralia*: 'it is part of morality not to be at home in one's home' (Adorno 1978: 39).

Note

1   It is worth noting here Said's prescience in highlighting the geographical or spatial elements in Foucault's thought: he refers to Foucault's interview with geographers in *Herodote* (1980), and anticipates the work of writers such as Edward Soja (1989), Stuart Elden (2001) and Derek Gregory (2004), as well as Foucault's concerns in his 1970s Collège de France lectures (2003, 2007).

References

Adorno, T. (1978) *Minima Moralia: Reflections from Damaged Life*, Verso, London
Althusser, L. (1971) *Lenin and Philosophy and Other Essays*, New Left Books, London
Chomsky, N. (1983) *The Fateful Triangle: the United States, Israel and the Palestinians*, Pluto, London

Deane, S. (1997) 'The pathos of distance: Edward Said and the intellectual class', *Suitcase: A Journal of Transcultural Traffic*, Vol. 2, nos. 1 and 2

Elden, S. (2001) *Mapping the Present: Heidegger, Foucault and the Project of a Spatial History*, Continuum, London

Foucault, M. (1980) 'Questions of geography', *Power/Knowledge: Selected Interviews and Other Writings*, Harvester Wheatsheaf, Hemel Hempstead

Foucault, M. (2002) 'Governmentality', *Essential Works of Michel Foucault 1954–1984 Volume 3: Power*, Penguin, London

Foucault, M. (2003) *Society Must Be Defended: Lectures at the Collège de France 1975–1976*, Picador, London

Foucault, M. (2007) *Security, Territory, Population: Lectures at the Collège de France 1977–1978*, Palgrave Macmillan, Basingstoke

Gramsci, A. (1971) *Selections from the Prison Notebooks*, Lawrence and Wishart, London

Gregory, D. (2004) *The Colonial Present: Afghanistan, Palestine, Iraq*, Blackwell, Oxford

Nairn, T. (1997) *Faces of Nationalism: Janus Revisited*, Verso, London

Poulantzas, N. (1978) *State, Power, Socialism*, Verso, London

Said, E. (1978) *Orientalism*, Pantheon, New York

Said, E. (1983) *The World, the Text, and the Critic*, Faber and Faber, London

Said, E. (1985a) *Beginnings: Intention and Method*, Columbia University Press, New York

Said, E. (1985b) 'Opponents, audiences, constituencies and community', in H. Foster (ed.) *Postmodern Culture*, Pluto Press, London

Said, E. (1992) *The Question of Palestine*, Vintage, London

Said, E. (1994a) *Representations of the Intellectual*, Pantheon, New York

Said, E. (1994b) *The Politics of Dispossession: The Struggle for Palestinian Self-Determination 1969–1994*, Chatto and Windus, London

Said, E. (2000) *Reflections on Exile and Other Essays*, Harvard University Press, Boston

Soja, E. (1989) *Postmodern Geographies: The Reassertion of Space in Critical Social Theory*, Verso, London

White, H. (1987) *The Content of the Form: Narrative Discourse and Historical Representation*, Johns Hopkins University Press, Baltimore and London

Anaheed Al-Hardan

13 Understanding the Present Through the Past: Between British and Israeli Discourses on Palestine

'This country of Palestine belongs to you and to me. It is essentially ours. It was given to the Father of Israel in the words "Walk the land in the length of it and in the breadth of it, for I will give it unto thee"... We mean to walk through Palestine in the length and the breadth of it because that land has been given unto us' – Archbishop of York, in a speech given at the inaugural meeting of the Palestine Exploration Fund, 22 June 1865 (Moscrop 2002: 70–71).

'The land of Israel is the open Bible, the written testimony, the identity and right of the Jewish people... I say these things to you because they are the essence of my Jewish consciousness, and of my belief in the eternal and unimpeachable right of the people of Israel to the Land of Israel' – Israeli Prime Minister Ariel Sharon, in a speech given at the United Nations General Assembly, 15 September 2005 (Sharon 2005).

I have chosen the two quotes above in order to begin with a comparative illustration of my guiding premise that the contemporary discourse on Palestine, as recycled at the highest echelons of world power, is marked by a conspicuous genealogical resilience and continuity. This choice is also driven by the quotes' betrayal, despite their separation by 140 years, of a consistent relationship between 'non-vision and vision within vision' (Althusser and Balibar 1997: 21) that necessitates my own Palestinian Arab ontological displacement and erasure, dual when gendered, which is only evident if rescued from the margins by the woman-narrator of an embodied, 'situated knowledge' (Haraway 1991: 190) (dis)located across 'our' Palestine of 1865 and the 'land of Israel' of 2005.[1]

236

The three-dimensional axis around which the 'Question of Palestine' has been framed – since the British occupation and final geopolitical delimitation of the three Ottoman sub-provinces that came to constitute Palestine, namely, '(1) land; (2) people (3) political sovereignty of the people and the land of Palestine' (Abu-Lughod 2001: 193–4) – continues to be the central tenet around which the protracted colonial and its correlative anti-colonial struggle on the ground unfolds. However, what is of particular interest is the discourse on Palestine woven around the continued *a priori* justification of colonial-settler Zionist domination of the land between the Mediterranean Sea and the Jordan River by the pertinent international power players, and, in particular, how this discourse resonates in a commonsense, taken-for-granted way with Anglophone public audiences, marked by distinct '*amnesiac* histories of colonialism' (Gregory 2004: 9).

The contemporary facets of this discourse on Palestine revolve around exclusive colonial-settler Zionist Jewish claims to the land, differentiated on a gradation of control that ranges from 'covert' political exclusion within the State of Israel's 1948/49 armistice lines, to – the Gaza Strip's novel political status notwithstanding – overt military rule within the state's 1967 armistice line (Cook 2006). Furthermore, these exclusive claims 'to complementary noble missions', which 'embody every conceivable cliché about pioneers, ingenious scientists, intrepid humanitarians, and noble fighters' (Said 2001: 4) within Israel's 1948/49 armistice lines, become necessary, in terms of containing '[terrorists], fanatics, irrational murderers, contemptible hypocrites' (Said 2001: 4) within its 1967 armistice lines.[2] And, finally, the outcome of this discourse, the international sanction of colonial-settler Zionist Jewish dominion (the exclusive beneficiaries of Zionism) of an indigenous Palestinian Arab population whose total number between the Mediterranean and the Jordan is now more than that of Israeli Jews (Brown et al. 2005).

With these considerations in mind, I explore specific facets of this discourse created around the *a priori* justifications for the domination of Palestine, as elaborated by high-ranking British government officers during the early years of British rule, when the civilian administration came under Colonial Office jurisdiction in 1921 and the 'mandate' with which Britain would rule over Palestine, or colonialism acting on behalf of the principle of the 'sacred trust of civilization' under the guise of self-rule tutelage (Northedge 1986), was in the process of being approved and affirmed by the League of Nations in 1922, coming into force a year later. This allows for a comparative assessment of this discourse in relation to its contemporary counterpart, in the form of speeches given on international political platforms, which justify and reconfirm the post-*Intifadat al-Aqsa* guiding cornerstones of Israeli policy. This comparative assessment, I argue, reveals how the contemporary discourse on Palestine, as reiterated at the highest echelons of world power, is, *mutatis mutandis*, heir to a discourse born out of a specific Western European historical experience and concurrent world-view. Its *a priori* justifications for the domination of Palestine were manifested physically and materially with the British occupation of 1917, and it continues to serve as an *a priori* justification of exclusive colonial-settler Zionist Jewish rule over the same land at the expense of the indigenous Palestinian population.

The British in Palestine: the Balfour Declaration and the British 'mandate'

The British discourse that sought to justify its symbolic and strategic domination of Palestine, like the discourse of its Israeli successor, was not born *ex nihilo*. Though exploring its antecedents is beyond the scope of this chapter, it is worth noting that the British entered Palestine in 1917 as the bearers of a complex historical cultural, economic and political process that began to take shape over the previous 500 years in Western Europe. The most relevant parts of this process are the religio-cultural sixteenth-century Christian Reformation-led shift in emphasis on the Old Testament, the Covenant, the Restoration, the Second Coming, and so forth (Sherif 1983; Suleiman 1995); the politico-economic 'transmutations' that led up to the 'age of technicality', which in turn culminated in the Industrial and French Revolutions (Hodgson 1977; Hourani 1991); and their spread economically and politically, as Europeans made their early-nineteenth-century *de facto* presence a reality in and around the Ottoman Empire (Hourani 1991).

Born out of these multi-dimensional historical processes, the British entry into Palestine used an already constituted repertoire of an orientalist 'corporate institution for dealing with the Orient' (Said 2003: 3) and, by extension, Palestine. This repertoire, at the same time cultural and political, was marked by an internal consistency and corresponded to the reality of the gradual encroachment on the Ottoman Empire and final domination of its former Arab provinces (Said 2003). In this repertoire, Palestine, unlike the Franco-British post-war Arab colonies of Iraq,

Syria, Lebanon, and Transjordan, occupied an exceptional place, as the 'Holy Land' whose Arab presence in the present tense had already been temporally erased in favour of a Western European post-Reformation Judeo-Christian biblical understanding of a past that violently displaced, and severed links with, the present lived reality (Silberman 1991; Davidson 1996), and in whose patrimony's service the British would later justify their symbolic and strategic domination of Palestine.

It is within this context that British officials' *a priori* justification of the 1917 Balfour Declaration must be understood. This justification became the *raison d'être* of Britain's colonial rule via a 'mandate', granted at the 1920 San Remo Conference and eventually coming into force in 1923 (Wasserstein 1991). The overlooking of the 'existing non-Jewish communities of Palestine' (Lacquer and Rubin 2001, 16), inherent in the Balfour Declaration, has been extensively elaborated in terms of negating the indigenous Palestinian Arab population, both politically and culturally, in relation to the fulfilment of a colonial-settler Jewish 'national home' via the British *chose jugée* of Zionism (Khalidi 1996: 22–23; Abu-Lughod 2001: 201).

What is of interest is the discourse created around this Declaration. When read in terms of a structured system of meaning, embodied in, and reinforced by, language implicated in non-discursive practices of power (Foucault 2005), this discourse reveals its own world of meaning that was implicated in the creation of a sense of mission and purpose to British rule. This was grounded in the exceptional place of Palestine in a biblical world-view, and shrouded in pretences of universality for the purposes of enforcing this Declaration.[3]

Thus, for example, in minutes of a meeting that British Prime Minister David Lloyd George had with an Indian Muslim deputation that came to Britain in order to attend the Near Eastern Conference in March 1921, Lloyd George elaborated various aspects of this discourse. The deputation, consisting of Muslim members of the empire who had sacrificed for, and taken part in, the 'Great War', pressed the prime minister on, amongst other 'Muslim'-related issues, Britain's policy with regard to Palestine in relation to the Balfour Declaration. The prime minister was clear when he stated that:

> On Palestine, I do not think we can alter the policy we have adopted there. It is a very mixed population, it is of course traditionally a great Jewish country, and although the Arabs are undoubtedly the majority and should have their vote in the Government of the country, I think in

view of the great international place which Palestine holds – it holds a different position from any other country in the world, it has a great international position where Jews, Mohammedans and Christians meet, all regard it as a sacred country, and they got their sacred shrines there – therefore, Palestine is in a very different position either to Mesopotamia or Constantinople (PRO, CO, 737 4, 28 April 1921).

In this tautological logic, the Balfour Declaration, that, both in its wording and in its implementation, negates the indigenous inhabitants of Palestine, is symbolically justified primarily in terms of Palestine *traditionally* being a 'great Jewish country'. The fact that this 'tradition' is specific to a Western European Judeo-Christian biblical world-view, which marginalizes both a historical and contemporary Arab Muslim and Eastern Christian presence, is compensated by an acknowledgement of their 'majority position'. This is immediately displaced, however, in view of Palestine's exceptional 'international place' that is not and cannot be universal, since the Declaration clearly spells out the establishment of a 'Jewish national home' in view of this very *tradition* that Lloyd George refers to. When translated materially, therefore, in terms of Britain's strategic location as the protector of this exceptional 'universal' patrimony, or, 'in view of its international character,' as Lloyd George later continues, 'we cannot change our policy and make it an Arab state' (PRO, CO, 732 4, 28 April 1921).

Lloyd George's remarks therefore make necessary rhetorical concessions to the 'Arabs' and the derogatory 'Mohammedans', that are not concessions at all, but a reinforcement of British rule in view of Palestine's exceptional place in relation to his pretences of a universal 'tradition'. By contrast, Secretary of State for the Colonies Winston Churchill, a month after the above meeting, was not so generous in his public rhetorical concessions. As the jurisdiction over the British Arab colonies was passed to the Colonial Office in 1921, Churchill travelled to Egypt, where he set the basic cornerstones of British post-war policies with regard to the newly acquired spoils, and from where he continued onto Palestine (Wasserstein 1991).

In an address to members of the Arab Executive Committee, an organization set up as the representative of the Palestinian Arab Muslim and Christian population, but not granted the same representative status as that granted to the Zionist Organization under the 'mandate' with which Britain would rule over Palestine (Wasserstein 1991; Pappe 2004), Churchill directly alluded to the British strategic direct continuity of the very same world-view. Furthermore, this world-view was disguised in the same symbolic pretences of an international, universal 'tradition' set out by Lloyd George, in relation to the fulfilment of the colonial-settler enterprise inherent in the Balfour Declaration, under the auspices of British protection, and thus provided an *a priori* justification of British rule.

In his address, Churchill made it clear that with regard to the Balfour Declaration

> It must therefore be regarded as one of the facts definitely established by the triumphant conclusion of the great war [sic]. It is upon this basis that the Mandate has been undertaken by Great Britain; it is upon this basis that the Mandate will be discharged; I have no doubt that it is on this basis that the Mandate will be accepted by the Council of the League of Nations (PRO, CO 733 2, 8 April 1921).

The establishment of a 'Jewish national home' inherent in the Balfour Declaration, therefore, is a 'fact' in whose service Britain has undertaken its altruistic rule over Palestine. That this fact, articulated by both Balfour and Churchill, may be far removed from the historical experience or world-view of the members of the Arab Executive Committee is irrelevant. Furthermore, it is precisely because of this fact and, more importantly, Britain's relationship to this fact, in terms of fulfilling a patrimony grounded in a British world-view, that Britain intended to undertake its rule. Only once this fact was established by its enforcement on the ground would Britain have fulfilled its truly noble mission. Finally, that this fact was inevitable, desirable and necessary, despite the prejudices of an irrationally intransigent 'native' bunch that stood between Britain, indeed, the world, and the fulfilment of a 'universally' desired fact born out of an equally 'universal tradition', is confirmed by the 'international' character of the League of Nations. The latter, alongside Britain, allowed British rule over Palestine in the form of a 'mandate' precisely because of Britain's pivotal role in terms of fulfilling a 'universal' promise enshrined in a 'mandate' that incorporated the Balfour Declaration.

The 'benefits' of British rule

British government officials created a discourse around the Balfour Declaration that sought to justify symbolically British rule over Palestine by resorting to the exceptional place of Palestine as the 'Holy Land' in the specifically British post-Reformation Judeo-Christian biblical world-view. This discourse strategically justified British rule in terms of Britain's pivotal role in the fulfilment of a 'Jewish national home' in the service of this world-view. A further facet of the discourse on Palestine, which equally cemented an *a priori* justification of British rule, was Britain's paternalistic *mission civilatrice*, in all but name, which sought, along with its colonial-settler Zionist *protégé*, to selflessly bring light to an otherwise Conrad-like 'heart of darkness'.

Thus, in the same minutes of the meeting between Lloyd George and the Indian deputation, Lloyd George unambiguously stated that, with regard to the newly acquired spoils generally:

> As to the Arab states, some of them are absolutely free from control. I do not think however that any responsible Arab Chiefs would like to try the experiment of being absolutely without the support of a Great Western Power in Mesopotamia or Syria. They are people who have not for hundreds of years had control of those States. They are not a coherent people, they are tribal… if we withdraw altogether – which we have been thinking of doing many a time, and we are by no means wedded to remaining in Mesopotamia, and if we knew that there was a powerful Arab ruler who would keep the country together and protect life and property and commerce there, we are not in the least concerned to remain there – what we are afraid of is that the moment we withdraw, these tribes will be at each other's throats; they owe no allegiance to each other. If they accepted some great Arab Chief and recognized him as the ruler, I think he would be the last man in the world to ask us to clear out. He would want our support, and I have seen some of these Arab Chiefs, very able men, and never have they asked us to clear out altogether; they have asked us to remain and give them advice and such support as is necessary, and I have no doubt that support will be required for a good many years to come […] We have given them free choice of their own ruler (PRO, CO, 737 4, 28 April 1921).

Lloyd George is reiterating a political vision of reality, which both created and served a relationship of British hegemony over the post-war Arab colonies, grounded in 'the essence of Orientalism… the ineradicable distinction between Western superiority and Oriental inferiority' (Said 2003: 42) in relation to the Arabs in general. Churchill, however, was more specific when translating this to Palestine in particular, when he stated that,

If a national home for the Jews is to be established in Palestine as we hope to see it established, it can only be by a process which at every stage wins its way on its merits and carries with it increasing benefits and prosperity and happiness to the people of the country as a whole. And why should this not be so? Why should this not be possible? You can see with your own eyes in many parts of the country the work which has already been done by Jewish Colonies; how sandy wastes have been reclaimed and thriving farms and orangeries planted in their stead. It is quite true that they have been helped by money from outside, whereas your people have not had a similar advantage, but surely these funds of money largely coming from outside and being devoted to the increase of the general prosperity of Palestine is one of the very reasons which should lead you to take a wise and tolerant view of the Zionist movement (PRO, CO 733 2, 8 April 1921).

In contrast to Lloyd George, who limits the 'benefits' of colonial rule to Britain, Churchill extends this Kiplingesque 'white man's burden' rhetoric to a vision of the fulfilment of Britain's *imperio in imperium*, the emblem of the white pioneer settlers bringing 'Reason', 'Truth', 'Liberty' and 'Progress' to an otherwise uncharted wilderness that stands in a dichotomous opposition to all these enlightened, indeed, *Enlightenment,* values. This should not only be accepted by the 'native' population, but rather *ought* to be accepted as it is synonymous with modernity, progress, civilization and so forth. And if it is not accepted, it is only testament to their 'backward' minds that are incapable of adopting 'wise' and 'tolerant' views. In the same visit, Churchill also addressed representatives of the Zionist Commission, reiterating the same underlying logic when he informed them that Zionism 'will also bring with it prosperity and contentment and advancement to the Arab population of this country' (PRO, CO 733 2, 8 April 1921).

It is therefore not only Palestine's exceptional place in Britain's world-view, and Britain's strategic responsibility in terms of the fulfilment of this world-view in relation to the Balfour Declaration, that justify British rule over Palestine. Britain's rule is also justified owing to Palestine's place in relation to the 'white man's burden', in the necessarily good and just cause that the British-Zionists will deliver to the 'natives' in their *mission civilatrice*. In fact, these *a priori* justifications can be read in relation to each other. Given that Palestine has a special place in Britain's world-view, which by extension obligates the latter to rule over Palestine in order to fulfil this world-view's patrimony in relation to the Balfour Declaration, it is necessarily also the mission of those who hold this world-view to take part in the divinely-ordained 'restoration' of the ancient (biblical) glories of the 'Holy Land', whose present reality is testament to an equally divinely-ordained 'desolation' (Silberman 1991), at the hands of 'orientals', once again rubber-stamping British rule.

If the discourse created around the *a priori* justifications of British rule over Palestine was indeed part of a tragic, yet closed, chapter in human history, one would be extremely tempted to keep this past locked away in the archives of the Colonial Office, relegated to an unfortunate, yet definitely sealed, episode, never to be repeated.

In retrospect, however, the catastrophe that befell Palestine and the Palestinians in 1948, and that is ongoing well into the present, with no end in sight, is testament to the force of the crude 'imaginative geography' (Said 2003: 73) which, in pitting 'West' against 'East', hermetically sealed off Palestine's exceptional place in Britain's world-view from both the contemporary and the historical Arab Muslim, Eastern Christian and Judeo-Islamic reality. This imaginative geography, whose discursive cartographies were materially and physically imposed after World War One, continues to map the world today, when lines of struggle are (re)drawn between 'us' and 'them' in a war against, we are told, an abstract notion of 'terror' that signifies 'them'.

In retrospect, too, the symbiotic relationship between the discursive colonization of Palestine, which ontologically marginalized Palestinians, and the non-discursive practices of power implicated in the colonization of Palestine, which eventually did erase both Palestinians and Arab Palestine from Palestine, also bears witness to the power of these imaginative geographies and the untold horrors that they have wrought upon Palestinians and Palestine for the past six decades.

I now turn to this ongoing relationship, as manifested by the colonial-settler Israeli state, which, in two instalments became the *de facto* successor to British rule over the whole of Palestine.

Israeli rule in Palestine: the Jewish State and the non-Jewish Palestinians

The arrival of former Israeli Prime Minister Ariel Sharon at the United Nations General Assembly in September 2005, and his successor's arrival at the American Congress eight months later, provided both men with an opportunity to outline to the international community and the seat of world power the post-*Intifadat Al-Aqsa* guiding cornerstones of the Israeli state's policy with regards to the people and the land under its dominion.

This policy began to be manifested physically during the Intifada, and is ongoing in several ways. It includes the building of the fence-cum-wall around the West Bank of the Jordan River, while carving the land into three disconnected cantons under military rule with an extensive system of military control in and between these areas; the withdrawing of the Israeli settlers and military from the Gaza Strip, while retaining military control over the area; and, finally, the further political and civil clampdown on the non-Jewish Palestinians living as non-citizen 'citizens' within the Jewish state's 1948/49 armistice lines. Examples of the latter are the 'Black October' shootings of thirteen unarmed protestors, the criminalization of inter-Palestinian marriages across fictitious Israeli one-way 'borders' (Cook 2006), and the recent political persecution of Azmi Bishara (Bishara 2007; Cook 2007; Pappe in this volume). What interests me here is the discourse on Palestine that revolves around the *a priori* justifications of these policies, especially those in direct genealogical continuity with their predecessor discourse, and which translate materially into the domination of Palestinians living under a gradation of exclusive colonial-settler Zionist Jewish rule between the Mediterranean and the Jordan.

Sharon's 2005 speech before the United Nations General Assembly began by laying a territorial claim, implicitly based on a sense of historical continuity, to Jerusalem, 'the capital of the Jewish people for over 3,000 years, and the undivided and eternal capital of the State of Israel' (Sharon 2005). In this one statement Palestinians are entirely dropped out of history. Moreover, in what is essentially a spiritual claim followed by a national-territorial claim, addressed to representatives of the political international community in English and in New York, Sharon is directly appealing to a specific Western European Judeo-Christian biblical world-view which serves ontologically to erase both a past and a present Palestinian presence in a Jerusalem that is strictly and exclusively posited in relation to *the* 'Promised Land'.

He continues his speech by quoting 'G-d's commandment to our forefather Abraham ... and the wanderings of the children of Israel in the desert, led by Moses, on their journey to the promised land, the land of Israel' (Sharon 2005). Sharon then, in logical succession, goes on to state that he was 'born in the Land of Israel', that same land of the Bible that he had already conjured. In this time-space collapse, the audience is taken from a biblical past, whether real or imagined (Whitelam 1996; Thompson 2000), to the twentieth century of Sharon's birth, in which the history of both the Palestinians and Arab Palestine, absent from this discourse, is erased from the annals of history for the purpose of justifying Israeli rule, and in which the Israeli state is posited not as the colonial-settler enterprise that it is, but rather as the natural continuation of biblical prophecies.

Using this same logic, Sharon continues along the same biblical lines, explaining to the audience that the withdrawal of the settlers and the military from the Gaza Strip is tantamount to 'relinquishing any part of our forefathers' legacy [which] is heartbreaking, as difficult as the parting of the Red Sea'. In this picture that Sharon paints, his 'Promised Land', in itself an annex to the Western European Judeo-Christian 'Holy Land', not only grants colonial-settler Zionist Jewish rule legitimacy, but, more importantly, allows him to invite the audience to empathize with the pain he feels, not so much in ending a military occupation, but in withdrawing settlers, deemed illegal under international law, and moving back the Israeli military beyond the prison bars of the Gaza Strip. The closing of the circle of this logic is the appearance of the Palestinians in Sharon's speech, not as a people indigenous to a land that his speech has thus far immersed in a biblical world-view in which there is clearly no room for anyone else but Zionism, but as 'neighbours', to whom lip service is paid in the form of 'respect' and 'no aspirations to rule over' (Sharon 2005).

The 'benefits' of Israeli rule

A few months later, Sharon's successor, Ehud Olmert, also firmly posited the *raison d'être* of Zionist rule within this discursive rhetoric of the 'Promised Land', 'Holy Land', etc., when he stated, 'I believed, and to this day still believe, in our people's eternal and historic right to this entire land' (Olmert 2006). Olmert further elaborates to his American Congress audience on the 'benefits' of Israeli rule by resorting, on the one hand, to the good and brave 'pioneer settlers versus savage natives', and on the other, to 'democracy and freedom versus tyranny and hate' dichotomies that in the context of the 'war on terror', both evoking deep resonances in his audience.

Olmert first discusses the benefits of Israeli rule within Israel's 1948/49 armistice lines, when he outlines the commonalities between the State of Israel and the United States, grounded in the 'profound belief in the importance of freedom and a common pioneering spirit deeply rooted in optimism. It was the energetic spirit of our pioneers that enabled our two countries to implement the impossible: to build cities where swamps once existed and to make the desert bloom' (Olmert 2006). Implicit in this story is an association of 'not just the good, the true and the beautiful, but a definite human image of the White settler hewing civilization out of the wilderness, an image that itself drew upon cultural sources in American Puritanism (with its strong philo-Semitic biases), in the nineteenth-century adventure narrative by Europeans about Africa and Latin America, and in the great modernist epics of the self-made hero' (Said 2001: 5–6). This discourse, with its *mission civilatrice* undertones, like that of its predecessor, first erases any 'natives' that might have existed in the past tense, and also provides an *a priori* justification of the continued erasure of these very people in the present tense, culminating in the justification of the continued domination of the people and the land, whom the bearers-of-civilization justly deserve to rule by virtue of their exceptional efforts and success. In Olmert's words, '[we] have succeeded in creating an Oasis of hope and opportunity in a troubled region' (Olmert 2006).

Within Israel's 1967 armistice lines, Olmert provides the *a priori* justifications for Israeli policies by positing the Palestinian struggle against the military occupation within the context of the 'war on terror': 'the enemy turned even more inhumane due to the scourge of suicide terrorism... Israel, America, Europe and democracies across the globe unfortunately face this enemy' (Olmert 2006). Olmert's dichotomous reasoning is not only explicit in its construction of the Palestinian as the 'savage other' in the context of the 'war on terror' (Mullin 2007). He also firmly aligns Israel's military occupation with the democratic, and thus civilized and modern, American and European 'us' in contradistinction to 'them', the Palestinian ('Islamic') 'terrorist', 'tyrannical' and 'backward' world. He continues with this identification, when he states, 'our countries do not just share the experience and pain of terrorism, we share the commitment and resolve to confront the brutal terrorists that took these innocent people from us' (Olmert 2006). These 'brutal terrorists', in this logic, are in contrast to 'us', justifying

Israeli military rule in the Occupied Palestinian Territories, because
they raise their children in 'a culture of hate', and they need to 'replace
a culture of hate with an outlook of peace' (Olmert 2006), which only
the free, modern, and democratic world can deliver to 'them'.

Thus, in Sharon's and Olmert's world-views, like their British pre-
decessors', claims to Palestine as a land are primarily articulated along
the lines of the 'Holy Land' in order to provide an *a priori* justification
for colonial-settler Israeli rule. Within this biblical discourse, there are
common themes between British and Israeli discourses on Palestine,
especially in relation to the appearance of the civilization-bearers
restoring this exceptional wilderness, whose restoration is divinely
ordained, making it a different wilderness to any other. By virtue of the
changed historical and material circumstances on the ground, the
present-day discourse, which serves to provide an *a priori* justification
for the continued colonial-settler Zionist Jewish domination of the
people and the land, also firmly posits the Israeli 1967 occupation of the
remainder of Palestine as good, just and necessary, since Palestine has
become yet another front in the 'war on terror'.

The past, the present, and spaces of resistance

The importance of the genealogical continuity of the discourse on
Palestine lies in its potent grip on Anglophone audiences, due to the
collision of Anglophone information sources with rhetoric recycled at
the highest echelons of world power (Berry and Philo 2004; O'Connor
2007).

The contemporary uses of the (European Jewish) Holocaust by the
Israeli state aside (Hass 2007), the confusion and misinformation arising
out of the interaction between the political and popular discourse on
Palestine are exemplified by a survey commissioned by the Open
Bethlehem Foundation. This survey interviewed 15,000 Americans and
1,000 Palestinian Muslims and Christians from the three urban centres
of Bethlehem. Approximately 60% of Americans interviewed thought
that Bethlehem was located in Israel, and that its inhabitants were either
Muslim or Jewish or a mix of both. Furthermore, although approximately 40% of the Americans interviewed were not aware of the wall in
and around Bethlehem, an approximately equal number thought that
the wall was there for Israel's security. In contrast, approximately 90% of
Palestinian interviewees believed that the wall was a systematic Israeli

land confiscation plan. While almost half the Americans blamed the increasing Palestinian Christian emigration on the rise in 'Islamic extremism', and less than 10% on Israeli policies, almost 80% of the Palestinian Christians interviewed blamed emigration on the Israeli occupation or the wall (Open Bethlehem Foundation 2006).

Another example of the result of the interaction between the political and popular discourse on Palestine can be found in the Glasgow University Media Group's study, *Bad News from Israel*. This study examined television news coverage of Palestine shortly before and during the early stages of *Intifadat al-Aqsa*, as well as how this coverage interacted with people's understanding of what they saw on the news. It was conducted over a two-year period and involved both extensive television news analysis and an audience sample of 800 respondents.

In the audience studies part of the research, which involved a mixture of focus groups and questionnaires that canvassed the opinions of 100 respondents selected on the basis of income, age and gender, the Media Group found that in the 'main sample of British students [surveyed] only 9% in 2001 and 11% in 2002 knew that the Israelis were occupying and that the settlers were Israeli. In the first of these samples there were actually more people who believed that the Palestinians were occupying the territories and that the settlers were Palestinians' (Berry and Philo 2004: 217). Although these percentages increased to 26% and 29% amongst German and American students interviewed, there was still a great deal of confusion; 'for example, over half of those who had written that the Palestinians became refugees on the formation of Israel or were "forced from their homes by Israel" also thought that the Palestinians occupied the occupied territories' (Berry and Philo 2004: 218). Furthermore, the general perception in the focus groups with regard to the Occupied Palestinian Territories was one based on the land 'not seen as having been subject to a military occupation and the settlements were not understood as being part of this. The army was there simply to keep the Palestinians back... even people who were sympathetic to the Palestinians had absorbed the message of the settlers as small embattled communities' (Berry and Philo 2004: 219–20). Furthermore, 'most participants in this research had little idea of the history or origins of the conflict' (Berry and Philo 2004: 212). For example, in 2001, only 4% of British students 'wrote that the Palestinians had been forced from their homes on the formation of Israel', (Berry and Philo 2004: 212), and a year later, the figure rose to a mere 8%.

Finally, perhaps nothing demonstrates better the potency of the interaction between the political and popular discourse on Palestine than the ability of the US and the EU to collude overtly with the four-decade-old Israeli military occupation of the Occupied Palestinian Territories, especially after the Hamas election victory in January 2006; this collusion rubber-stamps an economic siege of an occupied people that dares to resist, a siege illegal under the very rules of war of the self-proclaimed members of the political international community (Bomsey and Manor 2006). At the same time, while this community's international political status quo revolves around a principle of secular civic democracy, so much so that wars are waged on behalf of this desired norm, the Israeli state continues to be the normative exception, and its status as a Jewish state remains unquestioned (Cook 2006).

The implications of all this for those of us in the international Palestine solidarity campaign are immense. First, continuities between past and present colonialisms must be brought to the fore. In order to do this, it is self-defeating to continue to talk about the Israeli occupation of the West Bank and the Gaza Strip. Instead, we must start talking about the Israeli colonial-settler project that occupied Palestine in two waves, first in 1948/49 and later in 1967. Second, highlighting these continuities can shed light on the relationship of Israel's military occupation to the unfinished war of 1948/49, which in turn highlights the State of Israel, not as a continuation of biblical prophecies, but as a colonial-settler project born out of the darkest annals of European colonial history. In this way, religio-ethnic claims to the land between the Mediterranean and the Jordan can be better understood, bringing to the fore the centrality of the Palestinian refugees and the right of return to the Palestinian struggle against Zionism. Therefore the solidarity campaign must be reframed in order to fight Zionism in all its facets, whether in its belligerent regime of occupation in the Occupied Territories, or in its racist colonial-settler regime in the State of Israel, with a clear understanding of the present in view of the past.

Notes

1 This chapter benefited from a presentation at the 22nd Annual Middle East History and Theory Conference at the University of Chicago. I wish to thank Richard Farrow and Diren Valayden for comments on various drafts.
2 This is not to suggest that the two are mutually exclusive, or that there aren't

contemporary added extensions to these *a priori* justifications that vary from the need for a Jewish state, because of the (European Jewish) Holocaust, or, within the contemporary 'war on terror', Israel being a necessary and desired model beacon of democracy and light in an otherwise barbaric and totalitarian Arab world. However, I emphasize here the story of the pioneers and its correlative barbarity because of the stark commonalities in emphasis by British colonial officers ninety years ago, and their contemporary equivalents.

3   There is a clear discrepancy that strikes the researcher in the archives of the Colonial Office with regard to the Declaration between the internal discussions, which are clearly based on a policy born out of *realpolitik*, and the justifications based on a specific world-view as externally related by officers of the British government in general, and those of the Colonial Office in particular.

Archives

Public Records Office (PRO), London
Colonial Office (CO), Middle East Correspondence 732
Colonial Office (CO), Palestine Correspondence 733

References

Abu-Lughod, I. (2001) 'Territorially based nationalism and the politics of negation', in E. Said and C. Hitchens (eds) *Blaming the Victims: Spurious Scholarship and the Palestinian Question*, Verso, London and New York

Althusser, L. and E. Balibar (1997) *Reading Capital*, Verso, London and New York

Brown, M., A. Abunimah and N. Parry (2005) 'EI exclusive: Palestinian population exceeds Jewish population says US Government', *Electronic Intifada* «http://electronicintifada.net/cgi-bin/artman/exec/view.cgi/11/3649»

Berry, M. and G. Philo (2004) *Bad News from Israel*, Pluto Press, London and Sterling, VA

Bishara, A. (2007) 'Why Israel is after me', *Los Angeles Times*, 3 May

Bomsey, A. and Y. Manor (2006) '*Li Maslahat al-Hamajiya al-Israiliya al-Itihad al-Orobi wa Amrika Yantahikan kol al-Qawanin al-Dowaliya: al-Hisar al-Iqtisadi Yaqtol al-Filastiniyin*' ('The EU and US Violate International Law for the Benefit of Israel's Barbarity: The Economic Siege is Killing the People of Palestine'), *al-Talea* «http://www.taleea.com/newsdetails.php?id=8266&ISSUENO=1736»

Cook, J. (2006) *Blood and Religion: The Unmasking of the Jewish and Democratic State*, Pluto Press, London and Ann Arbor, MI

Cook, J. (2007) 'Defending Israel from democracy: The Shin Bit and the persecution of Azmi Bishara', *Znet* «http://www.zmag.org/content/showarticle.cfm?ItemID=13007»

Davidson, L. (1996) 'Biblical archaeology and the press: Shaping American perceptions of Palestine in the first decade of the Mandate', *The Biblical Archaeologist*, Vol. 59, no. 2, 104–14

Gregory, D. (2004) *The Colonial Present: Afghanistan, Palestine, Iraq*, Blackwell Publishing, Oxford

Foucault, M. (2005) *The Archaeology of Knowledge*, Routledge, London

Haraway, D. (1991) *Simians, Cyborgs and Women: The Reinvention of Nature*, Free Association Books, London

Hass, A. (2007) 'The Holocaust as political asset', *Ha'aretz*, 1 May

Hodgson, M. G. S. (1977) *The Venture of Islam: Conscience and History in a World Civilization: The Gunpowder Empires and Modern Times, Vol. 3*, University of Chicago Press, Chicago

Hourani, A. (1991) *A History of the Arab People*, Faber and Faber, London

Khalidi, R. (1997) *Palestinian Identity: The Construction of Modern National Consciousness*, Columbia University Press, Columbia

Lacquer, W. and B. Rubin (eds) (2001) 'The Balfour Declaration, 1917', *The Israel–Arab Reader: A Documentary History of the Middle East Conflict*, Penguin Books, London

Moscrop, J. J. (2002) *Measuring Jerusalem: The Palestine Exploration Fund and British Interests in the Holy Land*, Leicester University Press, London and New York

Mullin, C. (2007) 'Constructing the savage other: The 'War on Terror' and its impact on the discourse of political Islam', paper presented at First Annual Doctoral Symposium on Arab and Muslim Media Research, London

Northedge, F. S. (1986) *The League of Nations: Its Life and Its Times, 1920–1946*, Leicester University Press, Leicester

O'Connor, P. (2007) 'Buying the war on Palestinians: The US media, the *New York Times* and Israel', Electronic Intifada, 2 May «http://electronicintifada.net»

Olmert, E. (2006) 'Address by PM Olmert to a Joint Meeting of the US Congress', Israel Ministry of Foreign Affairs, 24 May «http://www.mfa.gov.il»

Open Bethlehem Foundation (2006) 'Americans back Bethlehem – But are not sure where it is', Friends of Sabeel – North America: Voice of the Palestinian Christians electronic mail list correspondence

Pappe, I. (2004) *A History of Modern Palestine: One Land, Two Peoples*, Cambridge University Press, Cambridge

Said, E. (2001) 'Introduction', in E. Said and C. Hitchens (eds) *Blaming the Victims: Spurious Scholarship and the Palestinian Question*, Verso, London

Said, E. (2003) *Orientalism*, Penguin Books, London

Sharon, A. (2005) 'Text of Ariel Sharon's speech to the UN General Assembly, September 15', *Ha'aretz* «http://www.haaretz.com »

Sherif, R. (1983) *Non-Jewish Zionism: Its Roots in Western History*, Zed Books, London

Silberman, N. A. (1991) 'Desolation and restoration: The impact of a biblical concept on Near Eastern Archaeology', *The Biblical Archaeologist* 54 (2): 76–87

Suleiman, M. W. (1995) 'Palestine and the Palestinians in the mind of America', in M. W. Suleiman (ed.) *US Policy on Palestine: From Wilson to Clinton*, Arab American University Graduates Press: Normal, IL

Thompson, T. L (2000) *The Bible in History: How Writers Create a Past*, Pimlico, London

Wasserstein, B. (1991) *The British in Palestine: The Mandatory Government and the Arab-Jewish Conflict, 1917–1929,* Basil Blackwell, Oxford

Whitelam, K. W. (1996) *The Invention of Ancient Israel: The Silencing of Palestinian History*, Routledge, London

Contributors

Nahla Abdo, an Arab feminist activist, is professor of sociology at Carleton University, Ottawa, Canada. She has published extensively on women, racism, nationalism and the state in the Middle East, with special focus on Palestinian women. Her recent publications include *Women and Poverty in the OPT: Some Conceptual and Methodological Notes* (2007), *Violence in the Name of Honour: Theoretical and Political Challenges* (2004, with Shahrzad Mojab) and *Women and the Politics of Military Confrontation: Palestinian and Israeli Gendered Narratives of Dislocation* (2002, with Ronit Lentin).

Anaheed Al-Hardan is a doctoral student in the Department of Sociology at Trinity College Dublin, where she is researching Palestinian refugees' practices of memory and remembrance of the 1948 Palestinian Nakba.

Gargi Bhattacharyya is professor of sociology at Aston University, UK. She is the author of *Traffick: The Illicit Movement of People and Things* (2005), *Sex and Society* (2002), *Race and Power: Global Racism in the Twenty-First Century* (with John Gabriel and Stephen Small, 2001), and *Tales of Dark Skinned Women* (1998). Her latest book, *Dangerous Brown Men*, will be published by Zed Books in 2008.

Honaida Ghanim is a postdoctoral fellow at the Center for Middle Eastern Studies, Sociology Department, Harvard University. Her Ph.D. at the Hebrew University Sociology Department focused on the social role of Palestinian intellectuals in Israel, 1948–2002.

Between 1998 and 2004 she was a visiting lecturer at al-Quds University, Bir Zeit University, Bethlehem University and the Hebrew University of Jerusalem. Her main interests are political and cultural sociology as well as gender studies. In her forthcoming book, *Intellectuals Reinventing a Nation: Israeli-Palestinian Persons-of-Pen Crossing Boundaries and Struggling Liminality*, she focuses on a comparison of three generations of Palestinian intellectuals and idea producers and disseminators in Israel.

David Theo Goldberg is the director of the system-wide University of California Humanities Research Institute and professor of comparative literature and criminology, law and society at the University of California, Irvine. His authored books include *The Racial State* (2002), *Racial Subjects: Writing on Race in America* (1997) and *Racist Culture: Philosophy and the Politics of Meaning* (1993). His edited books include *Anatomy of Racism* (1990), *Multiculturalism: A Critical Reader* (1995), *Race Critical Theories* (2001) and *A Companion to Racial and Ethnic Studies* (2002). His latest book is *The Threat of Race* (2007).

Sari Hanafi, a sociologist with a Ph.D. from EHESS–Paris (1994), is associate professor at the American University, Beirut and former director of the Palestinian Refugee and Diaspora Centre, Shaml. He is the author of numerous journal articles and book chapters on economic sociology and network analysis of the Palestinian diaspora; relationships between diaspora and the centre; political sociology and sociology of migration (mainly about Palestinian refugees); and sociology of the new actors in international relations. His books include *Here and There: Toward a Deconstruction of the Relationship Palestinian Diaspora from a Social and Political Perspective* (2001, Arabic); *Between Two Worlds: Palestinian Businessmen in the Diaspora and the Construction of a Palestinian Entity* (1997, Arabic and French); *La Syrie des ingénieurs. Perspective comparée avec l'Egypte* (1997). He has edited books on Arab NGOs (2002; 2004) and *Palestinian Sociology of Return* (forthcoming). His book (with Linda Taber), *The Emergence of the Palestinian Globalized Elite: Donors, International Organizations and Local NGOs*, was published in 2005 in Washington and Ramallah.

Laleh Khalili is a lecturer in politics and international studies at the School of Oriental and African Studies, London. Her book, *Heroes and*

Martyrs of Palestine: The Politics of National Commemoration, was published in 2007.

Alina Korn is a lecturer in the Department of Criminology at Bar-Ilan University and Ashkelon College, Israel. Her research interests include social control, sociology of law, and the links between crime, politics, and the media. She has published articles on rates of incarceration in Israeli prisons (in *Criminal Justice*), and on the reaction to political crime in Israel in the 1950s (in *International Journal of the Sociology of Law*). Her recent publications include a chapter on the Israeli press reporting of the Intifada (for *Muslims and the News Media*, edited by Elizabeth Poole and John E. Richardson, 2006), an article on the reporting of Palestinian casualties in the daily *Ha'aretz* (in *Journalism Studies*), and an article on the press coverage of Israel's policy of assassinating Palestinian militants suspected of terrorism (in *Crime, Law and Social Change*).

David Landy is a doctoral student in the Department of Sociology, Trinity College Dublin, having written an M.Phil. in ethnic and racial studies on 'The Role of Zionism in the Production of Irish-Jewish Identities'. His doctorate examines the mobilization of Israel-critical diaspora Jews. He has contributed to C. Barker and M. Tyldesley (eds) *Eleventh International Conference on Alternative Futures and Popular Protest: A Selection of Papers from the Conference* with 'Jewish involvement in Israel-critical groups: Identity politics, solidarity movement'.

Ronit Lentin is director of the postgraduate programme in ethnic and racial studies at the Department of Sociology, Trinity College Dublin. She has published extensively on gender and genocide, racism in Ireland, and Israel/Palestine. Her books include *Conversations with Palestinian Women* (1982), *Gender and Catastrophe* (1997), *Israel and the Daughters of the Shoah: Reoccupying the Territories of Silence* (2000), *Racism and Anti-racism in Ireland* (with Robbie McVeigh, 2002), *Women and the Politics of Military Confrontation: Palestinian and Israeli Gendered Narratives of Dislocation* (with Nahla Abdo, 2002), *Re-presenting the Shoah for the 21st Century* (2004), *After Optimism? Ireland, Racism and Globalisation* (with Robbie McVeigh, 2006), *Race and State* (with Alana Lentin, 2006), and *Performing Global Networks* (with Karen Fricker, 2007).

Conor McCarthy is a lecturer in English at NUI Maynooth. He is the author of *Modernisation, Crisis and Culture in Ireland 1969–1992* (2000) and of *The Cambridge Introduction to Edward Said* (forthcoming).

Ilan Pappe is the chair in history at Exeter University. He is the author of several books on the history of Palestine, including *The Making of the Arab-Israeli Conflict, 1947–1951* (1992), *A History of Modern Palestine; One Country, Two Peoples* (2003) and *The Ethnic Cleansing of Palestine* (2006).

Raef Zreik completed his SJD thesis at Harvard Law School. He holds an LLM from both Columbia Law School and the Hebrew University and an LLB from the Hebrew University. He practiced law for several years in Israel and, as a political activist, he established several NGOs that deal with human rights issues. Among his publications are 'Palestine as exile: Notes on the dialectic of sameness and difference' (*Global Jurists*), 'The Palestinian question: Themes of power and justice' (*Journal of Palestine Studies*) and *Exits from the Scene* (forthcoming). He has published articles on citizenship, identity and space.

Index

3, 53, 72, 74, 101-13, 119, 121, 124-8,
148-68, 173, 179, 231, 237, 245;
minorities 40, 46, 162-3; as *mukhabarat*
(security) state 17, 148-68; and multiculturalism 58-9; New Right in 153; in
Occupied Territories 14, 19, 31-2, 40-
1, 65-80, 83, 92, 96, 105, 116-29, 153,
159-60, 173-87, 193, 202, 222-3, 248-
50; as racial state 2-3, 6-15, 25-45, 46,
48-9, 153, 156-7, 159-60, 208, 216;
religious right in 30, 47, 74, 137, 142;
security apparatus 157, 159, 162-8; siege
policy 69; and 'war on terror' 46-60;
'whiteness' of 33; Zionist Left 153
'Israeli Arabs' 8
Israeli Committee Against House
Demolitions (ICAHD) 191, 196, 202
Italy 157

Jacobson, Alexander 159
Jaffa 25, 177
Jenin 117
Jenin refugee camp 128
Jerusalem 25, 37, 66, 127, 167, 191, 245;
East 75, 117, 124, 167, 191
Jewish National Fund (JNF) 9
Jewish self-criticism 29-30
jihadists 93
Jordan 40, 83-5, 96, 229
Jordan Valley 117
Judea 35
Jund al-Sham 82

Kant, Immanuel 34, 132
Karmi, Raed 125
Karsh, Ephraim 41
Kasher, Assa 74-5
Katzav, Moshe 72
Kenya 109-110
Keret, Etgar 210
Kfar Etzion 206
Khaled, Laila 184
Khalili, Laleh 16, 101-13
Khan Younes 126
Kierkegaard, Søren 132-3, 135
Kitson, Frank 109
Klein, Claude 153
Korn, Alina 16, 116-29
Kufr Hittin 214

labour 31, 40-1, 84, 86-7, 89, 122-3, 231
Labour Party 54-6
land 9, 11, 15, 32, 39-40, 47, 49, 68, 71,
121-2, 139, 144, 160-1, 167, 175, 196-
7, 207, 210, 216-17, 222-3, 228-31,
236-7, 248; laws 9, 161, 167
Landy, David 18, 189-203
Langer, Laurence 210
Lawrence Inquiry 49, 56
League of Nations 42, 237, 241
Lebanon 16, 42, 57, 82-97, 101-13, 163,
239; civil war 87
Lebanon War (1982) 3, 86-7, 101, 232;
(2006) 163-4, 217
Leibowitz, Yeshayahu 34
Lentin, Ronit 1-20, 206-17
Levi, Primo 214
Levinas, Emmanuel 42
liberalism 132, 135-7, 154-5
Lidd 177
Lincoln, Abraham 155-6
Lloyd George, David 239-43
Lobieh 94
locality 42, 192
Locke, John 40, 132-3
Lorde, Audre 11

Ma'ale Adumim 40
MADA al-Carmel (Arab Centre for Applied
Social Research) 164
Madrid bomb attacks 152
Malaya 109-10
Mamdani, Mahmood 37-8, 175
Mandela, Nelson 39
Maoris 192
Mau Mau rebellion 109
McCarthy, Conor 19, 221-34
Medécins san Frontières 127
media 54, 152, 154, 160, 174, 249
Meggido prison/interrogation centre 103
Meir, Golda 28
Memmi, Albert 42
memory 18-19, 93, 135, 206-17
Meridor, Yaakov 106
Middle East 3, 13, 31, 33, 160-1, 164, 174,
217, 221
migration 55, 59, 87, 89, 122, 211
Milansky, Moshe 73
Mizrahim see Arab Jews